Mar

SOCIAL INEQUALITY

Dedicated to:
All of the women in my life who remain a constant source of support and strength, especially Mum, Leanne, Lynsey and my three daughters Maia, Milana and Meadow.

SOCIAL INEQUALITY

Louise Warwick-Booth

Los Angeles | London | New Delhi
Singapore | Washington DC

Los Angeles | London | New Delhi
Singapore | Washington DC

SAGE Publications Ltd
1 Oliver's Yard
55 City Road
London EC1Y 1SP

SAGE Publications Inc.
2455 Teller Road
Thousand Oaks, California 91320

SAGE Publications India Pvt Ltd
B 1/I 1 Mohan Cooperative Industrial Area
Mathura Road
New Delhi 110 044

SAGE Publications Asia-Pacific Pte Ltd
3 Church Street
#10-04 Samsung Hub
Singapore 049483

Editor: Chris Rojek
Editorial assistant: Martine Jonsrud
Production editor: Katherine Haw
Proofreader: Derek Markham
Indexer: Charmian Parkin
Marketing manager: Michael Ainsley
Cover design: Lisa Harper
Typeset by: C&M Digitals (P) Ltd, Chennai, India
Printed by: Replika Press Pvt Ltd

Library of Congress Control Number: 2012954795

British Library Cataloguing in Publication data

A catalogue record for this book is available from
the British Library

ISBN 978-0-85702-917-1
ISBN 978-0-85702-918-8 (pbk)

CONTENTS

ABOUT THE AUTHOR

Louise Warwick-Booth is a sociologist with specific interests in health policy and social policy. She is located in the Centre for Health Promotion Research, having joined the Leeds Metropolitan University in September 2005, and teaches on a wide range of modules, including sociology, health policy, research, community and global policy, and health care. Louise was also the course leader for the BSc Public Health – Health Studies programme, from 2007–2012.

Louise's PhD explored lay research conducted within a community development setting. Louise has numerous research interests, including community development, community research and social inclusion. She has recently project managed a commissioned evaluation of the Sunderland Health Champion Programme and is involved in other evaluation research.

Louise (with Ruth Cross and Diane Lowcock) has recently published a major textbook, *Contemporary Health Studies: An Introduction* (Polity Press, 2012), and is also the author of *Researching with Communities* (VDM Verlag, 2009).

ACKNOWLEDGEMENTS

The author would like to thank the following people:

- The reviewers for providing helpful and constructive comments on the development of the book proposal and the final manuscript.
- The members of the Health Promotion Group in the Faculty of Health and Social Sciences at Leeds Metropolitan University for their support and encouragement.
- The many students that I have taught who have helped me to develop and refine my ideas.
- My assistant editor, Martine Jonsrud, for all of her advice, support and generally keeping me on track.

INTRODUCTION

The overall aim of this volume is to enable the reader to enhance his or her understanding of the dynamics of contemporary social inequality. The book examines what inequality is and how it is defined, explored and measured in a number of ways, and then takes the reader through numerous well-documented social divisions and associated relationships that are all fundamental aspects of social inequality. The book also considers inequality within a global framework in terms of conceptualising the issues and solving them, examining the relationship between social inequality and globalisation, as well as critically discussing the role of global governance and its impact on social inequalities. Policy at the national level is also examined to illustrate the ways in which social policy can be used as a tool to tackle inequalities, as well as the manner in which policies also serve to perpetuate inequalities. The reader is then introduced to a range of potential solutions for inequality within the final chapter.

As the scope and dynamics of contemporary social inequalities are extremely large, this book enables the reader to focus on the central tenets of inequalities by exploring the human experience of social divisions across several dimensions, for example, social class in Chapter 3, gender in Chapter 4 and ethnicity in Chapter 5. The book also critically discusses and analyses the many factors that are influential in relation to current social inequalities, such as definitional and measurement issues, global influences and the social policy environment. Some key aspects of the contemporary dynamics of social inequality are weaved throughout several chapters, such as measurements, definitions, policies and ideologies. Indeed, as there are many diverse discourses and huge debate in this area, each chapter uses a detailed case study to analyse the issues in more depth. Understanding and exploring social inequality requires an interdisciplinary discussion. Thus, this book draws on sociology, anthropology, health, social policy and economics throughout the chapters. Through the examination of these different disciplines and influences, social inequality is shown to be overwhelmingly structurally influenced, and is situated within a multidisciplinary critical framework.

In summary, this book explores the human experience of social inequality as it is mediated by individual, societal and global contexts, particularly highlighting the social and political dimensions of the problem. The book deals with a variety of influences and determinants of social inequality, taking the reader on a journey through a range of areas, such as policy environments, the processes associated with globalisation, and the importance of global society. Each chapter:

i starts with key learning outcomes to help the reader to understand the purpose of each chapter while navigating the book;
ii includes a number of tasks for readers to complete, to encourage reflection and deeper understanding of the issues;
iii summarises key points at the end, poses questions to stimulate debate and reflection, and suggests further reading for those wishing to explore further.

As this book illustrates, social inequality is an important component of contemporary social life. This book aims to encourage you to think about this and open your eyes to the very unequal and unfair world in which we all live today.

Detailed outline of the book

Chapter 1 opens the book by considering the concept of social inequality in critical depth, exploring it as a complex issue that is often taken for granted. The chapter outlines how social inequality can be defined and conceived in different contexts – historically, globally and subjectively. The chapter provides many examples of inequality and encourages the reader to explore their own understandings and ideas about inequality, including how these are culturally shaped and maintained.

Chapter 2 provides an overview of social divisions and their relationship with social inequality. It introduces readers to the key issues and critically discusses age, social exclusion, area effects, health, disability and sexuality. The chapter shows that social status and individual social characteristics relate to experiences of inequality in very different ways. The relationship between social divisions and social inequality is illustrated as complex, with the chapter constantly touching upon these complexities as well as the importance of status in relation to societal position and inequality. Power and powerlessness are also key considerations when exploring inequality and so the chapter critically explores how power is related to social divisions and larger structural influences within society through the introduction and discussion of a number of different theoretical explanations for the existence of social divisions. This chapter discusses inequality within various contexts and guises to show that inequality arises in all places across the globe and this is represented in numerous social divisions.

Chapter 3 then moves into a more detailed analysis of the social division of class, providing discussions about definitions of class and exploring its relationship with social inequality. This chapter explores how social class is related to social status and the ways in which social class divisions permeate many contemporary societies. The chapter discusses social class within various contexts and guises to show that inequality associated with class position arises in all places across the globe and that many explanations are offered as to why class is still an enduring social division.

Chapter 4 is a more detailed analysis of the social division of gender. Again, definitions and measurement are explored, social status is analysed and the persistence of inequalities in this area are outlined, despite recent progress that has been made in terms of increased gender equality. The chapter explores the complex relationship between gender and social inequality and outlines the importance of the global context in relation to gender inequalities. The chapter also discusses the explanations offered in the literature that tell us about why gender inequalities remain a problem within contemporary societies across the world.

Chapter 5 is the final chapter dealing with social divisions. It focuses on ethnicity as a contemporary social division remaining within a range of contemporary contexts. This chapter outlines some progress that has been made in terms of reducing inequalities associated with ethnicity. However, despite this, many inequalities remain, linked to social inequality, status and power in complex ways. The chapter explores the complex relationship between ethnicity and social inequality, highlighting the explanations offered in the literature that tell us why inequalities associated with ethnic classifications remain a problem within contemporary societies across the world.

Chapter 6 moves the reader into the territory of broader analysis by focusing on inequality within a broader global context, showing that inequality cannot be understood without a global perspective. The chapter examines the key question of how globalisation has affected and altered inequality by discussing the concept of globalisation and exploring its relationship to inequality. The chapter illustrates competing opinions about whether globalisation is beneficial for creating a more equal society as well as introducing discussions and evidence suggesting that it actually worsens inequality. The chapter addresses key questions such as how current global economic trends are affecting inequalities as well as discussing lessons from the 2008 'global' recession in relation to inequality.

Given that the scope of the concept of globalisation is so large scale, Chapter 7 still focuses at the level of the global. However, the analysis here is about global governance and global social policy. The chapter builds on discussions started in Chapter 6 to examine the importance of global governance and the key global economic players that influence current patterns of inequalities. Thus key transnational players, such as the World Bank and the World Trade Organisation, are reviewed to illustrate and critique their role. Can these institutions be a force for creating a more equal world or is their agenda more complex? The chapter also discusses the key global challenges which policy makers need to tackle, and how these relate to inequalities.

Chapter 8 continues the focus on the role of social policy. The chapter critically explores specific examples of social policy at both the global and national level to assess their impact on levels of inequality within society. Under the New Labour government within the UK, there were specific policies implemented which aimed to tackle inequality and to reduce national poverty. So were these policies and interventions successful? What can the UK's efforts tell the rest of the world about social policy being used to address inequalities? What about policy in relation to finance and economics, given the current focus on these areas by both national governments and key global players – is finance fair? The chapter considers current policy strategies in a range of contexts to assess their impact on inequalities.

The final chapter brings together all of the previous discussions and weaves them into a solution-focused analysis. The chapter considers the question of how a more equal global society can be created. So is globalisation part of the solution? Can we effect better social policy both nationally and globally to change inequalities? Through a variety of critical debates, the chapter asks whether equality is actually possible within a capitalist framework and analyses what is attainable. The chapter explores a range of potential solutions for inequality, the ideological positions underpinning the proposed solutions and ends with an exploration of what the future holds in relation to likely patterns of social inequality.

1

WHAT IS SOCIAL INEQUALITY?

Key learning outcomes

By the end of this chapter you should be able to:

- Understand the complexities associated with defining the concept of social inequality

- Understand that many different types of social inequality exist

- Understand the different ideological positions associated with explaining inequality

Overview of the chapter

This chapter considers the concept of social inequality in critical depth, exploring it as a complex issue that is often taken for granted. The chapter outlines how social inequality can be defined and conceived in different contexts – historically, globally and subjectively. The chapter provides many examples of inequality and offers Learning Tasks to help you to explore your own understandings and ideas about inequality, including how these are culturally shaped and maintained.

Conceptualising social inequality

It is clear to most people that the world in which we live is unfair, unequal and full of inequality. However, when it comes to defining what inequality is, there has been much debate and as a result there are many ways in which inequality can be conceptualised. Inequality is often understood to be socio-economic, meaning it is based on income. This is just a single measure of inequality but one that is now closely associated with social inequalities in terms of outcomes (Ortiz and Cummins 2011).

> ### *Defining social inequalities*
>
> Social inequalities are differences in income, resources, power and status within and between societies. Such inequalities are maintained by those in powerful positions via institutions and social processes. (Naidoo and Wills 2008)

Social inequality and divisions within national contexts have been explored by sociologists for many years, although global inequality only became of interest to researchers in the 1980s, when the first calculations of such inequality were made (Milanovic 2006). Sociologists have historically studied stratification and inequality within societies but paid little attention to global disparities until relatively recently. Furthermore, data is required about the income of countries in order to calculate inequalities between them and this only became available during the 1980s. Despite the availability of such data, there remains confusion about how exactly to calculate and measure inequality and the same or similar terms are used within the literature to describe different things (Milanovic 2006). Differences in income distribution matter for a number of reasons, as this chapter clearly shows, but most importantly they matter for people because they represent social injustice (Ortiz and Cummins 2011). Social inequality is also culturally important because we compare ourselves to others. Wilkinson and Pickett (2009) argue that relative inequality is important in terms of our own levels of happiness. So if we see others who have much more than ourselves, even if we actually have many of our basic needs met, then this causes problems. Defining what we need is also complex and for many living in high-income countries, expectations are increasingly growing in terms of what we say that we 'need'. Complete the following Learning Task, which will help you to think about how you construct your needs.

Learning Task 1.1 – how do I define need?

Look at the following list. Which of these would you say that you 'need'?

- Water
- Warmth
- Shelter
- Food – two meals per day
- Fresh fruit and vegetables daily
- A hobby
- Savings
- Visits to friends and family
- Car
- TV
- DVD player
- Mobile phone
- Internet access
- Holiday every year

- Nights out socialising
- Fridge
- Freezer
- Microwave oven
- New clothes
- Two pairs of shoes
- Bed and bed linen for everyone
- Presents for family and friends
- Clothes for special occasions
- Medicines
- Access to health care as required
- Damp-free home
- A computer at home
- Celebrations on special occasions

1 Which of these are necessities of life?
2 Which do you think are the most important?
3 If you lived in a different place in the world, how do you think your perceptions of need may differ?
4 See www.jrf.org.uk/publications/poverty-and-social-exclusion-britain for a report that details the findings from the UK Poverty and Social Exclusion Survey in 1999, which incorporates the views and perceptions of members of the public. How do your views compare?
5 There are other useful websites from around the world that explore social exclusion in a range of contexts. Take time to explore these:

- The European Year for Combating Social Exclusion and Poverty http://ec.europa.eu/social/main.jsp?langId=en&catId=637

- The University of Michigan, School of Public Policy has a National Poverty Centre www.npc.umich.edu/poverty/

This Learning Task should have helped you to understand that defining need is difficult and context-dependent. Defining social inequality is difficult too and, as a consequence, measuring inequality is also problematic.

Measuring social inequality

Milanovic (2007) outlines how socio-economic inequality can be measured. First, he discusses concept 1, international inequality measured by comparing the average incomes of different countries, usually based on the gross domestic income of each nation. This definition, however, fails to measure and examine inequality within countries. This type of measure has generated a large amount of literature but is problematic because it does not accurately portray inequality across the world as it fails to take account of the population size of the countries being compared to each other. As a result of countries having unequal population sizes, increases in income have different effects, especially if a nation is highly populated (Milanovic 2006).

Global inequality can also be measured by taking into account the population of each country. Labelled concept 2, this measures the variables of gross domestic income and population size. This approach to calculating global inequality remains popular because little data is needed to make the calculations and the relationship can be shown in an equation called the gini co-efficient of national income distribution. However, there are problems with this calculation because it does not measure the inequalities that exist within countries, which is necessary to calculate 'true' global inequality (Milanovic 2006).

The third measure of global inequality (concept 3) is one that accounts for in-country differences in terms of individual incomes. Such data is often drawn from household surveys reporting disposable income because these are the only source of information from which individual income distribution can be calculated. However, a global survey of households does not occur, therefore the only way to calculate this third measure of inequality is by comparing data from individual countries' surveys. This is also problematic because there are differences between gross domestic income and disposable income in terms of how these are defined within individual countries (Milanovic 2006).

Given that income inequalities can be measured in a number of ways, it should not be surprising to hear that inequalities can also be conceptualised in a number of different ways. For example, within countries social class position is a common measure. The Indian caste system, in which people are divided into specific social categories that form a rigid hierarchy, is one such example of class inequality. The lowest classification of individuals is called 'the untouchables'. There are ongoing debates about the existence of social class within the UK, another form of stratification based on occupation, with the lowest group often termed 'the underclass'. There are many other social divisions related to inequality, including gender, age, ethnicity and disability, which are all explored in later chapters. It is important to examine different social divisions so that income distributions can be viewed in terms of how they affect different groups, such as women, children and the poor in general (Ortiz and Cummins 2011).

The human development index is another way in which inequality can be measured. The index measures the three dimensions of health, education and living standards to assess how countries are progressing in development terms and to offer international comparisons. This measure is broader than simply examining income but, despite this, has received criticism because there are still omissions. For example, the index does not include any measure of gender equity or environmental sustainability (United Nations Development Programme 2010). Human development is of course much more than just education, health and income: 'The chance to lead a meaningful life depends on the conditions people face, including the distribution of advantages in their society, the possibilities for participating in decision making and the way choices affect the well-being of future generations' (United Nations 2010: 25). Some countries, such as Norway, which is ranked as number 1 on the human development index, are rated much lower for their ecological footprint, which is the area of land and sea needed to replace the resources that a country consumes. So just because a country performs well according to one criteria or measurement tool does not mean it is without problems.

Sen (1999) similarly argues that it is important to use other measures when examining inequality. In his capability approach, he outlines standards of living as being important. This approach is also concerned with poverty, justice, quality of life and freedom within context. There are again measurement problems when trying to evaluate standards of living. Sen (1985, 1998) carried out empirical work from his capability approach analysing many inequalities, such as sex bias, hunger and development. Well-being is another useful measure of development and provides an alternative picture because countries that have the highest income do not necessarily have the highest levels of well-being. For example, the USA is the highest income country in the world but does not lead when measured according to well-being (United Nations 2009). The work of Sen has led to the development of the multidimensional poverty index, which is grounded in the capability approach. The index highlights deprivations at the household level across the same three dimensions used within the human development index: education, standards of living and health. The index looks at specific indicators within each dimension to report on deprivations. For example, in the living standards dimension, the index looks at the access that households have to a toilet, cooking fuel, water and electricity as well as assets. There are 10 indicators and a household is classed as multidimensionally poor if it is deprived in at least two of these. The index arguably provides a more comprehensive picture of the experiences of those who are deprived (United Nations 2009). When measuring using the index, the number of people categorised as multidimensionally poor is classed as higher than other measures. *The Real Wealth of Nations* (UNDP 2010) shows that 1.75 billion people are multidimensionally poor compared to 1.44 billion people estimated to be living on less than $1.25 a day in the same countries (United Nations Development Programme 2010). However, this still remains less than the 2.6 billion people who live on less than $2 per day, demonstrating the different figures that measurement tools produce.

'Social exclusion' is another term strongly related to inequality and again encompasses more than just a narrow focus on income.

Defining social exclusion

'Social exclusion is a shorthand label for what can happen when individuals or areas suffer from a combination of linked problems such as unemployment, poor skills, low incomes, poor housing, high crime environments, bad health and family breakdown.' (Social Exclusion Unit 1997)

Social exclusion is one of three often-used measures of poverty. Social exclusion can be understood in a number of ways and has three domains (Levitas et al. 2007: 117), as follows:

1 **Resources** – material and economic, access to services (both public and private) and social resources
2 **Participation** – economic (i.e. usually via work), social, education and political participation (i.e. voting)
3 **Quality of life** – health and well-being, the environment in which you live and crime levels in the area in which you live.

Levitas (2006) argued that non-participation in activities such as voting, employment and education are closely linked to poverty and a lack of resources. The measurement of social exclusion is carried out using a range of quantitative indicators. Given that there are many dimensions to social exclusion, different surveys will use different indicators, but the use of a broad range of indicators again serves to demonstrate the range of ways that inequality permeates all aspects of social life. The following example shows the many indicators that can be used to measure social exclusion.

Measuring social exclusion – a Scottish example

The initial set of indicators used to measure social exclusion included six dimensions and 16 indicators, outlined as follows:

Dimension 1 – Low incomes

Indicator 1 – Households below half average income
Indicator 2 – People dependent on income support
Indicator 3 – Children entitled to free school meals

Dimension 2 – Access to employment

Indicator 4 – People of working age not in employment
Indicator 5 – Long-term unemployment
Indicator 6 – Full-time employees on low pay

Dimension 3 – Housing quality and availability

Indicator 7 – Overcrowding
Indicator 8 – Homelessness

Dimension 4 – Education

Indicator 9 – Unauthorised absence from school
Indicator 10 – School leavers' qualifications
Indicator 11 – Working-age people with no qualifications

Dimension 5 – Health and fertility

Indicator 12 – Underage conceptions
Indicator 13 – Low birth weight babies
Indicator 14 – Premature deaths

Dimension 6 – Citizenship and community participation

Indicator 15 – Election turnout
Indicator 16 – Fear of selected crimes

Source: Scottish Parliament (1999)

Use the internet to explore other measures. For example, see discussions about the development of new measures of social exclusion in Australia:http://benews. unimelb.edu.au/2011/a-new-measure-of-social-exclusion-in-australia/

These indicators would not necessarily apply in all contexts and across all countries because of cultural differences and the lack of available information across some of these dimensions. Indeed, there is no point in establishing an indicator if there is a lack of available data to support it. The more complex measures of social exclusion, development and inequality all derive from the study of poverty. Poverty and inequality are unsurprisingly closely related and are both consequently still widely measured across the world.

Poverty remains widespread in many parts of the world, within both high and low income countries. Poverty is also most often measured according to monetary terms. There are absolute measures of poverty and relative measures.

Defining poverty

Absolute poverty refers to a set standard (usually income) that can be used to measure poverty across countries and time. The World Bank (2005) defines absolute poverty as those living on less than $1.25 per day. There is, however, evidence to suggest that measuring poverty according to poverty lines underestimates the actual extent of poverty (United Nations 2009).

In comparison, relative poverty is a standard that is used within countries and it is about a minimum standard that no one should fall beneath. Relative poverty is again usually represented by a figure.

Defining poverty is highly contested and judgements about need are difficult to separate from political opinion (Lister 2004) and subjective views, as Learning Task 1.1 demonstrated. Politicians often focus on work as the solution to both poverty and inequality. While there is little doubt that the absence of paid work is an important cause of poverty and social exclusion, there will always remain work that is low paid and individuals who are unable to work, resulting in the continued existence of inequality (Joseph Rowntree Foundation 2000). Chapter 9 provides an in-depth discussion of the range of solutions that can be considered to deal with inequality and poverty.

All of these measures are valid ways in which to define and measure poverty, but these have again been criticised for simply examining income when poverty is in fact much broader, as Sen (1999) indicates. Dorling (2009) similarly conceptualises inequality simply as injustice and outlines a variety of different types of inequality that are broader than income inequalities but are still strongly related to them. For instance, children who are labelled as delinquents, adults who are in debt and unable to manage financially, and households without a car in countries where car use is the norm, are all examples of contemporary experiences of inequality. He also discusses the socially excluded, including those suffering from mental illness and those politically inactive and unable to vote. Similarly, Bauman (2011) argues that income inequality is a conceptualisation that is too narrow because social inequality encompasses poverty, vulnerability, danger and the denial of dignity. In addition, social inequality has to be understood as encompassing the factors that include and, more particularly, exclude people from information, especially within a global world context that is increasingly information-driven.

Clearly, measuring inequality is complex and academics working in this area also debate the best way to represent inequality, with all current measures receiving criticism. Not everyone believes that measuring income is the most appropriate way to show global inequality. Other ways in which differences across the world can be shown have already been discussed and can also include the measurement of consumption or expenditure. Again, there are complexities here and methodological challenges (Milanovic 2006). Given these complexities, how do you think that you would measure social inequality?

Learning Task 1.2 – measuring social inequality

1 Revisit the measures of social inequality described in this chapter.
2 List all of the aspects of social inequality that you can think of (e.g. income inequality, poverty, other related deprivations such as food poverty, fuel poverty, social exclusion etc.)
3 For each of the areas that you have listed try to think about the questions you would ask on a questionnaire in an attempt to measure these different aspects of social inequality. If you were designing a questionnaire, what sections would you include?
4 Now use the internet to look at how other surveys measure aspects of social inequality. For example, the British Household Panel Survey has several questions that relate to living in Britain that you could use and adapt in your survey. See www.iser.essex.ac.uk/bhps/documentation/pdf_versions/survey_docs/ for the questions used in the survey. How does your questionnaire compare?
5 What are the strengths and weaknesses of measuring social inequality by using a questionnaire? Will the data that you would like to collect be available in all countries and locations?

The global context of inequality

Despite all of these measurement issues and the ongoing debates within the literature, there is a general agreement that global inequality exists and that there are groups across the world who hold more wealth than others, and groups who live in poverty. There are numerous statistics that demonstrate vast income inequalities across the world:

- A 2005 United Nations report describes 2.8 billion people living on less than $2 per day (United Nations 2005).
- In 2007, 1.2 billion people were living on less than $1.25 per day (Ortiz and Cummins 2011).
- The richest one-fifth of the global population consumes 86% of the world's goods and services (United Nations Development Programme 1998).
- The wealthiest 61 million individuals who make up just 1% of the global population had the same amount of income as the poorest 3.5 billion (or 56%) in 2007 (Ortiz and Cummins 2011).
- The 25 richest Americans have a combined income that almost matches the combined income of 2 billion of the world's poor (Sernau 2011).
- 20% of the world enjoys more than 70% of global income (Ortiz and Cummins 2011).
- It will take more than 800 years for the bottom billion to achieve 10% of global income if current levels of progress continue (Ortiz and Cummins 2011).

Inequality between people within the world is clearly demonstrable and is shown in various data sets. Therefore, there is an agreement among experts that global inequality is vast. The direction in which inequality is travelling is, however, much disputed (Milanovic 2006). Some argue that global inequality has been on the rise in recent decades both nationally, with more than 80% of the world's population living in countries in which income differentials are increasing (United Nations 2007), and internationally. These increases are not across all high-income countries (Wilkinson and Pickett 2009) and trends within countries are also changing. The current trend is towards rising inequality within countries (Firebaugh 2003). Other data shows that living standards are rising in some countries and poverty is declining too (United Nations 2009). Measurement problems abound, assumptions can be made when calculations are being done (Milanovic 2006) and the inclusion of some countries within the measurement of overall global trends also serves to skew and distort the larger picture (United Nations 2009a).

United Nations (2013) figures still depict large disparities and thus inequality between many countries, according to a variety of metrics. Table 1.1 demonstrates some of these contemporary inequalities.

Ortiz and Cummins (2011) examine global income inequality according to gross domestic product in US dollars, comparing the poorest and richest countries to demonstrate the severity of current global inequality (illustrated using selected examples in Table 1.2).

There are many complexities here because a country can be ranked high on one measure but then perform less well according to other categorisations. Indeed, measuring according to different exchange rates or by using the inter-country model will provide a different picture. But do not get confused by the tables and figures; you can see from simply comparing them that there are huge differences in terms of income, development and education levels across the world. Similarly, figures that show the number of people living on less than $1.25 per day across the globe are a further demonstration of the level of inequality experienced today, as Table 1.3 shows.

Table 1.1 Global comparisons in income and inequality measures (2012 data)

Country	Values in the Human Development Index	Education levels (measured by school enrolment ratio)	GNI per capita, 2005 PPP $
Australia	0.938	129.0	34,340
United Kingdom	0.875	93.0	32,538
Japan	0.912	85.9	32,545
Pakistan	0.515	40.0	2,566
Kenya	0.519	60.0	1,541
Ethiopia	0.396	36.0	1,107

Source: United Nations Development Programme (2013)

Table 1.2   Poorest and richest in the world in 2007, measured according to GDP (US dollars)

Poorest country	GDP per capita	Richest country	GDP per capita
Liberia	47	USA	96,946
Niger	50	Singapore	76,189
Guinea-Bissau	51	Norway	70,184
Malawi	52	UK	58,408
Central African Republic	60	Denmark	56,421

Source: Adapted from Ortiz and Cummins (2011)

Table 1.3 shows those with the highest levels of poverty at the top, according to 2005 measures, and then moves to those with lower levels. The table also shows some interesting trends by comparing the measures at two different points in time, demonstrating that progress has been made in some countries, with poverty rates declining, but in others rates have actually increased significantly. Again, this reflects the complexity of contemporary patterns of inequality.

There is an array of evidence cited in the contemporary literature that clearly shows social inequality across a range of countries, both high and low income, showing that the poor are present in all societies. Indeed, it is easy to present data which shows the extremes of poverty compared to high income levels, and while this is useful for illustrating large global differentials, it can mask the complexity of the overall picture.

Table 1.3   Proportion of the population living on less than $1.25 per day in 2005 in selected countries

Country	1990	2005
Liberia	83.2	86.1
United Republic of Tanzania	70.3	82.4
Burundi	84.5	81.3
Haiti	56.8	58.0
Cambodia	77.3	40.2
Uzbekistan	4.9	38.8
Papua New Guinea	43.0	29.7
Pakistan	58.5	22.6
Philippines	29.7	22.6
Honduras	43.5	22.2
Kyrgyzstan	4.8	21.8
Bolivia	4.0	19.6
Djibouti	1.8	18.6
Yemen	4.9	17.5

Source: World Bank, Development Research Group (2009)

Wilkinson and Pickett (2009) argue that inequality within nations can be shown to exist across the entire social gradient of many societies. Despite any similarities within the data, it is important to realise that countries are not uniform and should not be characterised as such; social inequality manifests itself in different ways within and between countries. Many countries have managed to develop at a great speed and so in part begin to address some social inequalities. However, there are still several countries that are falling behind, with countries stuck at the bottom of the development ladder facing a variety of traps that keep them in poverty (Collier 2008).

There is indeed powerful evidence that illustrates contemporary global economic inequality and overwhelming figures that can be quoted. Many commentators suggest that globalisation has exacerbated the problem (see Chapter 6 for further discussion of the relationship between globalisation and inequality). Despite this wealth of evidence about the existence of inequality, the solutions to inequality are hotly debated (see Chapter 9) and reading statistics does not allow us to understand its nature or impact. 'In particular, it does not show how ordinary people struggle to get by, or in some cases fail to get by, on limited means' (Held and Kaya 2007: 1). Living in extreme poverty is often accompanied by having unsatisfied material needs, being undernourished and facing a sense of powerlessness (United Nations 2009).

Patterns of contemporary inequality

The 2010 Human Development Report (*The Wealth of Nations,* United Nations Development Programme 2010) states that there is little evidence of progress in protecting vulnerable people against 'shocks' such as the 2008 economic crisis or in making the world more sustainable, indicating that inequality is still a significant problem within the world today. Inequality is also on the rise according to many analyses both nationally and internationally, with more than 80% of the population of the world living in countries where income differentials are widening (United Nations 2009). Within countries, inequality is increasing and for each country that has seen an improvement in recent decades, there are at least two in which the situation has worsened (United Nations 2009). Furthermore, according to many indicators, progress has been made since the 1980s but this has been slower than expected and, given the global financial crisis currently being experienced, inequality is likely to increase.

The most recent economic crisis has resulted in large price increases for both energy and food, with the Food and Agriculture Organisation (FAO) (2009) estimating that as a result another 115 million people were experiencing chronic hunger in 2007 and 2008, particularly in Africa. The World Bank (2009a) published figures estimating that the food and energy price rises had increased the global headcount of those in poverty by 155 million. Prices have declined since 2008 but still remain high. So there have been large price rises, with the cost of living increasing hugely, combined with a drop in per capita income growth (United Nations 2009). As a consequence of this, poverty reduction will be slowed and the impact of this will be experienced specifically within already poor areas such as Latin America and Africa. Given the difficulties already highlighted in measuring income inequality and poverty, current projections are likely to underestimate the true impact of the financial crisis on poverty levels (United Nations 2009). The projections, even as underestimates, make for foreboding reading, as a result of the most recent global economic crisis:

- Up to 100 million more people will remain poor or fall into poverty
- In East and South Asia between 56 and 80 million people are likely to be affected
- 16 million people in Africa are likely to remain in poverty when they would have moved out of it
- 4 million people in Latin America and the Caribbean are also likely to be unable to escape poverty (United Nations 2009).

Similarly, there has been a rise in inequality within OECD countries (the Organisation for Economic Co-operation and Development), which are higher income countries. Thus in a typical OECD country, the income of the richest 10% was almost nine times more than that of the poorest 10% (Chapple et al. 2009). Indeed, Britain has high levels of inequality despite it being a high-income country. A recent report by Hills et al. (2010: 1) presents an anatomy of economic equality across the UK and starts by stating that:

> Britain is an unequal country, more so than many other industrial countries and more so than a generation ago. This manifests itself in many ways – most obviously in the gap between those who are well off and those who are less well-off.

The report considers several aspects of inequality, not just income differentials. Thus, it examines educational outcomes, employment statuses, levels of earnings and wealth as well as individual incomes to demonstrate that inequalities are complex and represented in different ways. There is a wealth of data considered within the report and some interesting evidence summaries that show that both earnings and income inequality within any sub-groups of the population was greater in 2006–07 than it was in 1968. Thus, inequality within the UK is increasing when incomes and earnings are measured. This confirms an earlier report by Lawler and Nicholls (2008), who argue that despite much economic growth in the UK, for the 15 years prior to the publication of their report, inequality had widened and pockets of severe deprivation had continued to develop. They argue that economic growth has not resulted in reductions in inequality because the benefits that come with such growth are not equally shared across the whole of society. Their review of evidence suggests that benefit claimants are heavily concentrated in deprived areas, demonstrating that place, poverty and disadvantage are related. These issues are discussed in more depth in Chapter 2.

Given these analyses of inequality within the UK, it can be argued that just because a country has a high income in comparison to its global counterparts, does not mean that those who live within it do not experience social inequality or poverty. Reading these figures is depressing without even considering the impacts on the lives of the people in poverty and their experiences. Now complete Learning Task 1.3, which will help you to reflect on the experience of inequality.

Learning Task 1.3 – the experience of inequality

Think about your life and all of the things that you take for granted, such as where you live, what you choose to eat, access to water, heat, basic necessities and all of the other things that you do without thinking – for example, travelling, eating out, socialising, etc. Now imagine experiencing social inequality, living in poverty and not having money. How would this impact on the lifestyle that you currently have?

1 Draw a spider's web of causation, as shown in Figure 1.1, and list all of the ways in which you can think the experience of living with social inequality would impact on your life.

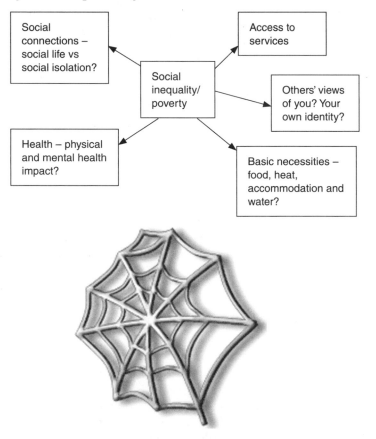

A spider's web of causation is similar to a mind map.

Figure 1.1   Spider's web of causation

Source: Adapted from Bhopal (2008)

2 Did you think about social exclusion, educational impacts, child poverty and fuel poverty? There are many dimensions to social inequality which result from poverty and income inequality.
3 Finally, consider the fairness of such a situation. If you were in such a position, would you consider it fair, given the structure of society, the level of wealth held by the minority and the powerless that is faced by many?

This Learning Task helps you to think about how the experience of inequality would affect your life as it currently stands but is no substitute for the actual situation itself, in which people struggle to survive on a daily basis and live in very difficult circumstances. Your needs and expectations may also be different if you lived in a different place in the world.

Subjective inequality

Completing the above Learning Task should have helped you to think about the experience of inequality. The experience of inequality is subjective and relational because it involves comparisons to others, for example in terms of income, education levels, health outcomes, political participation and consumption patterns, to name just a few criteria. It can be assumed that individuals compare themselves to their reference group and that this determines, in part, their well-being; therefore the same holds true for perceptions of inequality. For people to establish their own social position, they do compare themselves to others, such as those who live close by geographically like neighbours and friends (Runciman 1966). People also compare themselves to earlier generations, such as parents and grandparents. Most people have better-off lives than previous generations because of overall changes in living standards and consumption patterns. However, there is very little research about how people subjectively perceive and understand social trajectories (Kelley and Kelley 2009). It has been suggested that social change in affluent societies masks relative inequality because temporal comparisons lead to people feeling that the present is an improvement on the past (Bottero 2011). There may be more room at the top in societal terms but this is overlooked by many people, as are increasing income inequalities within societies, in part because of the comparisons that people make to the past.

Historical inequality

Inequality is nothing new; there are many examples of historical social inequality. For example, empire building in Roman times used slaves, feudal systems of land ownership existed with serfs working the land while kings owned it and ruled the kingdoms. Historically, then, inequality was related to land ownership but the industrial revolution changed the structure of society and the basis on which wealth was created, as documented by Marx (1906 [1867]). The work of well-known sociologists in the nineteenth century, such as Marx, reflects academics becoming interested in the existence of social inequality and theorising about it.

Karl Marx, a political economist, examined capitalism and wrote about two classes of individuals that made up society. The dominant and powerful social class, the bourgeoisie, were the ruling elite who owned the means of production. So the wealth of the ruling class is based not on land ownership; rather, it is related to production. Those in the lower social group were labelled as the proletariat, the subservient poorer individuals who work and produce by selling their labour. For Marx, this new structure of inequality within society brought many social problems, such as the increasing drive for profit, called the constant crisis of profit, the accumulation of wealth and the alienation of workers who are simply part of a machine of mass production. Marx hoped for the development of class consciousness, whereby those in the lower social class realise the need for a solution to their situation and therefore revolt. However, the revolution desired by Marx has never occurred. This analysis is called a conflict perspective.

Despite the obvious flaws with applying this theory to contemporary western society, in that it does not account for the development of the middle classes and a revolution has never occurred in the way that Marx envisaged, it offers useful insights. The financial power of corporations is indeed huge, with some companies earning more than some countries. Those at the top of the social spectrum are still those who have the most financial capital and social divisions remain evidently related to power across the world. The rich do maintain positions of power. For example, Owen (2010) showed that within the UK Coalition government elected in 2010, of the 29 ministers entitled to attend Cabinet meetings, 23 have assets and investments estimated to be worth more than £1 million. This has led to criticisms of the government and arguments that politics remains dominated by those who are wealthy.

Given the insights that historical sociological theory can provide, other sociologists have continued to develop the work of Marx and produce further conflict perspectives. For example, Max Weber (1946, 1978) drew heavily on the political economy perspective to produce an analysis which depicts an individual's societal position as dependent on their life chances in the market place. Weber also focused more on analysing power, concluding that prestige and status are as important in creating social hierarchy. He viewed social position as being less rigid than Marx and saw social mobility as a process by which individuals could move up the social scale. The idea of social mobility remains contemporaneous, as is often discussed within current policy approaches to inequalities. Some commentators and politicians suggest that social mobility is possible and that people simply find their natural place within the social order. However, there is less social mobility in more unequal societies, suggesting that the idea that those who are more talented are better rewarded is simply an ideology (Wilkinson 2011). Thus, sociologists have continued to study social class within contemporary debates, focusing on the changing structure of class within societies. Chapter 3 provides a more detailed analysis of how social class and inequalities remain interrelated.

Since then many sociologists have documented and many have explored social inequalities and there is a huge literature about social divisions, focusing not only on class, but on gender relations, race and ethnicity, power, politics and the state, education, work, health and illness, and crime. For example, female sociologists began to write about gender inequality in a number of areas, such as women who live in a man-made world (Gilman 1911), women re-negotiating the world of paid and unpaid work due to changing gender roles (Smith 1987), as well as women experiencing gendered power imbalances (Smith 1990). Feminist literature also describes women doing emotional labour and dealing with its impact (Hochschild 1983). In addition, feminists have explored the objectification of women and have developed standpoint feminist theory, examining the experience of black women, lesbian women and working class women too. Race and racism have also received much attention, with sociologists arguing that they still exist within contemporary society but that their meanings have changed (Gilroy 1987). Other theorists have examined educational inequality, using concepts such as the possession of 'capital', which can be economic, cultural and social (Bourdieu 1984). These issues are all explored in more depth in later chapters.

Indeed, social inequality has also been historically recognised as a social problem warranting political attention, for example in the UK. Whether inequality is recognised as a social problem by politicians depends on their ideological viewpoint and is context-dependent too For example, in post-war Britain, there was a political mandate to reward everyone for their efforts during the war and to recognise the deprivations and hardships that had been experienced, which resulted in policy developments to tackle a range of inequalities. Beveridge (1942), in his now seminal report, highlighted post-war social and economic inequality within the UK, describing the five 'giants' of want, idleness, squalor, ignorance and disease. Beveridge was a liberal thinker and his report led to the development of the UK welfare system which aimed to tackle the following problems:

- Want – people did not have sufficient income
- Idleness – there was unemployment because there were not enough jobs
- Squalor – poverty and poor housing conditions
- Ignorance – gaps in educational provision
- Disease – poor health was made worse by a lack of affordable and accessible medical care.

Despite the establishment of the UK welfare system, inequality persists and there is debate about the extent to which social policy can act as a mechanism through which to tackle such inequality. Chapter 7 explores the relationship between global social policy and inequality, addressing the question of whether it facilitates inequality or actually addresses it. Chapter 8 also explores social policy as a potential solution to inequality. In relation to more recent historical inequality, the evidence is that it is increasing. Milanovic (2009) shows that from 1820 to 2002 income inequality steadily rose and it seems very likely that, given the current global economic crisis, such inequalities are increasing. Given all of this evidence about inequality, why is it so important and of such concern?

Why does inequality matter?

1. Inequality results in health and social problems

Wilkinson and Pickett (2009) argue that within all societies both health and social problems are strongly associated with income. So ill health and social problems such as crime and violence are more common in the less economically well-off groups within all societies. Furthermore, the overall burden of these problems is much higher in the most unequal societies. The issue for Wilkinson and Pickett (2009) is that what matters is not poor material conditions *per se*, but the scale of differences between people within societies. Thus social gradients and the scale of inequality matter. Societies that are more equal generally do better, demonstrating that inequality matters. For Wilkinson (2011), social inequality is divisive and socially corrosive.

In addition, the problems associated with inequality are huge, with those in the lowest positions being the most detrimentally affected. Differential health outcomes are strongly correlated with inequality. The relationship between income and health is complex but, generally, individuals living in high-income countries tend to experience both better health and life chances when compared to those in lower income countries, as demonstrated by differential life expectancies in Table 1.4.

The evidence that poverty and inequality are associated with ill health is now overwhelming. In 2001, access to clean drinking water could have prevented the deaths of 2 million people – they simply needed access to uncontaminated food and clean drinking water (Kindhauser 2003). Put simply, within all societies death rates are typically highest among the poorest.

The mechanisms through which inequality affects health are still debated. For example, the psychosocial environmental interpretation explains that income affects

Table 1.4   Comparison of life expectancy across different countries

Approximate life expectancy (years)
Afghanistan – 42.6
Iceland – 80.1
Zimbabwe – 37.9
UK – 78.2

Source: http://www.worldlifeexpectancy.com/

health via the perceptions of place in the social hierarchy. These perceptions result in negative emotions which lead to poorer health outcomes. Marmot (2004) argues that autonomy, a sense of control over your life, and social connectedness are the greatest influences on health and both are related to social position. Comparatively, the neo-material interpretation suggests that health inequalities are the result of differential access to material resources within the social world (Lynch et al. 2008). These are all interesting debates but do not let them obscure the key message that social inequality results in health inequality.

The relationship between health and income is again complex. Wilkinson (1996) has demonstrated the importance of relative income in relation to health within societies. For example, although gross domestic product (GDP) is similar in Sweden and Britain, the poorest groups in Sweden can still expect to live longer than the poorest groups in Britain (Kunst et al. 1998). Wilkinson and Pickett (2009) also demonstrate how health outcomes fail to rise rapidly in countries when income reaches a certain point, showing that economic growth is not simply beneficial for health *per se*. Achieving good health in a low-income country can be made very difficult by poor sanitation, polluted water, lack of education, poor health care and a much higher risk of exposure to infectious diseases. The World Health Organization (WHO) has stated that extreme poverty is the most serious cause of disease. Indeed, 70% of deaths in low-income countries are attributable to five causes that can be easily and cheaply combated: pneumonia, diarrhoea, malaria, measles and malnutrition (WHO 1995). This is the true tragedy of inequality: that many preventable diseases lead to high death rates in poorer countries, and that 4,500 children die every day unnecessarily from avoidable diseases (WHO 2007).

Those who experience the worst inequality often find that their basic needs are not met. For example, they may lack access to water, shelter, clothing, sanitation and access to basic health care and education. Spending on health care is incredibly unevenly distributed across the world, with the poorest countries spending the equivalent of $11 per year per person, compared to an average US spend of $2,000 (WHO 2000). The 30 highest income nations account for 90% of the world's total health expenditure (WHO 2007). In addition, the very poor are also socially excluded, lack social and political rights and, most importantly, lack power (Pogge 2007).

2. Inequality generates political instability

Inequality is strongly associated with political instability. Ortiz and Cummins (2011) argue that unequal societies are much more prone to destabilisation, politically motivated violence and terrorism because conflict originates from social grievances and perceptions of inequality among groups. Inequality effects individual lives, results in more poverty and simply slows progress. This leaves more people feeling dissatisfied with their economic position and creates a society in which political consensus is hard to achieve. Justino (2004) analysed political conflict and rioting in India between 1973 and 2000. She concluded that redistributive policies are effective in diffusing conflicts which stemmed from the discontent experienced by those who were faced with persistent poverty and inequality. Therefore, societies need to be more equal in order to be more stable. Similarly, Alesina and Perotti (1996: 1225), after analysing 71 countries, conclude that 'income inequality increases socio-political instability which in turn decreases investment'.

Political instability also means that countries are less likely to secure investment and therefore development is often compromised and undermined. To achieve a favourable investment climate, political stability is highly important because investors do not want to face political changes that may result in economic changes, for example higher taxation rates. Countries that experience political instability often experience a vicious circle of low investment, then low or even negative growth, further poverty and social conflicts, and therefore further political instability (Soubbotina 2004). Given this, political instability is detrimental to the reduction of poverty levels, as has been seen in many African countries (Collier 2008).

3. Inequality impacts on the most vulnerable

In societies where there are high levels of income inequalities, more social inequalities exist. This is clear. Furthermore, these social inequalities are more likely to affect the most vulnerable members of society, such as children, the most. A UNICEF report (2011) analysing social inequalities demonstrated many negative outcomes for children living in lower income countries, as follows:

- They are less likely to attend primary school
- They are nearly twice as likely not to receive certain vaccinations, such as the measles immunisation
- They are twice as likely to die before they reach the age of 5
- They are significantly less likely to have access to clean drinking water
- Young girls are also three times more likely to be married before the age of 18.

Poverty is responsible for the deaths of 25,000 children each day. Indeed, the individuals who are socially excluded are powerless in being able to improve their situation because societal divisions reduce the possibility of accessing economic or political opportunities (United Nations 2009). As a result, many commentators argue that global inequality is an ethical issue (Singer 2002) and that governments should be charged with a moral imperative to tackle it. However, policy is not always an effective mechanism, as Chapters 7 and 8 discuss.

4. Inequality slows economic growth

Countries that have lower incomes and high levels of inequality tend to grow more slowly in economic terms (Ortiz and Cummins 2011). Economic growth is seen as necessary in neo-liberal theory in order to reduce inequalities. Neo-liberal approaches to economic policy, such as the promotion of free trade, deregulation, the removal of subsidies and often the privatisation of services, are seen to lead to economic growth, development and therefore poverty reduction. So, in theory, increasing wealth is seen to decrease poverty via a trickle-down effect. There is, however, contradictory evidence in relation to this theory, with some arguing that economic growth does not automatically result in reduced levels of inequality; rather 'it is a major factor in enriching the rich and further impoverishing the poor' (Bauman 2011: 50).

A study by the World Bank (2002) of countries developing between 1977 and 1997 showed that those who experienced economic growth did not demonstrate any significant changes in terms of income inequality. The World Bank (2005: 135) has also stated that 'the distributive effects of trade liberalisation are diverse and not always pro-poor'. Ortiz and Cummins (2011: 11) conducted a rapid review of global inequality and concluded that, given the clear levels of extreme inequality that exist in the world today, we need to question the current development model and ask 'development for whom?' Therefore, the current development model that is based on enhancing economic growth remains under critical scrutiny for some theorists. So while inequality may slow economic growth and therefore be seen as negative by economists, economic growth itself is unlikely to result in poverty reduction (see Chapters 7 and 8).

5. Inequality affects subjective well-being

Another important consideration is the question of whether inequality makes people unhappy – does inequality affect subjective well-being? The evidence is complex but interesting. For example, poor people gain more in subjective well-being from a dollar of extra income than rich people, but subjective well-being is also affected by a fall in income. What actually matters for subjective well-being are comparisons in income, with the general lesson being that comparing incomes can have a negative impact on well-being (i.e. if you earn less than your colleagues) but it may increase satisfaction when there are prospects for mobility (Chapple et al. 2009). Indeed, when income levels reach a certain point, well-being does not improve, even when income levels rise. Therefore, having more money does not result in greater happiness.

So overall, inequality clearly matters: it is divisive and socially corrosive (Wilkinson 2011) and has many negative effects. It is, however, still growing, particularly within nations, begging the question 'why does it persist?'

Why does inequality persist?

Dorling (2009) argues that there are many widespread beliefs that perpetuate inequality because there are enough resources for everyone; it is simply their distribution and associated control that is the real problem. He goes on to outline the key beliefs (the

five new evils that have replaced Beveridge's original evils) that he says are responsible for the persistence of inequality within contemporary society. These are:

- **Elitism is efficient** – the best succeed, while those who are limited do not. This ignores equality of opportunity and the benefits associated with privilege.
- **Exclusion is necessary** – those who occupy elite social positions argue that exclusion is necessary as part of achievement and success.
- **Prejudice is natural** – it is directed at those in the lowest social orders.
- **Greed is good** – this is because greed drives economic growth via purchasing and the demand for new goods, thus greed is the essence of successful capitalism. Mass car ownership is cited by Dorling (2009) as an example of such greed as it results in congestion, pollution and further selfishness.
- **Despair is inevitable** – this is seen in increased diagnoses of mental illness and happiness levels not being correlated with economic development, yet the demand for economic growth persists and is cited as the solution within political circles.

The central point that Dorling makes is that inequality continues because the dominant global ideology justifies it by locating the blame at the level of the individual and focusing attention away from those in the most powerful and richest positions. He is certainly not the only commentator to make this suggestion. Wade (2007) argues that income inequalities are assumed to be because of differences in effort and talent, or just luck, and so there is no moral need to have a more equal society. This has led many writers to suggest that it is more revealing to look at wealth and who holds it rather than examining poverty.

These debates are part of a broad academic discourse that explores how we account for global disparities, who we blame for poverty and what (if anything) should be done about inequality. Now complete the following Learning Task which explores the labelling of groups within the UK. Completing this Learning Task will also help you to reflect on Dorling's view that prejudice is constructed as natural.

Learning Task 1.4 – labelling those in powerless positions

1 Read the following extract from the BBC News website, published on Thursday 30 June 2005 (Wheeler 2005).

Leave chavs alone, say MPs

By Brian Wheeler

BBC News politics reporter

They are rapidly becoming the most vilified group in British society.

Lampooned by comedians, attacked by social commentators, portrayed by the media as loud, vulgar and abusive, and increasingly seen as a drain on the public finances.

Is there anyone out there who will take up the cudgels on behalf of that other much maligned social subset – the chav?

Since the word crossed over into the mainstream last year, after first appearing on satirical websites, chav has become a catch-all term for a flash or showy working class person.

Everyone from millionaire footballer Wayne Rooney and his girlfriend Colleen to the shoplifting single mother character Vicky Pollard, from BBC One's *Little Britain*, has been labelled a chav.

The Sun newspaper ran a 'proud to be chav' campaign.

'Underclass'

The word has even entered the dictionary, defined as 'a young working class person who dresses in casual sports clothing'.

But one chav-baiting website sums it up more succinctly as Britain's 'new peasant underclass'.

Michael Collins, author of *The Likes of Us*, a biography of the white working classes, says there is nothing new about the middle classes sneering at working class people who are a 'bit affluent' or showy.

But the difference with the chav phenomenon, he adds, is that much of the vitriol has come from people 'who consider themselves progressive'. 'It has become quite a jokey thing. But the white working class are the last acceptable group to demonise,' he says.

Liverpool MP Louise Ellman sees parallels with the way Liverpudlian youths were labelled 'scallies' in the 1980s.

'I think it is all too easy to label other groups with ugly-sounding words. I think it is negative and not very helpful,' she says.

2 Make a list of all of the negative labels that you can think of that are used to describe working-class people in the UK – there are many, including 'chav', as used in the article above.

3 Think about your own perspective. Do you use any of these words? Have you ever thought about why these words are so frequently used? Take time to think about the negative labelling of working-class groups in the UK, what purpose does it serve in your opinion?

What other labels can you think of that are negative? Labels do not just relate to class, they relate to gender, ethnicity and those who are disabled too.

Social inequality and poverty have received much attention from academics, the media, charities and global policy actors, with discussions always ongoing. However, there has been much less attention paid towards the wealthy, and while questions of deservingness are often asked about the poor, they are not applied to the rich in the same way (Rowlingson and Conner 2011). Put simply, poverty and social inequality are seen as significant social problems whereas wealth is not (Orton and Rowlingson 2007b). Indeed, several commentators argue that people do not make judgements about the rich in the same way that they do about the poor, and this is in effect part of the problem of the persistence of social inequality. George (2010: 70) argues that 'the economy, in our case the one that results from the preferences of those who are the richest and most powerful, decides how society will function.' She argues that it is the powerful and rich who ultimately create poverty and inequality.

There is stigma associated with social position in the UK, as defined by class. Stigma is also strongly associated with poverty across the world. Groups of people who experience poverty are often subject to 'othering' in that they are socially distanced from societal norms (Robertson 2011) and seen as being beyond normal hard-working people (Lister 2004). Those in poverty are often seen as a problem and are blamed for their poverty, resulting in stereotypes which do not represent the complex dynamics and experiences that are engendered by positions of poverty within contemporary society (Robertson 2011). This viewpoint has a purpose for those in powerful and rich positions in maintaining the status quo. It is a key belief that underpins neo-liberal ideology. Many commentators focus on neo-liberal ideology that underpins contemporary economics, arguing that it is this philosophy that results in the continued existence of social inequality.

Neo-liberalism is a school of thought that Giddens (2009: 1126) defines as 'the economic belief that free market forces, achieved by minimising government restrictions on business, provide the only route to economic growth'. The underlying assumption here is that free markets are positive and lead to economic development, which is also seen as good. Who holds power and manipulates the market is often overlooked within political circles, as are the consequences of neo-liberal policies which for many are the exacerbation of poverty (Stiglitz 2006).

There has been little research on public attitudes to economic inequality. Orton and Rowlingson (2007a) explored UK attitudes and found that the majority of people (73% in 2004) considered the gap between the rich and the poor as too large. People also thought that those on higher incomes were much overpaid. Interestingly, the values that people hold about luck and effort in determining individual success affects their attitudes. There were also complex opinions about redistributing wealth, so while people may recognise inequality as a problem, opinion, at least in the UK, is not clear in terms of how people believe it should be tackled. This remains the case globally, with academics debating the solutions and politicians on occasion ignoring the issue or offering different approaches (see Chapter 9 for further discussion about the solutions to social inequality).

Case Study: The silencing of inequality within policy circles?

Given the vast amount of research discussed in this chapter already, and the undeniable existence of social inequalities, what action is being delivered to try to tackle the issue? Chapters 7, 8 and 9 explore various aspects of policy and potential solutions to social inequality but a significant problem remains in that policy makers in many countries do not take action in relation to inequalities. Power can operate by excluding some ideas within the realm of political action (Bachrach and Baratz 1962; Lukes 1974). Smith (2007) argues that the work of Wilkinson is known in some political circles but it has been discussed in ways that reduce the importance of inequality. Stevens (2011) argues that Wilkinson's work has informed individuals who play a significant part in policy making, although, despite recognition of the harmful effects associated with inequality, there has been no significant action taken. Kingdon (1995) recognises the exclusion of information from policy streams, and Stevens (2011) argues that this is what has happened within UK policy circles. Policy programmes are not intended to address the causes of inequalities (Wilkinson and Pickett 2009). Stevens (2011: 252) concludes that, in telling policy stories and using evidence, UK civil servants '…were not encouraged to select evidence which challenged the status quo for use in telling these policy stories. These stories therefore ultimately supported the consolidation of power in the hands of the people who already hold it.' Problems with policy approaches used to tackle inequalities are not solely limited to the UK, as Chapter 7 discusses.

Summary of key points

- Defining and measuring social inequality is complex. Social inequality can be described and measured in a variety of ways but, despite debates about the approach used, there is a large evidence base demonstrating the existence of social inequality.
- Patterns of global social inequality are changing but the picture is complex, with some countries making progress and others falling further behind.
- Social inequality results in many negative outcomes, both at the level of the individuals experiencing the inequality but also at the level of society. Therefore inequality is bad *per se* for countries.

List of questions to stimulate debate and reflection

1 Think about the approaches to the measurement of social inequality discussed within this chapter. Which one do you feel is the most realistic in interpreting inequalities? Which measure or combined measures would you use if you were tasked with the job of measuring contemporary global inequality?

2 Think about your own subjective view of inequality. Who do you compare yourself to and how does this inform your thinking about your societal position? Consider the ways in which your own subjective construction of societal position influences your view about other people and their position.

3 Pay attention to the media, watch the news, read newspapers and look at newspaper articles online. When there are stories that touch on social inequalities, how are these discussed?

Further reading

Held, David and Kaya, Ayse (eds) (2007) *Global Inequality.* Cambridge: Cambridge University Press.

This book contains chapters from many of the key names in the field of inequality. The book is a comprehensive overview, discussing the conceptualisation measurement and analysis of contemporary patterns of global inequality. It touches on social policy and goes on to highlight an intensive debate about whether and to what extent inequality matters.

The UC Atlas of Global Inequality, http://ucatlas.ucsc.edu/

This is a fantastic online resource which explores several aspects of inequality using maps and graphics. The Atlas explores debates among academics about whether inequality is rising or falling. It also focuses on inequality beyond income measures. It contains really useful sections on health, gender and economic crises. There is a student friendly glossary, providing an explanation of the issues and terms, which is directly linked to the reported research.

Wilkinson, Richard and Pickett, Kate (2009) *The Spirit Level: Why Equal Societies Almost Always Do Better.* London: Allen & Unwin.

This is an excellent book compiling information from over 200 sets of data to produce a wealth of evidence that shows that inequality exists and has detrimental effects. The book shows that inequality shortens lives, increases violence and affects relationships between different social groups within society as well as damaging the environment. It contains strong messages about social policy and the political will required to tackle inequality. The writers also have a website which makes for very interesting reading too. See www.equalitytrust.org.uk/

2

SOCIAL DIVISIONS AND INEQUALITY: AN OVERVIEW

> ## Key learning outcomes
>
> By the end of this chapter you should be able to:
>
> - Understand the relationship between social inequality and numerous social divisions
>
> - Understand that social divisions do not exist in isolation; rather they are interrelated
>
> - Understand the different ideological positions associated with explaining the existence of social divisions

Overview of the chapter

This chapter will provide an overview of the importance of how inequality operates and relates to different social divisions across society. Chapters 3, 4 and 5 offer more detailed discussion of the social divisions of class, gender and ethnicity, whereas this chapter explores age, social exclusion, area effects, health, disability and sexuality. The chapter shows that social status and individual social characteristics relate to experiences of inequality in very different ways. The relationship between social divisions and social inequality is illustrated as being complex, with the chapter constantly touching on these complexities. The chapter also demonstrates the importance of status in relation to societal position and inequality. Power and powerlessness are also key considerations when exploring inequality, and so the chapter critically explores how power is related to social divisions and larger structural influences within society through the introduction and discussion of a number of different theoretical explanations for the existence of social divisions. This chapter discusses inequality within various contexts and guises to show that inequality arises in all places across the globe and this is represented in numerous social divisions.

Overview of contemporary inequality

As Chapter 1 highlighted, there are many areas in which social inequality arises and this occurs across various social divisions. Despite the many debates that exist about how to define and measure the different aspects of social inequality, it remains the case that the world today is depicted as more unequal than ever before, with evidence showing how patterns of inequality are worsening, particularly within countries. Given the many types of inequality highlighted in Chapter 1, this chapter examines a number of social divisions in more depth, illustrating how they are important in relation to inequality and how they are explained within the contemporary literature. As this book demonstrates throughout, social inequality and social divisions are ever-present within the world today and affect us all. Now complete the following Learning Task which will help you to explore the social divisions that your life encompasses.

Learning Task 2.1 – exploring how social divisions intersect in your life

Think about the social world that you inhabit. For example, as a student, are you at university? Have you ever considered the types of social stratification evident at the university where you are studying? Take some time and make some notes on the following questions:

1 What categories of people are unequal? Are there gender or ethnic differences in your class, school, living accommodation, etc.? What does your teaching team look like and what divisions are evident there? Who holds the most powerful positions within your institution and what divisions can you see within the hierarchy of management?
2 If you were to rank the people in your class in terms of social divisions, where would they be? Does categorising them in such a way obscure more nuanced social divisions and mask the complexity of the divisions that are visible in everyday life? What divisions are evident in your everyday life?

---

3 In what ways are you advantaged when compared to other people? Also think about the ways in which you may be disadvantaged in comparison to others within your social network, such as friends, family members and colleagues?
4 In what ways are the people that you know unequal? On what basis are you making these decisions?

What about the stratification evident within other areas of your life, for example, your work environment and your family? Consider the ways in which your experiences of stratification may change as you move through your own life course.

In completing the Learning Task, you will have been able to develop your thinking more critically in relation to your own social circles and how social inequality is manifested throughout them. Table 2.1 gives an overview of many of the social divisions explored in the current literature and demonstrates the many divisions that are recognised as existing today. Did you think about all of these divisions when completing the first Learning Task? Table 2.1 includes suggestions for further reading to allow you to explore each social division in more depth.

Table 2.1 An overview of many recognised social divisions explored within the contemporary literature

Social division	Description	Suggestions for further reading
Social class and stratification (see Chapter 3)	• Social class is defined as 'social stratification resulting from the unequal distribution of wealth, power and prestige' (Macionis and Plummer 2008: 238). • This division is based upon economic divisions and individual occupations. • It is also related to social status – higher social classes have more status.	• Rosemary Crompton's (2008) *Class and Stratification* (Cambridge: Polity Press) is a comprehensive description of class analysis, measurement and related debates. • Wendy Bottero (2010) 'What is social stratification?', in Anthony Giddens and Phillip Sutton (eds), *Sociology: Introductory Readings* (Cambridge: Polity Press), pp. 137–43 is a good introduction to the concept of social stratification.
Income, wealth and poverty	• The world's wealth is concentrated in the hands of a minority (see Chapter 1). • Those in the richest sections of society are arguably increasing their wealth. • Absolute poverty remains a significant problem for many individuals across the world (see Chapter 1).	• Ruth Levitas (2006) writes about social exclusion in Christina Pantazis et al. (eds), *Poverty and Social Exclusion in Britain* (Bristol: Policy Press), which is an interesting read overall. • Jeremy Seabrook's (2003) *No-nonsense Guide to World Poverty* (Oxford: New Internationalist) is a short but excellent introduction to the problem of poverty across the globe.

(Continued)

Table 2.1   (Continued)

Social division	Description	Suggestions for further reading
Education and qualifications	• There are large educational divisions within society, between those who achieve different qualifications as well as between those who gain qualifications and those who do not. • The measurement of educational success according to outputs serves to socially divide and exclude. • Educational inequalities are evident along gender lines, between different ethnic groups and between different social classes.	• Yossi Shavit et al. (eds) (2007) *Stratification in Higher Education* (Standford, CA: Stanford University Press) compares educational inequalities across 15 different countries. • A.H. Halsey et al.'s (eds) (1997) *Education: Culture, Economy and Society* (Oxford: Oxford University Press) is a collection of key papers from the sociology of education field.
Gender (see Chapter 4)	• Men and women are socially divided. • Inequalities exist between men and women. • Men and women have different social roles and occupations but these are not natural; rather they are structural and based upon power differentials. • Notions of masculinity and femininity influence and constrain both men and women in different ways.	• Judith Lorber's (2009) *Gender Inequality: Feminist Theory and Politics* (Oxford: Oxford University Press) is an interesting read, focusing upon feminism across global contexts. • Jacqueline L. Scott and Clare Lyonette (2010) *Gender Inequalities in the 21st Century: New Barriers and Continuing Constraints* (London: Edward Elgar) looks at the global economy and changing gender dynamics experienced by both men and women.
Ethnicity (see Chapter 5)	• There is no universal definition of the concept of ethnicity but there is recognition that boundaries are created and maintained between different ethnic groups (Jenkins 1997). • Ethnicity is associated with cultural identities. • Ethnic identity results in social divisions between societal groups. • Different ethnic groups are clustered in specific occupations and geographical areas, signifying social division.	• John Hutchinson and Anthony Smith's (eds) (1996) *Ethnicity* (Oxford: Oxford University Press) covers the key debates. • Steve Fenton (2010) *Ethnicity* (Cambridge: Polity Press) comprehensively and critically discusses the concept.
Age	• Globally, people are generally living longer. • Existing social divisions, such as gender and class divides, become exaggerated in later life, while age remains a division in its own right. • Material deprivation is a significant social division for many older people. • Older people can face negative attitudes in some societies. • Childhood is also socially constructed and affected by power differentials.	• John Vincent's (2003) *Old Age* (New York: Routledge) covers the key aspects of ageing and shows age as a social division in its own right. • Karl Mayer (2009) in *New Directions in Life-Course Research* discusses the life-course approach and how this relates to the social division of age in *Annual Review of Sociology*, 35: 413–33.

Social division	Description	Suggestions for further reading
Social exclusion	• This term is used to describe the ways in which individuals may find themselves excluded when facing multidimensional barriers to participation within society.	• John Hills, Julian Le Grand and David Piachaud (eds) (2002) *Understanding Social Exclusion* (Oxford: Oxford University Press) is a good introduction to the concept of social exclusion, exploring definitions of the concept and how it can be measured.
Location, housing and geography	• The area in which you live can act as a social division and lead to social exclusion. • The type of housing that you occupy is associated with social status. • Area effects are well documented in the literature as associated with numerous social problems.	• Lynsey Hanley's (2007) *Estates: An Intimate History* (London: Granta Books) is an interesting chronicle of social housing within the UK, demonstrating the importance of policy and status associated with housing. • Diana Wilkinson's (1999) *Poor Housing and Ill Health* (Edinburgh: Scottish Office Research Unit) is also UK-focused but is a clear summary of research evidence linking poor quality housing to ill-health, and to social divisions.
Social status	• Status is a social division within contemporary society, associated with money, prestige, material possessions, home and lifestyle. • Status is a marker of position within a consumerist world. • Those with the least social status are socially excluded and viewed negatively.	• Richard Sennett's (2003) *Respect* (New York: W.W. Norton and Co.) discusses the relationship between respect and inequality. • James Owen's (2011) *Chavs* (London: Verso) is an interesting discussion of the negative labelling of the working class within contemporary Britain.
Disability	• Disabled people are effectively excluded from many areas of social life and society. • Disabled individuals are less likely to be employed when compared to able-bodied individuals. • Disabled people are more likely to experience poverty and discrimination (Hyde 2000).	• Colin Barnes and Geoff Mercer's (2003) *Disability* (Oxford: Wiley-Blackwell) provides a clear and concise introduction to the issues associated with disability. • Lenard Davis (ed.) (1997) *The Disability Studies Reader* (London: Routledge) is a collection of critical analyses and discussion from the field of disability studies.
Health	• Vast health inequalities exist across the world. • The poorest sections of society are those that are most likely to die younger, experience more ill health and face difficulties with access to health care, and indeed the cost of such care. • Ill-health can socially exclude people from society by affecting their identity and ability to engage in usual societal activities.	• The Marmot Review Team's (2010) *Fair Society, Healthy Lives* (London: The Marmot Review) is an independent review of health inequalities in England, reporting key data. • Jim Yong Kim et al.'s (2000) *Dying for Growth: Global Inequality and the Health of the Poor* (Monroe, ME: Commons Courage Press) is a clear account of the connection between poverty and illness.

(Continued)

Table 2.1   (Continued)

Social division	Description	Suggestions for further reading
Sexuality	• Heterosexuality is viewed as normal within society at many levels, such as via the institution of marriage, social security systems and popular culture. • Sexuality is commodified within contemporary society, which serves to mask the inequalities that exist within gender relations and sexual practices (Scott and Jackson 2000). • Gay and lesbian sexualities are marginalised, resulting in discrimination (Scott and Jackson 2000).	• Stevi Jackson and Sue Scott's (eds) (1996) *Feminism and Sexuality: A Reader* (Edinburgh: Edinburgh University Press) is a collection discussing feminist contributions and debates in the field of sexuality. • Steven Seidman's (1996) *Queer Theory/ Sociology* (Oxford: Blackwell) is a nice introduction to the sociology of sexuality.

Table 2.1 shows the range of social divisions that are recognised within the literature but is by no means exhaustive. Furthermore, while the table depicts divisions in isolation, this is not the case. In reality, many overlap and are interrelated. These divisions are explored in depth in this and later chapters. Now complete the following Learning Task which will help you to think about how your own characteristics are related to unequal opportunities, particularly in relation to work opportunities.

Learning Task 2.2 – your own personal characteristics and inequalities

Have you ever considered how your personal circumstances may affect your life chances? In completing this Learning Task you can explore how your individual characteristics are likely to affect how you progress in your career?

1 Use the internet to access the following website: www.open.edu/ openlearn/money-management/management/leadership-and-management/leading/boardroom-lottery
2 Complete the board room challenge, entering your own personal data.

Now consider what the challenge told you. Were you surprised by the results? What did completing this challenge tell you regarding social inequalities in general?

Now that you have explored how you may experience stratification in your own personal life, related to work and your life circumstances, it is time to consider some of the many ways in which societies are socially divided, based on the summary offered in Table 2.1.

Age

Age is an individual characteristic resulting in social division across societies because life is periodicised through age strata sequences. The life course leads to moving from one side of the division to the other. Older age is accompanied by retirement and therefore exit from the labour market, which results in lifestyle changes and associated changes in status. Age is perceived differently across societies – old age can be highly valued or viewed as low status. Definitions of old age also vary cross-culturally and within societies, so again there are complexities here. This means that the ageing experience is very different for people within differing social contexts. Globally, society is simply greying, with all societies ageing, but this is not happening equally and there are massive inequalities in terms of life expectancy, as highlighted in Chapter 1.

The United Nations (2011a) chronicles the demographic changes resulting in older populations everywhere. Fertility rates are declining and the proportion of people aged 60 and over is expected to double between 2007 and 2050. In most countries, the number of those aged over 80 is likely to quadruple to almost 400 million by 2050. This transition has massive implications for the organisation of society and so will bring many related challenges. For example, increasing life expectancy does not necessarily result in healthy life expectancy. There may be an increased need for health and social care as a result of ageing populations and this poses funding challenges. Social class intersects the division of age in that groups of people of the same age have distinct sets of life chances as a result of their position in the social strata. The material deprivation and inequality structured by class and gender, become exaggerated in later life. Therefore, those who found it difficult to enter the labour market and who achieved poor rewards for their labour tend in their old age to be among the most materially deprived in the population. This is borne out in global data with United Nations' (2011b) analyses demonstrating that:

- In OECD countries 13.3% of people aged over 65 are poor, on average, compared to 10.6% of the general population.
- In nine out of 15 countries in Sub-Saharan Africa, poverty levels in households that included an older person were significantly higher than the population average.

Where data is present and analysed, it demonstrates that poverty among older persons tends to be higher than for the rest of the population. The relative risk of old-age poverty is also higher when compared to the rest of the population (United Nations 2011a). As women outnumber men in the older population, there has been a feminisation of poverty in older age. However, this trend is changing, with more men living longer (Office for National Statistics, *Social Trends*, 2004).

The challenges of an ageing society are raising humanitarian concerns in lower income countries because change is occurring rapidly and many older people have low incomes, poor health and little social protection, such as welfare or health care services. Consequently, older people within these societies are much more likely to be ignored because of the multitude of other problems that exist, resulting in age being a more significant social division for inhabitants of these countries (Harper 2006). There are many social implications of ageing, including changes in health status, changes in work status, the experience of inequalities and challenges such as isolation.

Explaining age-based divisions

Functionalist theorists suggest that older people have to adjust to their changing role within the broader societal context. Parsons (1960) argued that roles for older people that could utilise their wisdom and experience do not exist within western society because of the dominance of a focus on youth and the avoidance of death. While he recognised that older people would have to psychologically adjust to their new circumstances, he also said that new and productive roles needed to be found for them. Disengagement theory builds on these arguments by suggesting that older people should disengage from society when they are no longer useful, as this enables society to function more effectively (Cumming and Henry 1961). However, this is a very negative conceptualisation of the ageing process and not necessarily how older people view themselves or their age-related transitions (Howard et al. 1986). Furthermore, with many countries re-examining the age of retirement and extending it, as well as the non-paid roles assumed by older people such as volunteering and caring, the idea that older people are less useful is neither valid nor acceptable. Theoretical interpretations have developed more positively, with the life-course perspective viewing ageing as a process that continues from birth to death (Giddens 2009).

Political economy interpretations have also analysed ageing as part of economic and political systems that reproduce power and inequalities (Estes et al. 2003). For example, women who are unable to participate fully in the labour market due to caring responsibilities earn less and therefore contribute less to pension schemes, if they contribute at all. At retirement they are further disadvantaged and face more financial hardship, showing how inequalities in older age are related to social forces within society. However, on a more positive note, attitudes to older people are shifting and becoming more positive. A recent report (Humphrey et al. 2011) explored people's attitudes towards old age (i.e. beyond the age of 70) as well as experiences of ageism across 28 countries. The key findings of the report showed that:

- Respondents in countries where there is a higher proportion of older people held more positive attitudes, suggesting that societal attitudes shift as populations age.
- Older people's status was perceived to be higher in countries that had later state pension ages.
- Age discrimination is still an issue because it had been experienced by approximately one-third of all respondents.
- Age discrimination is complex and affected by a variety of individual characteristics. Thus, ageism was experienced more by younger people, the less educated, those who perceived themselves to be poorer, the unemployed, and those who live in cities.

Old age is by no means the only age category in which disadvantage is an issue. Evidence also demonstrates how younger people are often excluded and face many social divisions. *The State of the World's Children* report (UNICEF 2011) highlights some of the challenges faced by young people and focuses particularly on the vulnerability faced by adolescents, especially disadvantaged young girls. The report stresses the importance of the rights of young people as well as outlining the challenges that they face. Indeed, Jackson and Scott (2000) show that children experience the social divisions of gender, ethnicity and class while also facing the major division between their childhood status and that of adulthood, in which power relations are central. Social divisions often result in some form of social exclusion. For example, given global trends in technological development, and the pace of change in the postmodern, hi-tech world, older people will be faced with a form of exclusion from the contemporary world if they are unable to participate in social life due to their lack of technological capability. Thus, technological exclusion is just one aspect of social exclusion.

Social exclusion

There are many aspects of social exclusion identified within the contemporary literature, and there are many debates about what social exclusion is not. For example, it is not just about poverty, and is often complex in that social class position can result in social exclusion, as can age, gender, ethnicity, employment status and location. See 'Defining social exclusion' page 6.

Clearly, social exclusion is a complex concept. Furthermore, the relationship between social exclusion and the distribution of income is not the same in all societies because it is affected by the extent of commodification as well as the costs of public and private services (Barry 1998). Dorling (2009) highlights a range of people who experience social exclusion within contemporary Britain, and therefore conceptualises the experience of exclusion in a broad framework, summarised in Table 2.2.

Table 2.2   Overview of the many diverse aspects of social exclusion

Area of exclusion	Summary of what the exclusion entails	Evidence
Education	Within the affluent world young people are often seen as: • Failing to meet specific standards defined by uniform measures. • Being unsuitable for higher education such as university.	• Labels are applied to those who are least able. • Certain and specific types of knowledge are seen as more valuable. • Universities recruit the elite – those who attend private schools are more likely to gain university places, especially at the more prestigious institutions.
Excluding people from society	Changing societal dynamics has led to the development of the new poor who: • Lack the necessities required to be socially included. • Become indebted to keep up appearances and participate in perceived essentials such as holidays and other possessions.	• Taking holidays is a social norm within Europe. • Debt is accrued mostly by those who receive lower than average wages in Europe as these groups are attempting to keep up their social standing through consuming.
Racism	• Racism was clear in Europe in the 1970s but attitude surveys now demonstrate that younger people's attitudes to racism are changing, as they view it as less acceptable. • Racism still exists and contemporary patterns of racism are changing.	• Those who have no choice over the work they do are often seen as less able despite this being a myth. • Attitudes to work have changed massively, with certain types of job being deemed unsuitable for people of specific social standing. • Fear of immigration and asylum seekers is commonly seen in the world's media.
Greed	• Greed has been constructed as good within contemporary society despite its role in perpetuating inequalities and damaging the world.	• The rich increasingly take greater shares of what is valued in society. • The people most likely to need goods are the ones least likely to have them. • Rising inequality is seen as good. • The cult of celebrity and watching the super-rich demonstrates shifting societal values that continue to perpetuate inequality.

Area of exclusion	Summary of what the exclusion entails	Evidence
Despair	• People are not immune to inequality and all of the associated problems that it results in.	• Rising rates of depression within unequal populations, including among young people. • The increasing rates of anxiety that are being reported are a result of the way in which we live and contemporary values. • The mass medicating of the rich population is part of profit-making.

Source: Adapted from Dorling (2009)

Dorling (2009) shows how individuals are excluded within society in many ways and have little choice. Many analyses have depicted social exclusion as something that happens to minority groups, but Dorling's (2009) illustration is one in which many members of society face exclusion. Indeed, Barry (1998) cites the example of Apartheid in South Africa as a regime in which the minority of whites successfully excluded the rest of the population from accessing education, occupations and political positions. He also argues that the rich in society can be socially excluded but they achieve this through choice in that they are able to erect barriers to keep out others. This can clearly be seen within gated communities, in which like-minded people live together in secure and well-protected communities. Thus, there are different levels of social exclusion which are more evident in some societies than in others. Table 2.3 shows the different

Table 2.3   The different levels of social exclusion evident within the USA

The lower level of social exclusion	The higher level of social exclusion
• Inhabitants of poor areas receive little or no police protection.	• The inhabitants of gated communities need little police protection because they can afford to employ their own security guards.
• The inhabitants of poorer areas have little contact with state schools because of truancy and early drop-outs.	• The inhabitants of richer areas have little contact with state schools because they attend private schools.
• Those in the poorer sections of society do not take part in ordinary politics and often do not vote.	• Those in richer social groups do not take part in ordinary politics because they have direct access to the decision makers through their financial contributions.
• Those in the poorer social groups lack access to specific types of health care and treatment.	• Those in the richest social groups have access to all of the health care services and treatment that they can buy.

Source: Adapted from Barry (1998)

types of exclusion experienced in the USA through power (choice) and power-less (lack of choice).

The existence of gated communities shows the importance of location and neighbourhood dynamics. Indeed, the area in which you live can also result in social exclusion as a result of area effects, inequality and close relationships between areas and social status.

Area effects

In analysing contemporary social divisions, attention has increasingly become focused on place as well as employment relations, social class, gender and all of the other divisions that are described in this chapter. The relationship between space and stratification is therefore receiving much more attention within the literature for a variety of reasons. Chapter 1 outlined the extent of global inequality that exists and the indisputable evidence to support this. Inequality is thus tied to place because the global context in which we are geographically located influences our lives and experiences of inequality. Inequality within countries is also visible across geographical divides.

In a recent publication called *Bankrupt Britain*, Dorling and Thomas (2011) provide a geographical analysis of inequality depicted through maps of the social changes that are affecting Britain. Chapter by chapter, they produce a fascinating insight into the spatial inequalities that permeate Britain today, showing areas that have the highest rates of unemployment, areas experiencing high residential repossessions, differential crime rates across areas as well as comparisons in well-being and environmental differences. The book is a fascinating insight into how inequality in a number of guises is geographically located, demonstrating the importance of place within contemporary analyses. Dorling and Thomas (2011) focus exclusively on Britain, but there is a geographically broader evidence base that highlights area effects in relation to inequality globally.

The 'world cities' approach analyses how space occupation is changing within cities across the world. Many cities have become the cornerstones of the global capitalist economy and therefore face new and changing divisions of labour. However, some argue that the notion of a divided city is not a new idea. Marcuse (1993) argues that cities have been divided since the industrial revolution, with spatial segregation related to inequality being as clear in history as it is today. He usefully describes contemporary cities as being based on a number of divisions, which are summarised in Table 2.4.

Table 2.4 shows that patterns of social divisions are spatial as well as hierarchical. However, spatial patterns are not rigid and contemporary spatial inequalities can be differentiated from historical ones by increases in homelessness, the growth of certain areas such as the abandoned city and the gentrified city, and the role of the government in dividing the city for private interests (Marcuse 1993).

Table 2.4   Divided cities

Type of division	Description of the division
Luxury housing	• Often not really part of the city. • Those at the top of the social, political and economic scale live in these places. • Can be gated communities, to exclude the less socially desirable.
The gentrified city	• Parts of the city occupied by professional and managerial groups. • These may be young professionals, those who are married and includes those who have children.
The suburban city	• This is the housing that is occupied by skilled workers and mid-range professionals. • These types of housing are places in the outer city or apartments near the centre.
The tenement city	• This is the type of housing occupied by lower-paid workers, such as blue- and white-collar workers. • Often rental properties rather than owned. • Often includes social housing.
The abandoned city	• This is the accommodation left over for the poorest sections of society, such as the unemployed and excluded. • Includes homes for the homeless.

Source: Adapted from Marcuse (1993)

Explaining area-based divisions

Much analysis of the changing city has been conducted through the theoretical lens of social polarisation, in which changing economic demands have created new high-powered and well-paid jobs, such as those in the fields of banking and insurance. Other jobs, such as service sector occupations like security and cleaning, are less well paid. This has led to occupational polarisation, matched with associated changes in residential locations (Sassen 1991). Here the social divisions of class and area effects intersect. Not all agree with this analysis. Hamnett (1994, 1996, 1998, 2003) argues that while income inequality is growing, there is little evidence to support the polarisation thesis. His interpretation is that rather than the workforce polarising, there are groups of employed insiders and unemployed outsiders, that is, those who exist outside of the labour market. Hamnett (2003) describes 'socio-tenurial polarisation', recognising the growing distinction between home owners and those who rent accommodation. Broader analyses also examine area-effects in relation to inequality rather than just home ownership and location of residence.

There is a wealth of research that has examined area effects for many years. Wilson (1987) argues that poor neighbourhoods can be seen as systematically disadvantaging their residents as they isolate them from opportunity structures. Neighbourhood effects have been analysed in relation to child development, educational outcomes, teenage pregnancies, health, employment and delinquency, with research generally showing that poor neighbourhoods lead to poor outcomes (Jencks and Mayer 1990). This area of research remains important for area-based policy (Lupton 2003).

Area effects have more recently been analysed through the conceptual framework of social capital. Social capital is a concept defined in a variety of ways, for example as levels of trust (Fukuyama 1999), networks (Putnam, 2000) and family relationships (Coleman 1998). While ongoing debates exist in the academic literature about what social capital is and how it can best be measured, some commentators argue that all forms of social capital matter because the processes that prevent poverty and social exclusion depend on capital in many forms (Piachard 2002). In relation to area effects Atkinson and Kintrea (2004) cite empirical evidence to demonstrate that deprivation and routes out of it within British cities are clearly linked to the range of social networks, the reference groups of individuals and the values held within them. Similarly, network characteristics arguably help shape individuals' responses to structural constraints and opportunities (Cattell 2004). Narayan (1999) pays particular attention to the potential for the less powerful and more socially excluded groups to benefit from bridging ties. She argues that effective bonding and bridging ties are required to avoid social exclusion. The following Learning Task will help you to explore how social capital is important in your own life.

Learning Task 2.3 – understanding your own social network

Draw a diagram like the one in Figure 2.1 to map out your own social networks.

1 Think about the interactions you have had with other people, associations and organisations over the past month.
2 List the types of networks you belong to. Do you play sport? Belong to other clubs? Religious groups? What about your family networks? Your local community networks?
3 Think particularly about the area in which you live and the networks that you are a member of there.
4 Below is an example to help you think about your network.

Finally, think about how the picture might look if you lived in an area that was socially isolated, where you did not have social support. Imagine that the area faced a variety of social problems, such as anti-social behaviour, poverty and lack of employment. Now redraw the diagram. Take time to consider area effects as part of the problem of social inequality, viewing these through the lens of social capital as networks.

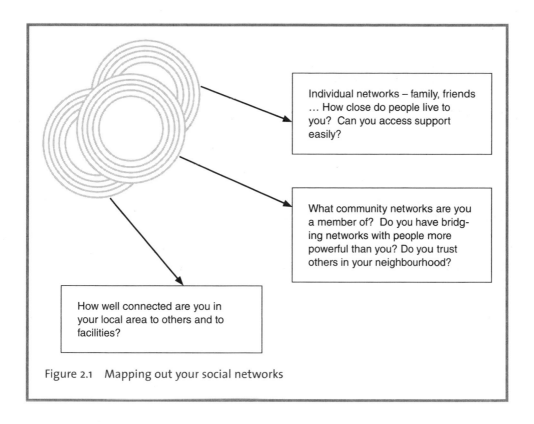

Individual networks – family, friends … How close do people live to you? Can you access support easily?

What community networks are you a member of? Do you have bridging networks with people more powerful than you? Do you trust others in your neighbourhood?

How well connected are you in your local area to others and to facilities?

Figure 2.1   Mapping out your social networks

The above Learning Task is to help you to think about how social inequality can be explored through the concept of social capital in relation to area effects and neighbourhoods. The evidence is again overwhelming in clearly demonstrating inequality in relation to space – the place in which you reside is also important in terms of social status. Hanley's (2007) history of social housing in the UK shows the lack of status afforded to those who live on estates. She outlines how UK estates are symbolically associated with poverty, social problems such as drug use, graffiti and anti-social behaviour, including problem youth, and neighbour disputes. The lack of status afforded to living in such a place is shown to result in denial from many about the location in which they live. The central point of Hanley's (2007) book is that the place in which you live, your home, is the largest social division within contemporary society. Your home and all that is associated with it, such as whether you own it, the size of it and where it is located, are all related to social status as well as inequality. However, while the points raised by Hanley (2007) about housing and inequality are important, other theorists point to inequalities that can be seen to be as important in influencing social position. This includes disability.

Disability

Disability is defined as different by the medical profession because disabled bodies are seen to be outside the realm of normality by members of society and indeed the medical profession. Research into the experience of disability demonstrates that those who are severely disabled, who seem to have a poor quality of life to outsiders, actually report that their quality of life is excellent or good (Albrecht and Devlieger 1999). This demonstrates a lack of understanding within general societal perceptions and constructions of disability.

There has also been a body of research showing how dependency is constructed by society not adapting itself to the needs of specific groups of people, making it more difficult for them to get out of their homes (Grundy and Bowling 1991). There are many ways in which disabled people are socially excluded, stigmatised and treated as differently across the globe. Thus, disability is fundamentally related to social inequality, as demonstrated by the following statistics (DEMOS and SCOPE 2006):

- More than 40% of disabled people in England and Wales experienced difficulty with travel.
- While almost two-thirds of households that include a disabled person do not have access to a private car, only 27% of non-disabled households don't have a car.
- The report describes the lack of accessible housing in the UK as 'chronic'. While it is estimated that nearly 1.5 million people require adapted accommodation, almost a quarter of them don't have it. There is also a lack of reliable information about the availability of accessible housing and this contributes to the problem.
- In terms of status, disabled people are more likely to be the victims of hate crimes or mercy killings, but less likely to appear on television or occupy a prominent role in public life.
- *The Global Burden of Disease* statistics (World Health Organization 2008a) demonstrate that disability in a variety of forms is a significant global issue, and many countries have inadequate provision to deal with this. However, in 2006 only 45 countries had introduced legislation aimed at protecting the rights of disabled people (United Nations 2006).

The UK is still often heavily criticised for its approach to dealing with disabled individuals, despite having laws related to disability. There have been recent reports in the UK media discussing how more positive views of disability have been created through the 2012 Paralympic Games. However, whether these positive perceptions translate into social changes remain to be seen. Indeed, as transport issues were also reported for disabled competitors accessing the Olympic Park, clearly many barriers remain (Radnedge 2012).

Given that the UK has disability legislation, the existence of inequalities and discrimination related to disability is disappointing. Attitudes do, of course, take time to change, and there are many places around the world that remain much further behind the UK in both their attitudes towards the disabled and the way in which they support disabled individuals. Indeed, the disabled in countries without welfare provision and specialist support experience much more inequality than those in the UK.

Explaining disability as a social division

The academic field of disability studies has brought attention to the ways in which conventional understandings of disability have served to disadvantage those who are disabled. Traditionally, the medical model of disability locates the causes of disability in the individual body. This is linked to individualistic understandings of disability which have formed the dominant discourse of societal understandings. Those who are disabled have different bodies and it is these bodies that cause them problems. Comparatively, a social model of disability locates the causes of disability as a form of social oppression and discrimination. Individualistic understandings see disability as located in the individual – a tragedy – and thus disabled individuals need professional help. Comparatively, the social model suggests that disability needs to be seen as a consequence of social attitudes, design and a lack of civil rights (Oliver 1990).

This social model of disability has challenged traditional understandings and shaped contemporary ways of understanding disability. Furthermore, in focusing on civil rights, the social model of disability has provided impetus for political strategies, advocacy and social movements which attempt to effect positive change for those who are disabled. However, the social model can be criticised for overlooking pain and bodily experiences, as well as the importance of the label of 'disabled' for some individuals (Barnes 2003). There are indeed a wide range of experiences related to disability and these are shaped by social contexts in which people live. It remains the case that disabled people are one of the most disadvantaged groups in the world, even in higher income countries (Giddens 2009). They also experience health issues and related inequalities. Health, too, is linked to social inequalities, as this book demonstrates throughout.

Health inequalities

The existence of health inequalities within society has been of huge interest for many years, with a large bank of evidence demonstrating their existence. In the UK, the publication of the Black Report in 1982 (Townsend and Davidson 1982) detailed a social gradient in terms of health outcomes, demonstrating large differences between the social classes, genders and ethnic groups in terms of health outcomes (see Graham 2000). The report showed that those in the lowest social class are far more likely to die at a younger age irrespective of their other social characteristics, such as gender and ethnicity. Furthermore, the report and later evidence shows that the lower social classes are also more likely to experience higher levels of morbidity, which is greater ill health during their lifespan. Finally, the Black Report indicated the existence of inequalities in relation to the utilisation of health services, so despite the existence of the NHS within the UK – a service free at the point of delivery, allowing everyone equal access – it remains the case that those positioned in the lowest social classes actually make less use of the service than those located higher up the class scale. It is also interesting that evidence about health inequalities shows that even when worse-off individuals do use health services at the same rates as better-off people, the health of poorer individuals still remains worse, demonstrating that health service usage is not the key to addressing health inequalities.

Since the publication of the Black Report, there has been a plethora of research and related policy documents within the UK investigating health inequalities. The World Health Organization also held a Commission on the Social Determinants of Health (2008b). There is therefore an overwhelming amount of evidence to support the argument that health outcomes and life chances are heavily influenced by our societal position, with a bank of evidence now available indicating vast inequalities in health globally. The social divisions of class, gender and ethnicity also all impact on both morbidity and mortality:

- In 2002 UK figures show that the average life expectancy for women was 80.4 years, whereas men had a life expectancy of just 75.7. So there was a gender difference of 4.7 years (Gjonca et al. 2005).
- In 2007 UK figures show that South Asian men were 50% more likely to have a heart attack or to experience angina than men in the general population (Parliamentary Office of Science and Technology 2007).
- In 2010 UK national statistics show that professional males live an average of 12.5 years longer than those working in manual occupations. For women, the average gap was 11.4 years (Office for National Statistics 2010).
- A United Nations Commission set up in 1999 demonstrated that there is a disproportionate disease burden experienced by lower income countries (Brundtland 2003).
- Millions of poor people die from preventable and treatable conditions simply because of their societal position (Sachs 2001).
- One-fifth of all global deaths in 2004 were children under 5 years of age, often as a result of malnutrition (World Health Organization 2008a).

Explaining health inequalities

Despite the marshalling of large amounts of evidence to demonstrate health inequalities, explaining their existence is complicated. The Black Report (Townsend and Davidson 1982) began to debate explanations for health inequalities and offers the reader four potential answers as to why inequalities exist. Table 2.5 provides a summary of the explanations for the existence of health inequalities, including the four given in the Black Report.

Table 2.5   Summary and critique of explanations of health inequalities

Explanation for health inequalities	Key points	Critique
Artefact explanation	There are methodological flaws in the measurement of class differences in morbidity and mortality.	• Health and differing health outcomes have been measured in a variety of ways, for long periods of time. • The evidence is now overwhelming in demonstrating social class differences linked to health outcomes.
Social selection as a mechanism	This is linked to the concept of social mobility – those who experience ill health have downward social mobility and those with better health are therefore higher up the social scale.	• Research demonstrates a much more complex relationship between ill health and class position than this explanation suggests.
Cultural argument as a mechanism	Class-related differences in health outcomes are caused by behaviour patterns – lower social classes experience worse health because they smoke more, drink more, exercise less and eat less healthily when compared to those in higher social class positions.	• This argument does not account for the overall context in which behaviour takes place. • Evidence shows that even when risk factors such as smoking and poor diet are controlled for, social class differences in health outcomes still remain. Individualistic behavioural explanations are too simplistic. • This explanation has been criticised for being 'victim blaming'.
Material and structural factors as mechanisms	Inequalities are caused by the differences in material circumstances in people's lives, such as unemployment and poor housing.	• The debate about this explanation is still found in the literature. Many complexities exist in explaining inequalities.
Psychosocial factors	Inequalities are caused by psychological and social factors that pre-dispose people to higher risks in relation to their health.	• Debates continue about this explanation. Many questions about the evidence base for the 'psychosocial hypotheses' in leading to physical ill health remain unanswered.

The first two explanations given in Table 2.5 have been largely discounted, and the remaining explanations are still being both investigated and debated. The importance of place has also been brought into the debate. Popay et al. (2003) argue that lay knowledge about social context and the experience of health are also important in determining health outcomes, and this should not be surprising given the earlier discussions in this chapter regarding area effects and social exclusion.

Sociological explanations focus on how social factors can be linked into explaining health inequalities, with the social model of health being used to explore the relationship. The social model of health is argued to be a significant determinant of health as the model explores how social factors and not just biomedical issues are linked to inequalities. The model in general acknowledges that illness does not necessarily act as a clear biomedical indicator because some people can feel ill without any biomedical evidence of causation. Rather, health and illness exist on a continuum that individuals move along (see Ogden 1996). However, there is no single social model of health. Instead, the model is a broad umbrella concept which covers several different areas, such as the existence of social divisions and inequalities, lifestyle factors, psychosocial determinants and the social constructions of illness and disease. Busfield (2000) demonstrates the complexity of social determinants in relation to health by using a four-part typology to begin to explain health inequalities. Busfield (2000) contrasts individual behaviour with attributes and circumstances. She also points to the material environment and the distribution of resources 'mediated directly on the body' (2000: 33), while distinguishing them from social relations and subjectivity. Her main argument is that there has been too little attention paid to material and environmental resource distribution as causes of health inequalities. This position is supported by the social determinants of health explanation.

Social determinants and health inequalities

The social determinants of health explanation strongly suggests that material deprivation leads to disease and ill health because the poorest sections of society are denied what they need for good health (Wainwright 2009). Material deprivation is crucial in determining health outcomes. Wilkinson and Pickett (2009) marshal a range of international evidence to clearly demonstrate that inequality has more detrimental health effects for those found within the lower social classes. However, the mechanisms by which this occurs are complex and are only partly explained by lifestyle factors and psychosocial determinants of health. Marmot argues that to address health inequalities, social inequality across society must also be tackled (Marmot Review Team 2010).

Lifestyle factors

The lifestyle factors approach focuses on individual choices and responsibility in determining health outcomes, exploring the way in which individuals make unhealthy lifestyle choices and how these lead to health outcomes. Higher mortality and morbidity rates within lower social class groups are explained by individuals making unhealthy choices, such as smoking more, drinking higher levels of alcohol, and eating less healthy food. However, there has been much criticism of this approach for its tendency to blame victims while not recognising broader structural factors which influence individuals' daily decisions relating to smoking, drinking and dietary choices. It can be argued that many lifestyle choices are in part determined by the financial situation in which individuals find themselves. This explanation has also received criticism for not affording enough attention to the psychosocial factors that influence our lifestyles.

Psychosocial factors

The psychosocial explanation of health inequalities is concerned with the relativity of inequality within any context. Wilkinson (1996) argues that greater levels of inequality lead to lower levels of social cohesion, more insecurity and social isolation, and this is experienced disproportionately by those in lower social class positions. These negative experiences lead to chronic stress, which affects biological pathways and impacts negatively on health. Psychological health is an important component of this process, with those in lower social class positions having less control and power in their daily lives and work environments – a situation that is critical for health (Marmot 2004). Position in society and its relationship to ill health is a very complicated matter, although it is suggested that those higher up the social class ranks can compensate for their experiences of illness and the effects of any disability because of their better access to resources and support networks.

Clearly, the social model of health and illness is complex and multifaceted, yet despite this, it offers insight into how societal position and stratification systems influence health inequalities. Stratification is related to all of the contemporary social divisions that have been discussed so far in this chapter. A further area in which stratification is evident is sexuality in that societies across the world remain sexually stratified.

Sexuality

While ideas about sexuality and, in particular, sexual orientation have undergone rapid changes in recent years, for many theorists sexuality remains a key social division associated with inequality. Foucault (1978) argues that notions of homosexuality did not exist in Europe before the eighteenth century. When the term did begin to be used, homosexuals were defined as different individuals with a sexual aberration (Weeks 1986). Homosexuality was seen as a condition that needed medical treatment and, historically, in many countries it was regulated by social policy and seen as a criminal act. Historically, there has not been acceptance or indeed tolerance of different forms of sexuality and sexual preference, and while tolerance has increased, many social inequalities remain.

Sexuality has been defined as heterosexuality and linked to monogamy demonstrated through marriage. However, there are many different types of sexuality.

Lorber (1994b) identifies at least ten different categories or identities, including straight men and women (heterosexual), gay men, lesbian women, bisexual men and women, transvestite men and women, and transsexual men and women. Indeed, she also writes about how sexual practices themselves are incredibly diverse. However, societies have sexual norms, which often link to and perpetuate inequalities. Indeed, sexual norms differ across cultures, as do acceptable sexual practices and notions of sexual attraction (Giddens 2009). This has led to some theorists arguing that sexuality is a social construction and that normality is often defined as heterosexuality. Have you considered how dominant notions of heterosexual norms are within the UK? Complete the following Learning Task to explore your own ideas about this.

Learning Task 2.4 – exploring notions of dominant heterosexuality

The following questions are a reversal of the questions that homosexual people often get asked by others. Think about how you would feel if you were asked these questions or were talked to in the same way. What they say about the relationship between sexuality and inequality?

1 What do you think caused you to be heterosexual?
2 When did you first realise that you were heterosexual?
3 Do you think that you just need a good gay/lesbian experience to turn you?
4 Your sexual status doesn't offend me as long as you don't force it on me.
5 Why are heterosexuals so promiscuous?

These questions reflect a lack of understanding about homosexuality within the UK, which is comparatively liberal compared with many other countries.

This Learning Task should have helped you to understand that there is a lack of status and understanding associated with different sexual identities. Sexuality is influenced by society and, indeed, by social policy. In public policy, gender and sexuality are treated in either of two ways. First, they are not always seen as a relevant policy issue but rather they are seen as private issues. Second, notions of compulsory heterosexuality dominate policy making (see Chapter 8 for more about policy making). However, in the context of policy related to sexuality, it is clear that individuals who are not heterosexual are often disadvantaged by the policy process, and as a result experience inequality. In the UK it was only in 2004 that Civil Partnerships for same-sex couples were officially recognised in law, and Civil Partnerships still do not afford those in same-sex relationships the same status or legal rights as those available to heterosexual couples who marry.

There are other examples of certain groups being rejected in law and social policy. For example, Uganda is a very conservative country in which homosexuality is seen as unchristian. Many gay people have faced discrimination, being physically attacked, losing jobs and being socially rejected. The law is often used to support such approaches rather than promoting equality (BBC News 2012). The law is used in many countries to socially exclude and stigmatise homosexuality.

Homosexuality has been stigmatised in many contexts around the world, and remains so in many places. Homophobia is a description of the prejudice that many gay people experience and is demonstrated by verbal abuse, violence and hostility, even in more tolerant western societies. This is despite long-standing political campaigns for equal rights. On a global scale campaigners for these rights have worked to increase awareness of the inequalities associated with sexuality as a social division. However, much work still needs to be done to change attitudes, laws and practices related to sexual preferences within contemporary societies.

Explaining sexuality as a social division

Sexuality as a social division has been explored in relation to gender inequalities (see Chapter 4 for a detailed discussion). Jackson (2006) argues that while gender, sexuality and heterosexuality are obviously interconnected, they are not all phenomena of the same order. Indeed, there are different dimensions of the social here, complicating the issue and the way in which heterosexuality is normalised. Jackson (2006) identifies the ways in which gender and sexuality operate as social divisions, arguing that heteronormativity as a concept is a useful explanatory tool. The concept describes the variety of ways in which heterosexual privilege is woven into the fabric of social life, as well as how it orders everyday existence. However, the way in which the differentiation of gender roles and gender inequality operates is identified as very complex by Jackson (2006) and is in need of further exploration.

Certainly, culture and history also play a part in the dominant discourse of heterosexuality and thus in the perpetuation of inequalities related to sexual preference. These aspects of society are related to the concept of social construction, which explains how social processes and societal patterns lead to different cultural understandings, and thus inequalities. Gender and gender divisions are socially constructed (see Chapter 4), and so too is sexuality. Both are shaped by social, political and economic influences which operate within societies. These social and cultural influences serve to disadvantage oppressed groups by silencing their voices in a variety of ways.

Case Study – Religion can be divisive

Religious belief and practice are related to contemporary social divisions, stigma and inequality in a variety of complex ways. In the USA, 72% of Americans say the country is divided along religious lines (Campbell and Putnam 2011), although, in the American context, religion is seen as one of the less important social divisions. Campbell and Putnam (2011) argue that religion serves as a form of civic glue, uniting rather than dividing. However, this view may well be disputed and there are many inequalities related to religion that are evident in the world today, as well as many ongoing religious conflicts in various parts of the world. For example:

- In 2011 France implemented a 'burqa ban', which restricted Muslim women from covering their faces in the burqa or niqab. It was argued that the ban would free women of gender enslavement and help Muslims better integrate into French society. There have been further media debates about how such an approach is related to inequality. For example, the need for Muslims to integrate into French society, rather than for French society to become more tolerant is indicative of religious inequalities.
- Recent debates in the UK media have focused on the rights of Christians to wear religious items, such as jewellery in the shape of a cross. This has led to a challenge in the European Court of Human Rights in which two female Christians sought the right to display their crosses in work environments. The Court ruled that they should be allowed to.
- In the wake of the 9/11 terrorist attack on New York in 2001, there have been reports of increased Islamophobia in a variety of contexts. Anti-Islamic sentiments are reported as prevalent across America, and some UK media report similar trends and religious prejudice, resulting in inequalities.

Thus, religion is also a social division in many contexts, which intersects with many other divisions discussed throughout this book, such as gender, age and sexuality, to create different positions and experiences of inequality throughout contemporary society.

Summary of key points

- There are many social divisions within society and while this chapter has not been able to explore all divisions in depth, it has outlined how inequality permeates many aspects of contemporary society and the worlds that we inhabit.
- Social differences and divisions are related to social inequalities in complex ways, as this chapter has demonstrated. Social divisions intersect, overlap and change

throughout the life course. Social divisions are also fundamentally related to both power and status.

- There are a number of ways in which social divisions are analysed and explained. The theoretical lenses that are used to explain inequality and stratification include Marxism, feminism, gender theory and social capital.

List of questions to stimulate debate and reflection

1 Pay attention to the media, watch the news, read newspapers and look at news reports online. You should be able to regularly see reports that demonstrate the existence of many social divisions across the world, in a variety of contexts.
2 Think about the social divisions that affect your life, as you did in the first Learning Task in this chapter. Reflect on the ways in which your experience and your own social divisions shape both your identity and experiences.
3 Think about the explanations and theories that have been discussed throughout this chapter for each of the social divisions discussed. Which explanation resonates with you the most and why do you think that this might be the case?

Further reading

Giddens, Anthony and Sutton, Philip W. (2010) *Sociology: Introductory Readings* (3rd edition). Cambridge: Polity Press.

This is an edited collection of readings, including many classical sociological texts, which relate to exploring, understanding and explaining social divisions. While not all chapters are relevant to social divisions, many are, including Marx's human history as class conflict, Walby's structuring patriarchal societies and Sassen's global city. There is also a specific section that explores social inequalities, with five interesting chapters and suggestions for further reading. This is a theoretically challenging read but one that will engage readers with the key sociological debates about social inequalities and divisions.

Platt, Lucinda (2011) *Understanding Inequalities: Stratification and Difference.* Cambridge: Polity Press.

This book explores many social divisions. It covers social class, gender, ethnicity, age, and disability as well as others. The book comprehensively covers the key social divisions, as well as associated theoretical issues and usefully shows that we are all members of social groups within society and therefore we are all socially divided. It contains recent statistical evidence to demonstrate the continued existence of social divisions and takes the reader through the latest sociological debates about these, so it is an excellent up-to-date introduction.

Ridge, Tess and Wright, Sharon (2008) *Understanding Inequality, Poverty and Wealth.* Bristol: Policy Press.

This is an edited collection of chapters which aims to introduce students to critical analyses of poverty and exclusion in relation to wealth. It focuses on the links between wealth and poverty and is reader friendly with text boxes, chapter summaries and suggestions for further exploration of related material. All of the chapters are relevant to expanding the reader's knowledge of social divisions, but Parts One, Two and Four particularly link to the discussions in this chapter. The book tends to concentrate on the UK and so is limited in its global focus, but it is still an interesting exploration of the issues.

3

SOCIAL DIVISIONS AND INEQUALITY: SOCIAL CLASS

Key learning outcomes

By the end of this chapter you should be able to:

- Understand the way in which social class is defined
- Understand the relationship between social inequality and social class
- Understand the different ideological positions associated with explaining the existence of social class

Overview of the chapter

This chapter provides an overview of social class as an enduring contemporary social division, defining social class and exploring its relationship with social inequality. This chapter also explores how social class is related to social status and therefore illustrates how social characteristics relate to experiences of inequality in very different ways. Social class divisions permeate many contemporary societies and are ultimately linked to both social inequality and status in complex ways. The relationship between social class and social inequality is illustrated as complex and this chapter constantly touches on these complexities as well as the importance of status in relation to societal position and inequality. This chapter discusses social class within various contexts and guises to show that inequality associated with class position arises in all places across the globe.

What is social class and why is it important?

As Chapter 1 outlined, social class is an important form of social stratification and division within many societies.

> ### *Defining social stratification*
>
> Social stratification refers to the 'inequalities that exist between individuals and groups within human societies. … Stratification can most simply be defined as structured inequalities between different groups of people.' (Giddens 2009: 432)
>   It is 'a system by which a society ranks categories of people in a hierarchy.' (Macionis and Plummer 2008: 232)

The existence of social stratification means that individuals within many societies experience unequal access to rewards based on their position in the world. At the most basic, rewards are monetary, although, as this chapter illustrates, status is also related to social stratification.

Giddens (2009) suggests that all socially stratified systems share three features:

1 Individuals are ranked based on common characteristics, although this does not mean that they identify with each other. Individuals can change their rank in many societies and move into another category.
2 Individuals' opportunities and life experiences relate clearly to their social position and their ranking. Therefore, differences such as male versus female, black versus white and upper class versus lower class affect life chances significantly.
3 Social stratification categories can change over time, although if they do, this is a slow process. For example, many commentators suggest that women are now equal to men in many industrial societies as a result of changing social rankings. However, as Chapter 4 shows, many feminists disagree with this and cite evidence to demonstrate the ways in which women remain unequal in both high- and low-income countries.

Social stratification is not a new societal division, as Chapter 1 illustrates. Historically, there have always been such divisions. Table 3.1 summarises these different divisions.

As Table 3.1 shows, there are many types of social stratification system. However, most traditional systems of stratification, such as the caste and estate systems, have been replaced by class-based systems associated with industrialisation. Given the changes in the world associated with globalisation (see Chapter 6), social class is seen by many as the dominant mode of stratification within the world today. Given its importance, how do we define social class?

> ### *Defining social class*
>
> 'We can define a class as a large-scale grouping of people who share common economic resources, which strongly influence the type of lifestyle they are able to lead.' (Giddens 2009: 437)

Table 3.1   Historical social divisions

Type of social division	Features of the system
Slavery	• People are owned as property by others and slaves are deprived of many rights. • Slavery in the USA was seen on Southern Plantations, in which being owned meant no legal rights for slaves. • Slaves were also common in ancient Greece but their roles were less restricted than US slaves. • Today slavery is illegal in every country of the world, and for many is seen as unethical as well as a violation of human rights.
Caste	• This is a system in which your social position is ascribed at birth and remains with you for life. • Social position is based upon different characteristics, such as religion or parental caste position. • Castes are rigid systems and any contact between different castes is not permissible as castes are seen as needing to remain pure. Thus marriage to someone from a different caste in some places is not allowed in law.
Estates	• Estates were found in feudal Europe and contained classes such as aristocracy and gentry as higher classifications and serfs (such as peasants) as the lowest group. • Mobility and intermarriage was possible so this system was not as rigid as the caste system. • European estates tended to be locally organised, although Chinese and Japanese estates were organised nationally, and were related to religion.
Class	• Classes are large groups of people who share similar economic circumstances and associated lifestyles. • Class systems are more fluid and are not based upon religion. • Class position can be achieved through social mobility; people can move up and down the rankings. • Class is economically based rather than focused upon race, birth-right or religion. • Class systems are often large and impersonal.

Source: Adapted from Giddens (2009)

However, despite the changes associated with industrial development in relation to social class, there are still elements of old systems that remain visible, such as UK Asians seeking arranged marriages for their children based on caste divisions. This focus on economic and social positions is also somewhat limited as social divisions arise in many forms, as Chapter 2 has already outlined in summarising the key divisions that exist across the globe. The processes associated with these divisions and within any stratification systems are numerous. Young (1990) outlines a number of the key processes at work which all interlink to social inequality:

1 **Social exclusion** – This is a term which describes the ways in which people are excluded from participating in society, and thus become marginalised.
2 **Exploitation** – For Young (1990), exploitation is about one group benefiting from the labour of another group.
3 **Power** – Often people who are in lower social positions lack power and are thus defined as powerless. They have a lack of authority and status when compared to those in higher socio-economic positions.
4 **Cultural imperialism** – This is the dominance of a particular group's experience and culture, so that this is seen as normal.
5 **Violence** – This is often directed at one group simply because they are identified as belonging to such a group. This is seen in racist attacks, in homophobia against homosexuals, and for feminists can be seen too in violence against women.

Young's (1990) work recognises the complexity of social stratification and the types of inequality associated with this. Now complete the following Learning Task to explore another area of social inequalities.

Learning Task 3.1 – mapping social inequalities

Current social stratification can be mapped geographically (see Dorling 2012).

1 Use the internet to visit Social and Spatial Inequalities – www.sasi. group.shef.ac.uk/
2 Explore the website and the mapping of social inequalities. There are several reports and some interesting mappings of geographical inequalities. If you are interested in the UK, go to the section labelled, 'What is your neighbourhood like?' and check out your inequality rating. To look further afield go to the right-hand side of the web-page and the section labelled maps. Click on the worldmapper and look at the different portrayals of the world. For example, see the world according to income and views of the world, which looks at different countries' success in the recent 2012 Olympics.

What does the data tell you about social inequality in the world today? Are all inequalities mapped on the website? If not, which ones are omitted?

The above Learning Task will have helped you to explore the geographical mapping of social stratification. There are different perspectives about stratification, and thus there is a debate about how to measure stratification in all areas of social life, including how to measure social class.

Measuring social class

The measurement of social class has caused much debate within the literature because it is complex. Large-scale patterns of similar employment within industries such as mining, mills and factories no longer exist today. Therefore, analyses of class have had to develop to accommodate such changes because divisions cannot simply be described as vertical. Some measures of class are also problematised because they are based on the male head of household's occupation and so have received criticism from feminists. There is validity in this criticism as work patterns have changed, more women now participate in the labour market and some may have higher class positions than their husbands.

Crompton's work (Crompton and Jones 1984; Crompton and Sanderson 1990) is important in demonstrating the complexity of class and other social divisions. She argues that in order to understand class inequalities, gender inequalities also have to be explored. Other debates about the measurement of social class have centred on whether to make theoretical approaches (such as Marxism and Weberianism) implicit or explicit, how to assign occupations to groups or classifications and the importance of the father's and mother's occupation in constructing socio-economic measures (Marks 1999). The UK measurement system that is currently used is outlined in Table 3.2.

Table 3.2   The National Statistics Socio-Economic Classifications (NS-SEC)

Social class ranking	Occupation
1	Higher managerial and professional occupations
1.1	Employers and managers in larger organisations (e.g. company directors, senior company managers, senior civil servants, senior officers in police)
1.2	Higher professionals (e.g. doctors, lawyers, clergy, teachers)
2	Lower managerial and professional occupations (e.g. nurses and midwives, journalists, actors, musicians, prison officers, lower ranks of police)
3	Intermediate occupations (e.g. clerks, secretaries, driving instructors)
4	Small employers and own account workers (e.g. publicans, farmers, taxi drivers, window cleaners, painters and decorators)
5	Lower supervisory, craft and related occupations (e.g. printers, plumbers, television engineers, train drivers, butchers)
6	Semi-routine occupations (e.g. shop assistants, hairdressers, bus drivers, cooks)
7	Routine occupations (e.g. couriers, labourers, waiters and refuse collectors)
8	Those who have never had paid work and the long-term unemployed

Source: From Office for National Statistics (2011)

Table 3.2 shows class positions based on occupation and demonstrates the importance of occupation as a tool for determining social class position. Occupations are
related to economic earnings, with the highest earning individuals being further
up the ladder. Attitudes to occupations are often reflective of such class divisions,
with status being related to occupation in many societies. This class scale is based
on the work of a sociologist called John Goldthorpe (see Marshall 1988), who
devised a scheme based on relative labour market position and work, which has
now evolved into the scheme above. The scale in Table 3.2 has been criticised in
the literature because the scheme does not cover everyone; if you are reading this
as a student, then you might contemplate that the category that you fall into is
not listed. The scale also does not demonstrate the large-scale differences in wealth
that are evident within contemporary society (Giddens 2009). However, despite
these criticisms, Goldthorpe's class scale has been extended into a European classification scheme, listed in Table 3.3.

Class divisions are similarly based on occupation in many other societies. For
example, social stratification in Japan is based on a mixture of old divisions, such
as nobility and feudal classifications, to more occupation-based categorisations

Table 3.3   The European Socio-economic Classification (ESeC)

ESeC class	Common term	Employment regulation
Large employers, higher grade professional, administrative and managerial occupations	Higher salariat	Service Relationship
Lower grade professional, administrative and managerial occupations and higher grade technician and supervisory occupations	Lower salariat	Service Relationship (modified)
Intermediate occupations	Higher grade white-collar workers	Mixed
Small employer and self-employed occupations (excluding agriculture)	Petit bourgeoisie or independents	–
Self-employed occupations (agriculture etc.)	Petit bourgeoisie or independents	–
Lower supervisory and lower technician occupations	Higher grade blue-collar workers	Mixed
Lower services, sales and clerical occupations	Lower grade white-collar workers	Labour Contract (modified)
Lower technical occupations	Skilled workers	Labour Contract (modified)
Routine occupations	Semi- and non-skilled workers	Labour contract
Never worked and long-term unemployed	Unemployed	–

Source: Adapted from the University of Essex (2012)

that include social graduations such as upper, upper-middle, lower-middle and middle class. Japanese class divisions have less firm boundaries than UK classifications and family standing remains an important tool for assessing social status within Japan (Macionis and Plummer 2008), hence class divisions are slightly different but occupation is still part of the way in which class positions are determined. Some countries, however, determine social class position without the association with occupation.

Claims have been made both politically and within the broader literature that class divisions are dying and are no longer important. Class divisions are arguably changing because of societal changes. Paluski and Waters (1996) argue that the political, economic and social importance of class is changing because societies are organised around status rather than occupation. These claims and some counter criticisms are presented in Table 3.4.

Table 3.4   The death of class debated

Evidence for the death of class	Some considerations
The huge shift in property ownership with many more people owning property has restricted the privileges passed on to future generations by capitalists.	• Some individuals remain excluded from the property market entirely based upon their economic status and position within society. • Those in higher social positions can still pass on more privilege as property ownership is often in the form of portfolios rather than a single residential dwelling. • Property ownership may be achieved by some in lower social classes at considerable economic cost, such as debt.
Consumers have more power within contemporary society; thus, class is marked by the ability to purchase consumer goods, rather than by social class.	• Consumption patterns are based upon economic position and resources; thus, those in lower social positions are likely to have less consumption power due to their occupation. • The achievement of status via consumption is evident across social rankings but the recent financial crisis outlined the amount of debt held by individuals in high-income countries. Those in poorer paid occupations are more likely to accrue debt to achieve consumer status.
Globalisation has changed the occupational structure in higher income countries with fewer traditional manual jobs existing. Stratification therefore exists on a more global than national scale.	• Chapter 1 presents evidence to suggest the importance of national social stratification with the UK being a notable example of a largely unequal society based upon occupation and economic position.
Family structures are also changing, with greater geographical mobility, therefore the importance of the family in the reproduction of class is changing.	• Research shows that social factors, including family, affect our life chances and social mobility (see below). For many, social class position still brings disadvantage.

Source: Adapted from Abbott (2001)

As Table 3.4 demonstrates, class is not necessarily dead but changing societal trends are adding to the complexities associated with the concept. Class still remains important and is linked to inequality in a number of ways, although contemporary class divisions are often depicted as being based on a fairer system than previous historical divisions, such as slavery or feudal systems, because they arguably relate to individual achievement. Thus, if you work hard and achieve, then you can move up the social class scale and gain a better job than your parents. This fits with the concept of meritocracy, a term that has been used politically to describe how individual merit results in rewards, because everyone in society is presented with equal opportunities. Thus, if you achieve educationally, you move up the class scale. This process is labelled as social mobility.

Defining social mobility

'Social mobility is a tricky concept to define, but is often used to refer to the ability of individuals from disadvantaged backgrounds to move up in the world, akin to the notion of equality of opportunity.' (Crawford et al. 2011: 6)

While contemporary class societies do exhibit greater fluidity (mobility) than historical feudal or caste societies, social mobility is not as easy to accomplish as those in power and politics suggest. Indeed, reading Chapter 1 should have helped you to understand that equal opportunity is a problematic concept given the range of inequalities both within and between societies across the world. Research shows that the UK, as an example, is a country that exhibits low social mobility (Blanden 2009). Furthermore, Blanden et al. (2004), in analysing intergenerational mobility between cohorts born in 1970 and those born in 1958, found that mobility actually decreased. However, Goldthorpe and Jackson (2007) found no change in social class mobility for the same data sets that Blanden et al. (2004) analysed. This second analysis indicates that social mobility has remained static rather than decreased.

Despite different results, both analyses act as critiques to the claims that social mobility can be achieved with ease. Indeed, analyses of social mobility often focus on education as the route to class movement without an examination of the cultural factors that can play a part. Research has shown that there are strong links between scoring well in intelligence tests and in coming from more advantaged backgrounds (Breen and Goldthorpe 1999). Furthermore, socialisation in early childhood also plays a role in shaping class differences in ability (Scherger and Savage 2009), showing that notions of equal opportunity for all are misguided because social factors remain linked to the prospects of different groups (Jackson et al. 2005).

Class effects therefore work in a variety of ways in relation to upward mobility because the transmission of cultural capital in relation to encouraging and supporting children contributes to the reproduction of class (Scherger and Savage 2009). Analyses of social mobility also tend to focus on upward mobility, assuming that individuals always wish to improve themselves and achieve self-betterment. Those who do not ascribe to such beliefs are negatively labelled in many social contexts because dominant political arguments focus on equality of opportunity, responsibility and the need for us all to achieve our potential without focusing on barriers and structural impediments for many, as well as the multiplicity of advantages that come with higher social positions.

Indeed, in the UK context the increasing privatisation of higher education means that achieving social mobility is likely to be more difficult for those from the poorest social categories. From 2012 UK universities raised tuition fees to a maximum of £9,000 per year for each student completing an undergraduate degree. Despite policies being put into place to assist those from the poorest backgrounds, many suggest that gaining an undergraduate degree will become about who can afford the fees, rather than individual ability. Media debates have discussed how young people will have to turn to 'the bank of mum and dad' (Hardy 2011), but this is assuming that mum and dad have money to give.

These debates about social mobility have long been in existence and are not specific to the UK, nor are class divisions. Sociology as a discipline has explored global class divisions since industrialisation and now writers focus on the complexity of contemporary divisions, illustrating how they interrelate as well as their relationship to both power and lifestyle (Macionis and Plummer 2008). Understandings of social class positions have also been expanded in that they represent more than accent or modes of dress. The term 'class' refers to dynamic power relationships between people and control over various resources as well as occupational position.

Explaining social class divisions

Sociologists have also spent much time discussing and explaining social divisions through different theoretical lenses, demonstrating a variety of competing interpretations and explanations. These explanations are now outlined in relation to social stratification and the existence of social class. The consensus perspective, also known as the functionalist perspective, argues that social divisions are necessary within society because such stratification results in benefits in relation to how society operates. Societies have complex occupational systems in which jobs vary in terms of importance. Therefore, those in the more skilled positions are more talented and require higher rewards. Such positions are also the most functionally significant and therefore come with higher rewards attached to them, both economically in terms of higher wages and with associated prestige (Davis and Moore 1945). For Davis and Moore (1945) social stratification is simply about unequal rewards. Having a system that provides unequal rewards is about motivating people to achieve more and therefore gain higher rewards. This explanation fits with the notion of a meritocracy, already discussed. Both meritocracy and the notion of social stratification as a functional necessity have been widely criticised. Davis and Moore (1945) fail to explain the existence of very different systems of stratification within societies across the world and do not detail how functional importance can be measured. Furthermore, social stratification does not necessarily reward individual talent either, as is claimed here (Macionis and Plummer 2008). This theory fails to explain the culture of celebrity in the global north, which results in people who are not necessarily educated or, indeed, talented earning significant amounts of money.

Other theoretical perspectives are less positive in how they analyse social stratification, adopting conflict perspectives to explain the existence of class inequality. Marxism was introduced in Chapter 1 as a perspective that developed after the industrial revolution and depicted those in power owning the means of production (bourgeois), with the less powerful working for them (proletariat). This analysis may no longer be applicable to today's class systems because of the changing dynamics of work. Changes include the expansion of classes, the fragmentation of the labour market and the development of weightless economies due to technological advancement. In addition, more women now engage with the labour market, and some individuals spend less time in the labour market due to prolonged education and earlier retirement, and there has been a debated decline in class politics.

Despite these changes, Marxist theory still has some contributions to make in highlighting some still relevant points for consideration in relation to the existence of social stratification. For example, the key argument that differences in social and economic resources serve the interests of certain groups remains an important feature of contemporary debates about capitalism and inequality. Indeed, given the level of inequalities that exist within the world today, it is impossible to dispute the suggestion that capitalism perpetuates poverty and advantage. Many sociologists (Giddens 1982; Boswell and Dixon 1993) argue that despite the problem with Marx's revolutionary ideas, his theory is valuable for the following reasons:

- Wealth remains concentrated in the hands of the minority
- The global system is capitalist
- Work is degrading for many
- The law favours the rich.

Weber is another theorist who spent time analysing social stratification, providing a more nuanced analysis by examining status. Ultimately, Weber identified stratification as a multidimensional process (Macionis and Plummer 2008). Weber agreed that class was based on economics, but he also saw skills as being important because these affect the types of work that people can participate in and be rewarded for. Thus, the more skilled are able to gain employment with good conditions, including economic reward and better life chances, resulting in different lifestyles and perceptions of status. Clearly, this analysis is valuable because status remains important within contemporary society. Complete the following Learning Task so that you can explore your own ideas about social stratification.

Learning Task 3.2 – exploring social stratification

1 Go to the following web-page where Macionis (2001) provides a summary about social stratification from his book, *Society the Basics*: http://cwx.prenhall.com/bookbind/pubbooks/macionis9/chapter8/objectives/deluxe-content.html

2 Read the content on the web-pages, which is a summary of Chapter 8 about social stratification, and make brief notes. You will recognise some of the points as ones made earlier in this section exploring social class.

3 In what ways is your life stratified?

4 Now try to answer the following question: How is social stratification a creation of society rather than a reflection of individual differences?

5 Reflect on how you feel about the question to determine what your view of social stratification is. Having read the theoretical explanations described in this section, which explanation do you think is the one most related to your own viewpoint? How do you view power and powerlessness? What are your perceptions of status as a form of social stratification?

6 Visit the following website: www.sociologyguide.com/social-stratification/features-of-caste-system.php. Explore more about social stratification in India: how is this different from the forms of social stratification that you have experienced yourself?

7 Given that America is portrayed as the land of opportunity, now visit the website below which details reports from journalists working for the *New York Times*, exploring how stratification and class still matter within contemporary USA: www.nytimes.com/pages/national/class/

This Learning Task will have helped you to think more about social class and social status and its continuing importance within many contemporary countries. An American sociologist called Wright (1997) combined aspects of the work of both Marx and Weber to illustrate that there are different types of control over economic resources, such as:

1 Control over economic capital and money.
2 Control over the physical production of labour (such as factories, companies and land).
3 Control over labour power.

Those individuals who are located in the lowest social classes have no control over any of these areas. Other individuals occupy more complex positions, for example white-collar workers still sell their labour like manual workers but they retain a higher degree of control over their work setting. For Wright (1997), these workers are contradictory, with his analysis focusing on such workers' relationship to authority and their possession of skills. These workers are both the exploiters and the exploited, as they assist capitalists and are rewarded with higher wages and promotions. Therefore, they experience less inequality than others. Wright's (1997) focus on skills and expertise is useful in exploring how some individuals receive greater economic rewards than others within the labour market. He depicts those who have skills that are in short supply as being able to receive higher rewards for their work. These different job positions are also related to perceptions of social status; thus different occupations are related to economic rewards as well as perceptions of higher levels of status.

Social status

Increasingly, social status is important within contemporary society. Social stratification includes a subjective element based on how individuals judge themselves and others.

Defining social status

'The social honour or prestige accorded to a person or a particular group by other members of society. Status groups normally involve distinct styles of life – patterns of behaviour which the members of the group follow. Status privilege may be positive or negative.' (Giddens 2009: 1134)

Sernau (2011) describes the many different ways in which status can be determined. For example, hunter-gatherer groups may place greater status on the best hunters, leaders or healers. Occupation can offer prestige and many rankings of prestige across the globe relate to income. Generally, higher paid jobs which require educational achievement to secure them acquire perceptions of increased status. Thus, doctors, lawyers and professors achieve more status than bus drivers, cooks and waitresses. Status is conferred on occupations similarly across the globe: 'almost everywhere, more high ranked work that involves mental activity, free from extensive supervision, confers greater prestige than lower class occupations that require supervised manual labour' (Macionis and Plummer 2008: 303). There are many discussions about the lack of status associated with several occupations (Dorling 2009; Warhurst et al. 2009).

Family position can also be associated with status and prestige, especially for those who have titles and lineage. This is true in many societies; to be a member of the Royal family in Britain or in Spain, for example, ensures status. To be part of the aristocracy in many other societies is also viewed in the same way. Levels of education, too, can be associated with prestige. Being able to change your title from Mr or Mrs to Dr ensures an increased level of prestige being bestowed upon you by others (Sernau 2011).

In some societies, status is synonymous with honour. For example, fighting elites have achieved high levels of status in some cultures. Japanese Samurai warriors acquired status and respect for the way in which they lived their lives, following a strict code of honour. Contemporary representations of respect vary. For example, respect is a key component of status within gang cultures. Thus, status is not always awarded as a result of positive behaviour or outcomes. The culture of celebrity that is perpetuated by the western media also demonstrates changing perceptions of status.

Prestige can also be earned in other ways from those associated with income. Charitable giving, philanthropic endeavours and the presentation of gifts can earn prestige. Sernau (2011: 165) argues that 'those who have gained great wealth and now want prestige as well must return some of their wealth to the community to get it'. This is not just the case in high-income countries, but has also been associated with tribal communities, as demonstrated through anthropological analyses (see Mauss 1967).

Giving is not just about money and gifts, it can also involve donating time or expertise, for example, volunteering in community enterprises. In Britain this has become increasingly important in policy circles in recent years. Within their social policy discourse, the UK New Labour government (1997–2010) stressed the importance of volunteering in society, and this was developed further by the Coalition government's emphasis on 'The Big Society', in which volunteering is seen as being the central lynchpin in achieving social benefit and citizenship. While volunteering as a form of giving has received criticism in some quarters, in others it can be important in accruing prestige. UK media coverage of the 2012 Olympic Games, for instance, often praised the volunteers who supported the Games, crediting them with making the Games a great success, so that the title 'Games-makers' itself became an indication of the status given to volunteering in this context.

Prestige can also be gained by individual members of society achieving respectability within their social contexts. Prestige in the form of respectability is arguably more important for those in lower income groups. As Sernau (2011: 165) states: 'within their small communities of neighbours and co-workers, they (individuals within low income groups) held some measure of social honour for their moral standards, their hard work, their experience, and their practical wisdom.

They were also interested in distancing themselves from those they viewed as having none of these.' The final sentence of this quote is interesting and demonstrates that prestige is associated with social positioning.

Marmot's book, *The Status Syndrome* (2004), explores the relationships between health outcomes and status. Those with lower status, even within the same organisation, have worse health outcomes. Similarly, James's *Affluenza* (2007) depicts the constant push for the accumulation of possessions within contemporary western society to demonstrate both prestige and status. He describes this as an illness called 'Affluenza' in a clear critique of capitalism. Furthermore, in the wake of the recent UK riots, Bauman (2011), when commenting on causation, suggested that the riots were ultimately linked to status and were participated in by those who lacked social prestige.

In terms of your own lifestyle and how you view status, complete the following Learning Task to help you reflect on your own values.

Learning Task 3.3 – how is status constructed in contemporary society?

1 Think about status within your own society and social groups. What is important for status in your social circles? Is it about having possessions? If so, which ones? Is it about behaving in a specific way? Is it about how you present yourself and dress? List all of the ways in which you achieve status.

2 Now think about how you define social status? Think about the judgements that you make about others. List the ways in which you make judgements. For example, do you judge people's occupation? Which jobs hold more status for you? Is it about the area in which people live? Is it about the size of an individual's home, or perhaps the type of car that they drive? What about the possessions that you view as important?

3 Take some time to think about how your ideas about status are shaped – where do your ideas come from?

4 Finally, take some time to think about how status may be conceptualised differently across the world. How might status be achieved in Japan? What does status look like for an African woman?

The above Learning Task will have helped you to explore your ideas and attitudes about status. The mechanisms which position people into classes are limited by being based on just the occupations we undertake, but class is determined by so much more than the jobs we do. Values, status and judgements from peers are also important in constructing stratifications within contemporary society.

Explaining differences in social status

Negative labelling, as described in Chapter 1, is also important in constructing understandings of status associated with both class position and occupation. This type of labelling is not new. During the 1980s, Charles Murray, a right-wing sociologist from America, outlined a category of individuals termed 'the underclass'. His work gained political currency and media attention, as he was brought to Britain by *The Sunday Times* to investigate whether there was an underclass in the UK. Murray (1990) said that he investigated whether the 'disease' was spreading. The term 'underclass' has been used ever since by a variety of politicians and, more recently, within the UK context following the riots in 2011. The term 'feral underclass' was used in the media at that time (Lewis et al. 2011). This term is not unique to the UK; in the USA it has also been used, as has the label 'ghetto poor' (Wilson 1996). Interestingly, research findings from Morris (1993) suggest that there is no direct evidence of a distinctive culture of the underclass, as has often been described. Indeed, in Victorian England the poor were labelled as 'the great unwashed' and treated with disdain. Thus, negative attitudes to the lower social classes have existed for many years, albeit represented in different guises. Social stratification is therefore tied to attitudes about class position and status. These attitudes have long served a purpose and, for Dorling (2009), are a clear reason as to why inequality persists.

Status is embedded in many societal contexts and is reproduced via the socialisation process in which parents teach children work habits, expectations and consumption patterns. One theoretical interpretation of this is Bourdieu's (1984) 'habitus'.

Defining habitus

Habitus is a concept that is used to describe our socially learned dispositions, including our social skills and ways of acting, which we usually take for granted. These are acquired through the activities and experiences of our everyday lives. In basic terms, habitus can be described as our sensibilities, dispositions and tastes. (Scott and Marshall 1998)

Habitus is a complex concept, but is one which describes how individuals acquire a set of socially learned dispositions. This includes skills, ways of acting and habits. These are acquired through the activities and experiences of everyday life and are taken for granted. They relate to social status and position because taste and habits are conditioned by social class position and societal stratification systems. Largely generalising, Bourdieu (1984) argues that upper-class habitus is marked by an aesthetic disposition in which art and music are appreciated as part of the cultural capital possessed by such groups. Comparatively, working-class habitus is influenced by economics and conformity. Habitus operates to reinforce class inequality because individuals feel comfortable in their own habitus and perceive a higher-class habitus as being at odds with their own experiences and viewpoints. Therefore, taste simultaneously 'unites and separates' Bourdieu (1984: 56).

Turner (1988) also theoretically explores the different types of status that exist within contemporary society and argues that social stratification has three major components:

1 Politico-legal rights (status as entitlement)
2 Cultural distinction (status as lifestyle, similar to habitus)
3 Economic class.

Status is also important in understanding other social divisions as well as class, for example, the status of women in many places in the world is lower than that of men, which results in gender being a significant social division (see Chapter 4). Social status and social class are also strongly related to social exclusion. Social exclusion is associated with stratification and class position and is a relatively recent addition to the literature in this area. It is a concept that has gathered popularity within the political arena in the UK, with the New Labour government establishing a Social Exclusion Unit in 1997, the year in which they came to power. Social exclusion is a label for the ways in which people become cut off from wider societal processes and are denied opportunities to self-improvement as a result of the stratification of society. Chapter 1 explores the concept in depth. It is useful here to consider how stratification can lead to social exclusion for some groups, and the relationship between social stratification and exclusion. While some individuals in higher classes may seek to exclude themselves, for example, by living in gated communities (see Chapter 2), others may be excluded through their lack of power and low social position. Thus, stratification and social class position are inherently linked to inequality.

Inequalities and stratification in contemporary society

Throughout history, many societies have demonstrated inequalities and different forms of social stratification, as indeed is also seen in contemporary times. Indeed, as Chapter 1 outlines, some commentators argue that social inequality and stratification is actually greater today than it has ever been. Given the issues that exist in measuring social inequality and stratification, this is a hard claim to prove, although now routine data collection across the world makes it easier to chart more recent trends. For many, social inequality is increasing (see Chapter 1), and some explanations of these increases relate to globalisation (see Chapter 6) and the deregulation of financial markets (see Chapter 8). What is new is the large amount of evidence being gathered about inequalities. Measures of social inequality are improving and now encompass broader conceptualisations and the impact that stratification and inequalities are having on us all. Now complete the following Learning Task to explore this further.

Learning Task 3.4 – exploring how inequality is bad for us all

1 Use the internet to access the following website and listen to the talk by Richard Wilkinson: 'How economic inequality harms societies': www.ted.com/talks/lang/en/richard_wilkinson.html
2 What are you own views about social stratification and inequality? Are they necessary aspects of society, as some theorists and politicians suggest?
3 Do you agree with the perspective presented in the talk? Are inequalities bad for us all?

While social stratification still exists and inequalities remain tied to it, there are people who experience social mobility and are thus able to move up the social class scale, myself included, as a child of working-class parents who is now an academic. New societal developments are also slowly changing patterns of inequalities. For example, technological advancements can lead to social mobility for some and of course social exclusion for others. Have you ever considered notions of technological classes? Some classes are excluded from technological development, while other class differences can be seen in the use of certain websites and online social networking. BBC News (2007) reported on research which showed how technological divisions mirror stratification within the United States. White children of educated parents are more likely to use Facebook whereas users of MySpace were more likely to be from lower-class groups and have less educated parents. This is indicative of different social experiences related to the stratified nature of contemporary society. Macionis and Plummer (2008) suggest that the world is divided into three types of experience:

1 The very rich and high status groups whose lifestyles are completely different from most people and who have traditionally remained away from the gaze of researchers, although this is now changing.
2 At the opposite end of the social scale are those who have incomes of less than $1 per day. Collier (2008) labels them as the 'bottom billion'. They have poor life experiences, poor health outcomes and are socially excluded in multiple ways. Their lives are brutal and often 'wasted' (Bauman 2004).
3 And the majority, such as you and I. We still experience social divisions, such as those related to gender, ethnicity, economic position and access to resources, and we are still subject to social stratification, holding social class rankings.

Thus, social stratification is linked to inequality in numerous ways, as illustrated in Figure 3.1.

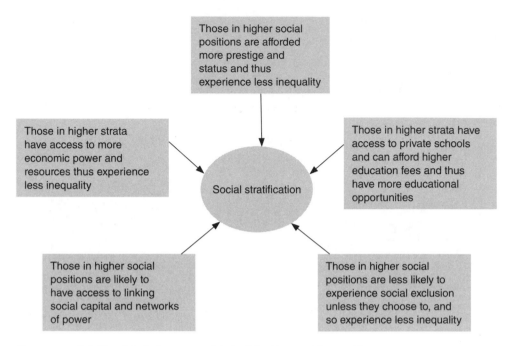

Figure 3.1   Relationship between social stratification and inequality

Case Study: The enduring prevalence of English social class

Fox (2005) wrote an anthropological analysis of the English in a book called *Watching the English*. Despite claims that social class is less important, she argues that 'class pervades all aspects of English life and culture' (2005: 15), and she illustrates this throughout the book. In a chapter about how the English speak, she shows how pronunciation and the words that we use are evidently linked to social class. If you are reading this from the perspective of someone who is not English, this may seem odd to you, but Fox (2005) suggests that English nationals have the ability to determine social class position based on the everyday words people use. She lists seven deadly sins:

1 Pardon – A lower-middle or middle-middle-class English person will say 'pardon', and upper-middle-class person is likely to say 'sorry', but an upper-class or working-class person will say 'what?'.
2 Toilet – The correct upper-class term is 'loo' or 'lavatory', whereas the working classes and middle classes tend to say 'toilet'.
3 Serviette – Those who use the word 'serviette' are lower class, whereas those in higher social positions say 'napkin'.
4 Dinner – Working-class people tend to refer to their mid-day meal as 'dinner', and their evening meal as 'tea'. Those in upper-class positions say 'lunch' for the mid-day

meal and 'supper' for the evening meal. 'Tea' for the upper classes is usually taken in the afternoon and involves cups of tea, sandwiches and cakes.

5 Settee – Those who call their furniture a 'settee' are working class and individuals in higher positions refer to it as the 'sofa'.

6 Lounge – 'Sitting room' is the most commonly used term for the room in which the 'sofa' is located. Those who refer to the location of the 'settee' in the lounge are middle-middles or below.

7 Sweet – The course at the end of the meal for those in working-class positions is known as the 'sweet'. For those in higher social class positions it is always called a 'pudding'.

Fox (2005) argues that these seven areas are the most common and reliable social class indicators. Why not test these in conversation with British people and rank their class position accordingly?

Summary of key points

- Social stratification systems are those which organise people into hierarchies based on differential characteristics. The dominant contemporary form of stratification is based on economic differences, with people being categorised into social classes according to their occupation. Status is also related to social class position. Lifestyle and cultural factors are also analysed within the contemporary literature.

- Despite debates about the death of social class and some changes in the way in which society is organised, social class remains a large influence on our lives. Social class position is clearly correlated with a variety of inequalities, such as economic resources, educational attainment and health outcomes.

- A range of theories exist which can be used to explain social class. This chapter has summarised analyses from Marx and Weber. Some focus on economic divisions, while others place more emphasis on status, but all see class as having a significant relationship with social inequality.

List of questions to stimulate debate and reflection

1 Where do you see social stratification in your life? Which social class do you feel that you belong to and how are you making the decision? For example, is it about your parental occupations, lifestyle and status?

2 What kind of power do you feel that you have in your life, and how does social stratification experienced by you limit your power, or indeed increase it? Do you have autonomy in your everyday life?

3 What are your thoughts on social stratification? Do you think that it is inevitable? Is inequality linked to the forms of stratification discussed in this chapter inevitable too?

Further reading

Bottero, Wendy (2005) *Stratification: Social Division and Inequality*. London: Routledge.

This book offers a different viewpoint on social stratification and so makes an interesting read. Bottero explores how our most personal choices, such as sexual partners, friends and consumption items, are influenced by hierarchy and social difference. She explains how hierarchy affects our tastes and leisure time activities, and who we choose and hang on to as our friends and partners. The book is very much European and American in the traditions and areas that it explores, and therefore it is of limited application globally. However, it offers alternative discussion in relation to global stratification.

Crompton, Rosemary (2008) *Class and Stratification: An Introduction to Current Debates* (3rd edition). Cambridge and Malden, MA: Polity Press.

This book introduces readers to the field and so is an excellent starting point to explore contemporary economic and social change in relation to social class and stratification. The book also explores 'cultural' approaches to class analysis, and key concepts in the field such as social mobility, educational opportunity and social polarisation.

Weis, Lois and Dolby, Nadine (2012) *Social Class and Education: Global Perspectives*. London: Routledge.

This book explores the intersections of class, social structure, opportunity and education within the global context. An edited collection, it has chapters covering the USA, Europe, China and Latin America, in order to explore how social class differences are made and experienced through school.

4
SOCIAL DIVISIONS AND INEQUALITY: GENDER

Key learning outcomes

By the end of this chapter you should be able to:

- Understand the way in which gender is defined
- Understand the relationship between social inequality and gender
- Understand the different ideological positions associated with explaining the existence of gender inequalities

Overview of the chapter

This chapter provides an overview of gender as a contemporary social division, defining it and exploring its relationship with social inequality. This chapter also explores how gender is related to social status and therefore illustrates how social characteristics relate to experiences of inequality in very different ways. This chapter outlines recent progress that has been made in terms of increased gender equality. However, despite this, many gender inequalities still permeate much of the world, linked to social inequality as well as status and power in complex ways. This chapter explores the complex relationship between gender and social inequality and outlines the importance of the global context in relation to gender inequalities. The chapter also explores the explanations offered in the literature that tell us about why gender inequalities remain a problem within contemporary societies across the world.

What is gender?

Gender is simply the social, behavioural and cultural attributes that are associated with being a man or a woman.

> ### Defining gender
>
> Thompson and Armato (2011) argue that gender is created and maintained through complex societal arrangements and practices; thus gender is socially constructed.
>   Gender is the system of beliefs and practices that refer to and create a sense of difference between men and women (Connell 1987).

Understanding what gender is and how it is created and operates within societies has led to arguments by many sociologists that gender is not about biological differences; instead, it is a phenomenon that is collectively produced and consequently has many powerful implications in people's lives (Thompson and Armato 2011). Gender is described by many sociologists as socially constructed. The idea of social construction is fundamental to modern Sociology, with the expression deriving from Berger and Luckman's (1996) book, *The Social Construction of Reality*. For social constructionists, every aspect of the social world has meaning and significance within society. Ultimately, there are no universal truths. To say that something is socially constructed means that it has been fashioned by society and made by humans. Butler (1990) argues that being female is not 'natural' rather it appears so because of the ways in which we repeatedly perform gender. These performances reproduce and define the traditional categories of gender. Some feminist theorists argue that biology indirectly influences women's destiny through the way in which it is socially constructed, while others argue that biology has a more direct influence on the destiny of women because of their reproductive capabilities (Sayers 1982).

   The concepts of structure, agency and culture are all relevant here too. Central to all theories within the discipline of sociology are debates about structure and agency. Sociologists focus on the structures of society, examining the features of the social world which constrain people or indeed force them into an action. Other theorists investigate the meanings that people attach to their actions (agency) and the events that occur in their lives. Structure refers to factors that help determine our experiences through the establishment of expected ways of behaving. Societal structures are not easy to see but do influence our behaviour. Thompson and Armato (2011) argue that how we dress defines our gender and that this is influenced by a range of social factors, such as our social location, historical context and the laws of our society. Social structures can also constrain our lives. For example, social discomfort is often caused by individuals who wear clothing that is not gender appropriate. Thus, social forces shape our behaviour and how we 'do' gender.

In contrast, the concept of 'agency' reminds us that individuals do not simply act out predetermined roles, but 'interpret' those roles in a way that is unique to them. Thus, individuals do gender but they take action to either sustain or indeed challenge gender arrangements. Sociologists also analyse how gender is created through interaction. The theoretical perspective of symbolic interactionism explains social phenomena from the perspective of its participants. This approach is a micro-analysis of individuals, examining behaviour on a small scale. Sociologists adopting an interactionist perspective have consequently attempted to understand these experiences from the perspective of those experiencing them. An insider's perspective concentrates on the subjective experiences of living within gendered frameworks and looking at how people interact with each other in different situations to create and maintain gender. An essential element of the interactionist perspective is the understanding of the unique nature of the social world, as made up of the actions of participants. For interactionist theorists, all encounters with others are what create both meaning and significance within the social world. Human action cannot therefore be observed or assumed, but must be 'interpreted' by studying the meanings that people attach to their behaviour.

So what meanings are attached to gender within society? Societies tend to recognise two genders, which is problematic for individuals who are transgender, who often conform to a specific gender role and attempt to perform it in line with societal expectations. We perform gender roles and feminist analyses of such performances have focused on the gendered division of labour within the household. Women often assume or are held responsible for the private sphere and the household, including taking care of children, cooking and cleaning. Women do gender, i.e. perform their roles by assuming household tasks. Oakley (1976) researched UK housewives and found that: (a) women worked long hours, (b) domestic tasks are repetitive and (c) that female housewives often found themselves to be socially isolated. Her description of women as domestic labourers is tied to gendered understandings of domesticity and the performance of gender. Caring, too, is often associated with gendered constructions. Thus, being a woman is about caring and parenting.

There are also many gendered assumptions that feminists have identified. In sports, for example, women are assumed to have less physical strength. Lorber (1993) cites that different rules and values for the same sport (e.g. basketball and gymnastics) are related to gender.

Put simply, then, we all do gender. Changing social constructions of gender can be seen over time and in different cultural contexts. Defining culture is difficult as it is a contested and debated concept. It has been defined in a variety of ways and is used differently across different disciplines. Culture can be understood as the collective beliefs, assumptions and values that are communicated between people within a society (Boyden 2004). Thus, culture is how we make sense of and understand the social world in which we live.

Defining culture

Helman (2000: 2) defines culture as 'an inherited "lens", through which the individual perceives and understands the world'.

We all live in a specific cultural context which functions as the context in which we perform gender, and thus has an influence on gendered performances, gender roles and understandings of gender. For most of us, gendered understandings are implicit within our social worlds as we often do not think about how culture influences gender. Culture is important in gender socialisation; we are all socialised from childhood to perform gender in specific ways. Different colours are identified with genders, toys are gendered and parents treat children in what are seen to be culturally appropriate gendered ways. Thus, gendered meanings are embedded in all areas of society across the world, and conveyed through social institutions. For example, in some contexts social institutions may urge women to stay at home and to raise children, and in some places laws are used to try to promote gender equality. A preference for sons (rather than daughters) is also common in a variety of cultures and is one of the strongest manifestations of gender inequality (Farre 2011). There are many examples of different gendered practices across the world related to gendered understandings, some of which are reinforced through policy and legislation:

- In Turkey, married women can only seek abortion when they have their husband's permission (Gursoy 1996).
- Child marriages are documented in many countries, such as Afghanistan and Bangladesh, where more than half of girls are married by the age of 18 (World Marriage Patterns 2000).
- In Burkina-Faso, women are not able to go to the dispensary themselves and need their husband's consent to do so (Nikiema et al. 2008).
- Education in some contexts is favoured for boys more than girls. In rural Pakistan, 91% of male-headed households are in favour of sending their sons to school, while only 63% wish to send their daughters to school (Sandhu et al. 2005). However, this trend is reversed in some places (Shafiq 2009).
- In Egypt, an unmarried woman who is younger than 21 needs her father's permission to apply for a passport (Farre 2011).

From these examples, it should be clear to you that gender is a feature of all societies and is fundamental to the way in which societies are organised and, indeed, operate. Gender is also central to global relations (Thompson and Armato 2011), as Chapters 6 and 7 illustrate in more depth. These different understandings and expectations are closely tied to gender inequalities.

Gender inequalities

Gender inequality is concerned with how the aspects of being either a man or a woman result in power differences, different life chances and different outcomes in a range of societal contexts.

> ## Defining gender inequality
>
> Lorber (1994a) argues that gender inequality can be defined as the devaluation of 'women' and the social domination of 'men'.

For Lorber (1994a), gender inequality has social functions and a social history, rather than being the result of sex, procreation, physiology, anatomy, hormones or genetic predispositions. Lorber (1994a) argues that gender inequality is produced and maintained via social processes and that it is built into the general social structure in which we all exist. She argues that gender as a modern social institution serves to construct women as a group to be the subordinates of men. Lorber is a feminist theorist. Broadly, feminism as a theory is an approach that explains social structures as being fundamentally based on inequalities between women and men. Men are seen to have greater power in both the public and the private spheres.

Feminists have different notions of the causes of gender inequality and these are discussed later in this chapter. In general, feminist ideas have addressed a number of issues, including the historical construction of knowledge, the social construction of gender roles, male dominance, and sexism within the sociological literature. Feminists have been central in highlighting gender inequalities across the world and there is now a large bank of evidence to demonstrate the extent of gender inequalities.

How can we measure gender equality?

The measurement of gender equality, similar to the measurement of social class, is complex and, as a result, there has been much debate in the literature about how to effectively measure it. There are, of course, many limitations when using statistics and the validity of some indicators has also been questioned because, as Wach and Reeves (2000) argue:

- Data is not available by gender in many countries.
- Comparing data between countries is challenging.
- Some indicators can be questioned in terms of their validity. For example, when looking at productive activity, this is often a measure of market activities and

therefore fails to take account of the productive activity of women in the informal sector and non-market areas, which is where women tend to be productive in many contexts.

One measure that has been used to explore gender disparities in development is that of the gender-related development index, which is closely related to the human development index. The gender-related development index looks at life expectancy, educational attainment and income. Another measure that can be used is related to gender empowerment, which looks at gender inequality in areas such as economic and political participation, decision making, seats held in parliament by women and managerial positions held by women. These measures are slightly different because the gender development index looks at basic capabilities but both were introduced in the *Human Development Report 1995* (United Nations Development Programme 1995). There are a variety of aspects of gender inequality that are currently measured, including:

- Poverty measures.
- Health measures, such as life expectancy, access to health services and health outcomes.
- Employment and pay indicators, such as opportunities for employment, pay, pension rights and working conditions.
- Educational measures, such as an opportunity to be educated, length of time in education and educational attainment such as literacy levels.
- Access to resources. These may be economic but also related to food and nutrition, water and sanitation facilities, property and land ownership.
- Governance, including social policies and the way that these affect women, women in political positions, and the right of women to participate in politics by voting.

This list of potential measures is by no means exhaustive and there may be other areas that you can think of too. What is clear is that the measurement of gender equality has produced a large amount of evidence demonstrating the significant inequalities experienced by women within the contemporary world.

Women and inequalities: the evidence

In 1911, women were allowed to vote in just two countries across the world whereas today the right to vote is almost universal (Turquet et al. 2011). Indeed, there are signs of gender equality in many areas, with the social situation of women much improved since the 1960s. Despite improvements, however, women still face economic, social and political barriers that men do not. Legal reforms in many countries are a positive change but do not always translate into equality or justice for millions of women worldwide. Historically, there were many gender inequalities, such as women not having the right to vote, women being classed as their husband's property and women being excluded from several societal domains, including education and the world of work. These are now distantly located in the past for many contemporary western women but many gender inequalities remain. Turquet et al. (2011) highlight several such examples:

- In many countries women are prohibited from working in the same industries as men.
- In 50 countries, the minimum legal age of marriage is lower for females when compared to males, which results in less educational opportunities and a higher risk of death and complications from early pregnancies.
- Violence (including sexual violence) against women and girls permeates the globe.
- Women globally tend to be employed in more vulnerable jobs, for example, in the informal economy, and so face worse conditions and often less remittance. Equal pay for women is still not a reality in many places despite legislation.
- Women do not always have the right to control their own reproductive health, for example, to use contraception or to choose abortion.
- Women face discrimination in many countries because of property laws, so they are unable to claim what is rightfully theirs.

Clearly, gender is important globally. Indeed, debates have abounded about the ways in which globalisation is related to contemporary patterns of gender inequality (see Chapter 6 for more about globalisation). A relational global feminist perspective links the relationship between the local and the global by showing how actions and policies in one country can affect both women and men in another country. Given that different countries have and exert varying degrees of power and influence, these gender effects are often more marked and disadvantageous in countries that wield less power on the global stage (Thompson and Armato 2011). Indeed, the globalisation of communication and the media has enabled the world to see the very marked differences that exist between men and women, depending on the context in which they are living. Venkatapuram's (2011: 1) starts his book, *Health Justice*, by saying: 'I am going to skip the usual graphic story describing the wretched life of some poor girl or woman in some poor country.' These images, then, are common place for many of us living in higher income countries.

The stark evidence of these and all inequalities should, however, not be ignored. The health outcomes of women across the world are demonstrative of the way in which inequalities are still a significant issue for contemporary women. Those in weak social, economic and political positions, such as women, are much more at risk of malnutrition, violence, sexually transmitted infections and respiratory conditions. Women and children bear the main burden of global health inequalities. In 2007, women made up 61% of HIV infections in Sub-Saharan Africa (UNAIDS 2007). In addition, there are many deaths from maternal mortality (Hill et al. 2007).

Sen (2001) has also contributed in this area, citing seven types of gender inequality, summarised in Table 4.1.

These are just a few examples of inequality; there are many others that are recognised and reported. For example, in Saudi Arabia in September 2011, a woman was sentenced to ten lashes for defying the ban on women being able to drive. This was after much media coverage reporting progress in women's rights in Saudi Arabia: from 2015 women will be allowed to vote for the first time (BBC News 2011a). Although the sentence was not carried out, inequality remains evident. Other examples of gender inequality in the literature are: women being employed in low-paid, low-status jobs; women being invisible carers, resulting in disadvantage; women being child-bearers and child-rearers as part of the ideology of domesticity; gender segregation in employment; and the feminisation of poverty. Furthermore, much development work has tended to ignore the rights and needs of women. There is still a long way to go before full equality is achieved.

Table 4.1   Different types of gender inequality

Type of gender inequality	Explanation
Mortality inequality	Inequality in many places involves life and death, e.g. in North Africa, Asia, China and South Asia there are high mortality rates for women.
Natality inequality	There is a preference for boys over girls in many societies, demonstrated in parents wanting newborns to be sons rather than daughters. Given the development of medical techniques to determine gender, sex-selective abortion is now common in many countries.
Basic facility inequality	Girls in many countries have far fewer opportunities to be educated.
Special opportunity inequality	Even in higher income countries, girls are denied opportunities to receive higher education, training and to work in some professional areas based upon gender provinces.
Professional inequality	In terms of employment in work and occupational opportunities, women face greater barriers than men.
Ownership inequality	Property ownership is very unequal in many societies even with basic assets, such as homes, not being shared.
Household inequality	Family arrangements are often unequal in terms of sharing the housework and childcare responsibilities. Thus, there are unequal divisions of labour, which impact upon employment opportunities and recognition in the outside world.

Source: Adapted from Sen (2001)

Complete the following Learning Task to explore the challenges that women face in relation to equality within contemporary society.

Learning Task 4.1 – gender equality: the greatest challenge of our time?

Use the internet to access Ted Talks and to listen to the following short presentation: 'Sheryl WuDunn: Our century's greatest injustice', which is available at: www.ted.com/talks/lang/en/sheryl_wudunn_our_century_s_greatest_njustice.html.

1 Do you agree with the arguments that are made? Is gender equality the greatest challenge of our time?
2 Give some thought to the ways in which gender inequalities have been visible to you in your everyday experiences? For example, in language used, in how different genders are described and labelled, and in how individuals are treated.

Given the arguments that you have just viewed in this Learning Task, it is clear that gender equality and development need to be attended to. Gender inequalities have recently been discussed in a World Bank Report.

Women, equality and development

The World Bank (2011), in its latest *World Development Report*, focuses on gender equality and its relationship to development (development as a mechanism to improve inequality is critically discussed further in Chapter 7). The report provides a comprehensive review of gender inequality today, arguing that progress has been uneven in many countries. For example:

- A wealthy child in Nigeria is likely to go to school for 10 years, whereas poor rural girls in Hausa receive less than six months' education.
- Death rates are higher for women when compared to men in low- and middle-income countries.
- Divorce or widowhood has profound implications for many women across the world as they often become landless and lose all of their assets.
- Women's occupations tend to be lower paid.
- Women are more likely to be the victims of violence at home and to suffer more severe injuries.
- Men are more likely to hold senior positions in business and in politics (see Learning Task 4.2 which explores work-related inequalities in more depth).

The report argues that gender equality is needed because it is important in economic terms: 'gender equality is smart economics: it can enhance economic efficiency and improve other development outcomes' (World Bank 2011: 3). The report argues from the outset that gender equality is important in relation to productivity. While this economic view and focus on development have resulted in criticisms (see Chapter 8), the report suggests more such as:

- Women's opportunities shape those of the next generation; thus greater gender equality has more positive outcomes for children in terms of investment in them.
- Increased female agency leads to better institutions and policies: for example, in India and Nepal, when women had more opportunities to manage forests, they improved conservation outcomes (Agarwal 2010).

The report argues for changes to achieve greater gender inequality, highlighting a range of high-priority areas for policy makers to consider. These include:

1 Reducing gender gaps in human capital (addressing female mortality and educational inequalities).
2 Closing earnings and productivity gaps between men and women.
3 Shrinking gender differences in voice, for example, increasing women's voice within households and within the political arena.
4 Limiting the reproduction of gender inequality over time.

Razavi (2011) analysed the World Bank report and its key arguments for achieving gender equality and, while discussing some positives, argues that the recommendations made in the report are too narrow in their focus and thus are not adequate as a mechanism to create a more equal society. Her analysis identifies both positives and weaknesses of the report, and these are summarised in Table 4.2.

For many, then, the promotion of economic development alone is not enough to change attitudes about son preference, for example, or to reduce discrimination against girls, because social structures also need to change. Traditions such as dowries, patrilineal living arrangements (where a wife lives with her husband's family) and discriminatory inheritances need to be eliminated (Farre 2011). Das Gupta et al. (2000) also point out that even where states are interested in promoting gender equality, their actions and social policies may be limited by strategies to maintain stable family structures. For example, the Chinese Communist Party attempted to eliminate arranged marriages, child-marriages and dowries through the creation of a marriage law. The implementation of the law was successful in the sense that arranged marriages did decrease and young women gained some autonomy. However, political dissatisfaction and concerns that this approach was threatening the family as a system led to the drive for change slowing. The family, then, and women's position within it, is key to exploring their unequal position, including in relation to socio-economic outcomes.

Table 4.2   An evaluation of the 2011 *World Development Report*

Positive aspects of the report	Criticisms of the report
It emphasises the intrinsic value of gender equality in line with basic human rights.	It fails to recognise the biases that exist within labour markets. Markets are not neutral; they are social institutions that contain bias, as seen in social norms and power inequalities.
The report comments upon the role of law and legislation, which both affect women's rights within the family.	It cites the public sector as an area which has given many women employment opportunities and, while this is of course undeniable, the public sector is under attack across the world, which will impact upon women.
It recognises gender inequality as a political project.	Employment recommendations are weak, focusing upon activation policies (see Chapter 8) rather than the current problems with the global economy.
It recognises that gender equality will not be achieved simply by countries getting richer through economic development.	The report does not mention the health hazards experienced by women in some occupations or female job losses due to changes in trade rules.
The report gives attention to the unequal division of unpaid domestic and care work that occurs between men and women.	The report is too vague when discussing the provision of services such as health and childcare, suggesting that both public and private funding streams can be used without acknowledging how privately funded provision is itself linked to inequalities.
It recommends the provision of clean water and sanitation, stressing the high social rate of return on such investments.	There are missed opportunities in terms of the social policy discussed in the report, e.g. there is no mention of gender bias in pension schemes or the problems associated with privatisation of services. Social policy is also reduced to single instruments, such as conditional cash transfers, which will have limited effect.
	There is no exploration of the relationship between gender inequality and macro-economic policy.
	There is no recognition of the current financial restraints that may well limit any policy changes in this area.

Source: Adapted from Razavi (2011)

Women and socio-economic outcomes

Much of the literature on gender focuses on the position of women in terms of socio-economic status and outcomes. Farre (2011) argues that there are still differences in the socio-economic position of women. Indeed, poverty disproportionately affects women across the world, as described by the label 'the feminisation of poverty'. This term is used to describe the way in which poverty is rising faster in the female population than in the male. Poverty is multidimensional, so simply looking at incomes and economic measures actually masks the true extent of poverty for women and for children too. Many analyses demonstrate that women are the majority of the poor. For example, the Global Poverty Project (2012) argues that women make up 70% of the world's 1 billion poorest people. Women are more likely to live in poverty, to earn less (if they earn at all) and to hold responsibility for more of the financial burden for children and other dependents. Now complete the following Learning Task to explore the link between women and poverty in more detail.

Learning Task 4.2 – exploring the array of gender inequalities

Use the internet and visit the following website: www.globalpovertyproject. com/infobank/women

1 Read the information about the links between gender and inequalities, including poverty.
2 Take time to watch the video called 'The Girl Effect' and reflect on what it tells you. Read the comments listed on YouTube after the video. What is your interpretation of these?
3 Finally, think about the solutions that are suggested on this website. Do you agree that these are the way forward? Can you see any limitations with these approaches?

Given the widespread attention now focused on women and the large bank of data about their unequal experiences, social policy measures are being used across the globe in attempts to tackle some of these issues (see Chapter 8 for further discussion). Not all countries are keen to tackle gender inequalities but some are trying. The Millennium Development Goals (United Nations 2007; and see Chapter 7) have raised awareness of the need to tackle poverty and gender-related inequalities.

One approach that has been put forward in the latest *World Development Report* (World Bank 2011) and has been used in lower income countries, is that of conditional cash transfers. One such scheme used in Mexico involves payments to women as long as certain conditions are met, including school enrolment, health check-ups and attendance at health-related seminars. These schemes do work to promote enrolment in school and improve health outcomes in some deprived areas, although they reinforce the role of women as childcare providers and do not tackle the issue of the home-related burden often experienced by women (Farre 2011).

In low-income countries, a well-evidenced barrier to women's economic success is that of their greater involvement in household duties and childcare (Farre 2011). Some research suggests that women are doing less housework now, largely as a result of women being involved in paid employment. However, there is mixed evidence as to whether the hours men spend on housework are changing (Hochschild 1989). Research about housework in Sweden shows that, regardless of access to resources, Swedish men do less housework than Swedish women (Evertsson and Nermon 2007), thus demonstrating gender inequalities in what is one of the most equal societies in the world. But even when women do gain access to employment, further inequalities are in evidence, in terms of job opportunities, the type of work available for women and pay. While women across the globe are increasingly taking up paid employment, labour force statistics underestimate their contribution by excluding work from the informal sector (Wach and Reeves 2000). Furthermore, despite increased involvement in formal economic activity, women tend to be paid less in many places in the world. For example, in the UK, female business and management graduates earned on average £3,400 per year less than their male counterparts four years after graduation. This represents a pay gap of 15% (Wilton 2011). Wilton (2011) argues that in the UK women earn less than men on average partly because they often work in the public sector. Now complete the following Learning Task to explore this further.

Learning Task 4.3 – women and work: exploring business and gender inequalities

Use the internet to access and watch 'Hilary Devey's Women at the Top' at www.bbc.co.uk/programmes/b01ml90w. This programme explores why so few women make it to the top in business, examining factors like maternity leave, the cost of childcare and women's leadership style.

1 Consider the idea of a glass-ceiling as an invisible area of gender inequality. Are you aware of other areas of work in which women are disadvantaged in terms of reaching top positions?
2 Use the internet to search for media reports about gender inequalities at work in a range of countries. Think about the places in the world where women are excluded from work or where they are forced to earn from the informal economy. Make a list of your conclusions.

Gender inequality within the work context has led feminists to call on policy makers to act and to challenge the role that women hold in the family. There has been some policy changes related to gender inequality within work in many countries. For example, the UK introduced an Equal Pay Act in 1970. However, despite this legislation there is still evidence of differences in pay and legal challenges to pay differences are complex and difficult. Other countries, too, have developed more gender equal family benefits through changing employment law and social policy. For example, Norway and Sweden both changed their maternity leave systems, extending leave periods and allowing time for new fathers to be away from work. This reduced the need for women to be the family carer on the basis that they usually earn less and therefore it is easier for them to reduce employment hours, or to become inactive within the paid employment sector. However, not all countries promote gender equality through employment legislation, and it is much more difficult to promote behaviour change in relation to housework and childcare (Farre 2011). Gender policies and any associated changes are linked to complex power dynamics within all social contexts.

Women and power

The concept of power is central to many feminist discussions of the position of women in contemporary society. Gender inequalities emerge for many feminists because women experience a lack of power due to their gender and social position. The powerlessness of women is demonstrated in the following examples:

1 Women and HIV/Aids

   Women are often powerless to negotiate safe sex; their economic dependency strips them of the right to protect themselves from infection. In many cultures, a sexual relationship is not a matter of choice but a matter of survival. Women are often not in a position to compel fidelity or contraceptive use. In times of destitution, prostitution is often the only means of support for single, deserted or divorced women in some areas of the world, which raises their risk of contracting HIV/Aids. The impact of HIV on women is not confined to them because women are often primary carers and have to care for the entire sick family. Finally, this caring role compounds the situation in that many infants born to HIV-infected mothers acquire the disease as a result of breastfeeding.

2 Women and famine

   Even in non-famine situations women are often deprived of food in that their powerlessness ensures that they have less eligibility. Women may choose to feed their husband and children before themselves. Therefore those in poorer circumstances are more vulnerable in general. Women in many contexts have weaker links to the labour market and fewer assets, and as a consequence their food entitlement often depends on men. Many studies show that this powerlessness means that in times of famine there is a higher mortality rate for women than men. Furthermore, in times of famine, marriages often break up, leaving women in an even more vulnerable position. The majority of the destitute in such times are women, who then have to attend relief centres for food or depend on grants for relief. Men in comparison can often pay cash for food (Agarwal 1994).

Dixey et al. (2013) argue in relation to powerlessness that individuals need to become empowered in order to address inequalities. They state that real empowerment only happens when a person makes the links between their personal position and structural inequalities, i.e. when they not only feel a sense of personal power, but when they begin to question their position in society. An example of this awakening is this:

> During the depression years of the 1930s, cookery classes were organised for women in poor communities in an attempt to help them to provide nutritious meals for their families despite low incomes. One particular evening, a group of women were being taught how to make cod's head soup – a cheap and nourishing dish. At the end of the lesson the women were asked if they had any questions. 'Just one', said a member of the group, 'whilst we're eating the cod's head soup, who's eating the cod?' (Quoted in Popay and Dhooge 1989: 140). (A cod is a fish commonly eaten in Europe.)

Powerlessness comes from three potential sources:

1 The systems which systematically deny powerless groups opportunities to take action.
2 The negative images that oppressed people have of themselves; this is a form of self-oppression.
3 The negative experiences that oppressed people undergo in their everyday interactions with systems, institutions or the media (Solomon 1976).

Experiencing powerlessness means that people feel further excluded, rejected, treated as inferior, and, in a downward spiral, then feel that they are inadequate, unworthy, and deserving of the role of 'second-class citizen'. There are many examples in which women now fight for further equality and aim to gain empowerment in a variety of ways, including on the global stage (see Chapter 6). Indeed, the following examples also indicate that empowerment can be gained in a variety of contexts by women who are attempting to address the structural inequalities which are affecting their lives:

1 Yuannan Women's Reproductive Health and Development Programme

Women participating in the Yuannan Women's Reproductive Health and Development Programme documented their life conditions using 'photovoice', a participatory strategy that uses photographs for creating discussion between people. The women used cameras to capture their lives as they saw them. The images collected were then used to promote dialogue, critical thinking and to identify causes of powerlessness. The images allowed the women to better advocate for change and resulted in an improvement in the reported levels of self-esteem and confidence. Positive outcomes of this project included the establishment of day-care centres, midwifery programmes and scholarships for rural girls (Laverack 2006).

2 New Zealand Prostitutes Collective (NZPC)

Laverack and Whipple (2010) report how a group of sex workers in New
Zealand were able to bring about reform in the legislation regulating sex work.
Through a process of community empowerment, the women achieved social
justice and equity for all sex workers in New Zealand. Although it took 15 years
to reform the legislation, started only by a small group of sex workers, NZPC
were eventually able to influence public policy and safeguard the human rights
of sex workers through building partnerships and alliances with agencies.

However, while it can be simple to identify the places and contexts in which women
are powerless, empowerment itself is a very complex process; even defining empowerment is problematic (Woodall et al. 2012). Furthermore, Baistow (1994: 40) argues
that 'problems' are often complex and interconnected, and a simple 'dose of empowerment' is unlikely to provide the full solution. Indeed, empowerment cannot be
simply given to women; as the examples in this chapter have shown, it comes from
individuals and communities empowering themselves. Thus, in order to facilitate
change, groups of women need to gain their own momentum, acquire skills and
advocate for themselves to fully realise empowerment (Rissel 1994; Wallerstein
2006). According to Nikkhah and Redzuan (2009), if power cannot change – for
example, if it is inherent in social structures – then it is not possible to achieve it.
Indeed, the decisions about who should be empowered are also complex and difficult. It may be the case that there are some groups who should become less empowered, rather than more powerful, but who should decide which groups? How can
such judgements be made, and who is best placed to make such judgements?
    While there have been many improvements in relation to the position of women,
as this chapter has already explored, there are still significant areas in which women
are powerless. This lack of powerlessness can be demonstrated by poor health outcomes, particularly for women in the poorest countries of the world. Women in
poorer countries often depend on men for survival, are not well educated and are
responsible for domestic chores. All of these factors combine to worsen their health
outcomes in general. Girls can be married young (from the age of 15) and will experience many pregnancies as they are often powerless to negotiate safe sex. Macdonald
(2007) argues that early marriages limit educational opportunities, increase health risks
due to pregnancies at a young age and put women at an increased risk of HIV exposure as they are often married to an older man, with a long sexual history.
    A 2007 report, 'Because I am a Girl' summarises evidence to show that female
foetuses are more likely to be aborted and female babies abandoned (Plan International 2007). In Asia it has been estimated that the female population is short of 60
million women as a result of such practices. Female babies are also less likely to be fed
as much, experiencing malnutrition, and are more likely to be illiterate by their teenage years, damaging their life chances later on. Indeed, social policy can also serve to
exacerbate such practices, as the 'one child' policy in China has shown, resulting in the
birth of many more boys with female foetuses again being aborted. Women in several

countries are seen as the property of their fathers until they are married, when they subsequently become the property of their husband. They do not get to choose when to have sex or indeed under what conditions. Younger women are also more likely to be sexually assaulted and face violence. Thus, there is a wealth of evidence to show that the powerlessness of women affects their physical and mental health, their access to health care treatment, and their right to control their own body and fertility. These inequalities are for many related to the social status associated with being female. Patriarchy constructs women as having lower social status than men, which serves to sustain gender inequalities. There are many different explanations offered for the existence of gender inequalities, so let's explore some of these now.

Explaining female inequality

Contemporary gender relations are increasingly complex, hence gender theories now emphasise the complexities of varied forms of masculinities and femininities. The work of Connell (1987, 2005) is concerned with explaining gender inequalities. She argues that gender relations are ultimately defined by patriarchal power and, as a result, various types of masculinity and femininity exist but they are all based on the dominance of men over women. Her analysis of the gender order is explained in Table 4.3.

The gender order, as depicted by Connell (1987) in Table 4.3, is not static and changes because gender relationships are the outcome of societal processes. She discusses the changing gender dynamics within contemporary society in the following ways:

1 Institutions within society are currently being undermined. Institutions that traditionally support men are becoming weaker because of legislation on divorce, domestic violence and rape, and economic questions in relation to women.
2 Hegemonic masculinity, the dominance of men maintained through cultural dynamics, is under threat and less dominant than it has been. Women's sexuality has grown in strength, as has gay sexuality.
3 Interest groups which pose challenges to the current gender order dominated by men are now forming or are already in existence. For example, women's rights movements, gay movements and movements generally changing attitudes towards sexism are resulting in social change.

Table 4.3   Connell's (1987) analysis of the gender order

Aspect of the gender order	Description of what it involves
Labour	• The sexual division of labour within the home and the labour market.
Power	• This operates through social relationships such as authority, violence, ideology in institutions, the state, the military and domestic spheres.
Cathexis	• This focuses attention on the dynamics within personal relationships, including marriage, child-bearing and sexuality.

Source: R.W. Connell, *Gender and Power: Society, the Person, and Sexual Politics* (1987) originally published by Polity Press in the UK and Rest of World; Stanford University Press in Canada, North America and its Territories; and Allen and Unwin in New Zealand, Australia, Fiji and Papua New Guinea. Reproduced kindly with permission © 1987 R.W. Connell.

Connell's (2009) more recent work has involved exploring gender within a global context because she argues that gender relations are now globalised. Transnational companies have male managers, international and non-governmental agencies such as the United Nations are mainly run by men, and the international media not only has a strongly gendered division of labour but also reports on gender issues which reflect specific understandings and interpretations.

Unsurprisingly, feminist theorists have widely contributed to the analysis and debate about women's gender inequality, as Chapter 1 outlined. As early as 1911, Gilman was writing about the man-made world which she described as an androcentric culture in which men monopolised activities such as work, confining women to the domestic sphere. Gilman (1911) argued that society needed to allow women to be both workers and mothers for progress to be achieved. So, progress has been made, although this has not resulted in full equality and critiques of contemporary gender relations continue. The gender order remains patriarchal for feminists in that it is seen to benefit and privilege men while marginalising and oppressing women.

> ### Defining patriarchy
>
> Thompson and Armato (2011) define patriarchy as rule of the father. They argue, however, that contemporary patriarchy is more than just the rule of individual men; it is about masculine institutions serving the interests and lives of men.

Connell (1987) argues that the central feature of the organisation of gendered power in western societies is the cultural association of masculinity with authority. When analysing gender, feminists use the concepts of femininity and masculinity to explore performances of gender and gender relations. Behaviours and objects associated with women and girls are considered feminine, while behaviours and objects associated with boys are considered masculine (Thompson and Armato 2011). Have you ever paid attention to the way in which gender is performed and how this might relate to concepts such as masculinity and femininity? Complete the following Learning Task to explore the notion of masculinities and femininities in everyday life.

Learning Task 4.4 – exploring the performance of gender

1 In one of the usual places that you occupy, for example, a classroom, a coffee shop or the student union, take some time to observe other people. Watch how women and men perform gender. Look at how

people dress, the way in which they speak and how this differs for men and women. Make some notes about your observations.

2 Now consider what this means in relation to the concepts of masculinity and femininity. Which aspects of the performance are masculine and which are feminine in your observations?

3 Finally, think about what this means in terms of gender inequalities. Can you see any gender inequalities in such performances? For example, some studies have shown that male students tend to dominate classroom talk, especially if there is a female tutor. Are there other examples of inequalities that you have observed in daily life?

Completing this Learning Task will have helped you to understand how complex gender is within the context of everyday life. Furthermore, what constitutes masculinity and femininity is different across social contexts, ages, races, ethnic groups and social classes. Gender theorists have developed the concept of hegemonic masculinity – masculinity as culturally ascendant (Connell 1987). This is the idea that masculinity legitimates male power. Femininity is not described in the same way. 'Emphasised femininity' is a concept that is used to explore the lower status of women, examining their bodily practices and the way in which they are encouraged to achieve feminine ideals by cultivating body image and appearance. Femininity in this conceptualisation is defined by heterosexual men's desires (Thompson and Armato 2011). Given these complexities, feminists argue that it is useful to understand masculinities and femininities – plural conceptualisations. Indeed, feminist theories are equally diverse, with the literature referring to feminisms as a way of capturing different explorations and understandings of gender inequalities. Table 4.4 summarises some of the many feminist explanations of gender inequalities.

Table 4.4   An overview of some of the contributions made by feminist theorists in analysing gender inequality

Feminist	Key points
Chodorow (1978)	• Analyses the reproduction of mothering. • Argues that masculinity and femininity are based in strong emotional structures that are established early in life, through socialisation. • Male children break away from the mother at an earlier stage, resulting in increased autonomy, inexpressiveness and hostility towards women.
Hochschild (1983)	• Focused sociological attention on feelings and emotions, in particular arguing that emotions are work. • She argues that there is a gendered division in terms of emotional labour; women are more likely to do emotional labour.

(Continued)

Table 4.4   (Continued)

Feminist	Key points
	• Culturally, women are expected to undertake specific aspects of emotional labour, such as caring, and to behave in emotionally appropriate ways, such as not showing anger. • She demonstrates that emotions also matter in the workplace, e.g. as part of the service economy, in which women dominate. • Emotional labour is more costly to the self because of what it encompasses.
Butler (1990, 1993, 1997, 2004, 2005; Butler and Weed 2011)	• Questions the ways in which gender is constructed as natural; rather it is a performance. • Gender as a natural objective thing simply does not exist; sex and gender are socially constructed. • Sexuality is used as a regulatory tool and therefore as a mechanism to perpetuate gender inequalities.
Collins (1990, 2004)	• Argues from a black standpoint perspective. • Non-white women's experiences are even more marginalised than white women. • The absence of black women's voices from power is part of the problem that exacerbates their oppression. • She recognised that different black women have localised experiences based upon the interrelationship of all of their social divisions, such as class, age and sexual orientation. • She draws attention to the powerful ideologies that exist in society, which serve to perpetuate inequality. • She argues that black women are culturally oppressed.
Smith (1987, 1990)	• Both knowledge in sociology and society is determined by men. • Women are excluded from knowledge creation through societal structures, expectations and institutional rules. • Ideologically powerful texts, such as the Bible, situate women as objects in society. • Sociology as a discipline is also written from the standpoint of men as it excludes women's realities. • Women's experiences need to be given attention to demonstrate how these are different from the 'objective' reality constructed by the ruling elite to produce transformative knowledge and therefore equality.
Walby (1990)	• Focuses upon patriarchy, which is the way in which social organisation is dominated by men, who then oppress and rule women. • Patriarchy, in her analysis, is composed of several structures that overlap: 1 Paid work – women are more likely to be paid less 2 Household – women are more likely to raise children and do housework 3 State – women are less likely to hold powerful positions 4 Violence – women are more likely to face abuse 5 Sexuality – women face more negative treatment in relation to this 6 Culture – women are misrepresented in popular culture.

Table 4.4 is a small selection of some feminist contributions. As the table shows, there are many types of feminist theories which seek to explain the social world in which gender is created. In general, it can be argued that feminism as a movement is an attempt to improve the lives of women (Lorber 1998). Feminists also try to challenge the often traditional ways in which we think about gender and understand it. Collins (1990) usefully highlights how dimensions of inequality are interrelated, arguing that race, ethnicity and social class intersect and interact with gender to form a matrix of domination. Social divisions are interrelated in the sense that people do not simply hold a position in the gender order; they also fit within other systems of segregation, such as racial and class systems.

Clearly, systems of stratification are complex and feminisms have sought to explore these complexities as well as attempting to achieve improvements too. Feminism is also linked to social movements, for example in the United States, feminists have fought to change the way in which women's lives were constructed, challenging property ownership laws, engaging women in education and extending women's rights across a range of sectors (Lorber 1998). Thus, women's civil rights movements have challenged female subordination and gender differences since the 1960s (Evans 1980).

There have also been analyses from male sociologists. For example, Parsons (1942) argued that gender differences serve as an important function for societal integration. Engels, in comparison, argued that capitalism intensified male domination by paying no wages for the work of women (Barry 1983). There are, of course, criticisms of all of these analyses, with not everyone sharing the same vision of how society operates. Feminists are also by no means in agreement about the causes or solutions of gender inequality, and have ideological divisions among themselves. For example, liberal, socialist and radical feminists all produce different analyses. Liberal feminists seek to expand the rights of women. Socialist feminists argue for the conventional family to be reorganised so that domestic subjugation ends. Radical feminists advocate for the eradication of the cultural notion of gender entirely. There is no scope to explore these debates in depth here. What is important is to understand basic feminist ideas, as outlined above in Table 4.2. These can be summarised as follows (Macionis and Plummer 2008):

1 Change is needed.
2 Choice needs to be expanded for women.
3 Gender divisions need to be eliminated.
4 Sexual violence should be ended.
5 Women's autonomy is important in all areas.

There have also been analyses of masculinity within the literature in terms of changing gender roles. Women are now more likely to work, men are generally more involved in caring and childcare roles and an increasing number of analyses examine how males experience disadvantage in relation to gender divisions. For example, there are complex analyses of the relationship between masculinities and health, with evidence documenting a range of health inequalities experienced by men. The relationships between social determinants, inequalities in men's health and masculinities are complex and arguably under-represented in both policy and practice (Gough and Robertson 2010). Mainstream gender theory is grounded in gender inequality, as Table 4.2 demonstrates. Men are seen to create gender inequality and therefore are a problem for women. However, gender also marginalises and disadvantages men in specific areas. Consequently, multiple power systems need to be examined to further understand the complexities associated with gendered social divisions (Bloomwood 2011).

Gendered inequalities are also fundamentally tied to different stages of the life course, with younger women facing specific gender-related challenges compared to those experienced by older women. This is another example of the intersection of social divisions.

What about men?

So far this chapter has exclusively focused on women and the inequalities that they experience. Feminists have drawn our attention to these issues over many years, and thus improvements are being made. While many challenges remain in relation to female inequalities, recent analyses of the literature show that men too experience inequalities, and that gender inequalities are themselves very complex. This can be demonstrated using the example of mental health.

Sociologists have examined many gender differences in terms of health, including mental health. The most common mental health problems, such as depression, are far more prevalent among women (see Foster 1995; Bebbington 1996). Despite this, men are more likely to successfully commit suicide (Biddle et al. 2008) as they often choose a more effective mechanism by which to achieve the end result. Research in this area has explored the social factors which play a part in the diagnosis of men with mental illness, for example looking at whether women are more health-seeking than men. Research has shown that men are less likely to use health services than women (Courtenay 2000) so, in the first instance, less contact with health services means less chance of diagnosis. Researchers have also analysed medical consultations between men and GPs, and argue that men relate their emotional experiences to expectations of being male, so they keep a 'stiff upper lip', do not cry, and control their emotions (Moynihan 1998).

Sociologists have also explored how important the notion of masculinity is in determining diagnoses of male mental illness. Being male and masculine is often culturally represented as being both independent and powerful (Newman 1997). This has led to suggestions that men are more reluctant to seek help for mental illnesses as they often do not wish to be viewed as less masculine. So, sociology offers some explanation of gender inequalities in mental illness rates by examining the complex interweaving of the influential role of culture and social influences, which combine to affect health-seeking behaviour, the attitudes of patients and diagnoses.

Gendered health inequalities are also evidenced for men across Europe. White et al. (2011) provide a comprehensive overview of the state of men's health across the 27 Member States of the European Union, the four states of the European Free Trade Association (Norway, Iceland, Switzerland and Lichtenstein) and the three candidate countries (Croatia, Turkey and the Former Yugoslav Republic of Macedonia). The report highlights the broad range of mortality and morbidity data arising from the many different health conditions that affect men in Europe, demonstrating marked differences between the health of men and women and, at the same time, large disparities in health outcomes between men in different countries. The report shows many ways in which men are disadvantaged in terms of health. For example:

- Although men's overall life expectancy in Europe is generally increasing, it has decreased in some countries in the past decade. However, life expectancy is lower for men than for women across the EU, with differences ranging from 11.3 years in Latvia to 3.3 years in Iceland.
- For the EU27, the death rate is higher for men in all age ranges, with particularly marked differences in the over 65 age range   a 50% higher death rate in the over 65 age group.
- Over 630,000 male deaths occur in working-age men (15–64 years) as compared to 300,000 for women.

White et al. (2011) also argue that men's health disadvantage is not a biological inevitability and that there is the need for further analysis and consideration of the broader socio-cultural factors underpinning the data. Men's perspectives need to be made visible and policy also needs to be gender-proofed. Thus, a main message from this report is that male health inequalities can only be addressed by targeted activity across the lifespan. Interestingly, these health inequalities are not evident across the entire globe, as female health inequalities are more significant in many lower income countries.

Clearly, work needs to be done in relation to health inequalities for both genders. Men have also come under scrutiny in recent years within policy-making circles in the sense that they are increasingly seen to have a role and responsibility in promoting gender equality. Given the control that men hold in many areas of society, their attitudes and behaviours cannot be ignored in the design of policy in this area. In patriarchal societies, gender equality cannot be promoted without the consent and involvement of men (Farre 2011). For example, men influence the reproductive health outcomes of women in societies where they make decisions or control women's reproductive roles. Ultimately, then, gender policies need to do more than simply target women.

Case Study: Gender inequalities and sexual violence

There is a wealth of global evidence showing that women experience violence at the hands of men, and that some of this is sexual violence. Feminists argue that the patriarchal structure of society acts as a mechanism to support and, in some senses, to justify violence. For example, the status of women is linked to such violence in many ways. Yodanis (2004) argues that when men dominate society through family, political, economic and other social institutions, these institutions are consequently likely to embody, reproduce, and legitimate male domination over women. Furthermore, violence is a tool that men can use to keep women subordinate, and to maintain male power and control. Finally, male-defined policies and practices developed through these institutions mean that often violence is not likely to be punished or stopped. In some respects such violence may be subtly or overtly condoned and encouraged. Men's attitudes to sexual violence within the UK have recently been scrutinised as several high-profile politicians have made gendered and inappropriate comments related to notions of real rape and consent. Women's fear is central to these processes, and it is through this fear that men are able to maintain control. Yodanis (2004) used a broad range of empirical data to explore the relationship between fear, women' status and sexual violence, concluding that:

- Structures of gender inequality are associated with a culture of violence against women. Women's status (measured by education and occupation) correlates with the prevalence of sexual violence, with higher status women corresponding with lower rates of sexual violence. Furthermore, where women hold positions of power and influence in institutions, associated policies and practices may be less tolerant of sexual violence.
- Sexual violence is associated with a culture of women's fear. Women do not have to be victims of violence to feel fear as they may hear about violence against other women. Thus, where there are higher rates of violence within societies, women have corresponding higher levels of fear.

This study, like other feminist research, supports the evidence that violence is not solely explained by men's individual characteristics, attitudes and experiences. Ultimately, male violence in relation to women remains related to societal structures of male dominance.

Summary of key points

- Gender is a clear social stratification system which affects the life chances, economic status and health of both women and men. Power and powerlessness, as well as status, are related to gender position. Cultural factors are also analysed within the contemporary literature in relation to gender inequalities.

- Despite some improvements in gender inequalities, there still is significant evidence of gender inequalities across the world. Gender position is clearly correlated with a variety of inequalities, such as lack of access to economic resources, educational attainment and health outcomes.
- A range of theories exist which can be used to explain gender inequalities. This chapter has concentrated on feminist theories, which not only analyse gender inequalities but also attempt to tackle these inequalities.

List of questions to stimulate debate and reflection

1 Consider gender inequalities in your own life. How do you compare your own opportunities to those of your parents? Do you think that you have more equality? Do you consider yourself to be a feminist (this is irrespective of your gender)?
2 What countries do you think are particularly challenged in terms of gender inequalities within the world today? Can you identify the issues within at least one country in terms of challenging gender inequality?
3 What do you think about the role of the women's movement in terms of changing gender inequalities? What successes do you think are important and what challenges remain? Can the women's movement change gendered inequalities within the current global context?

Further reading

Lorber, Judith (2009) *Gender Inequality: Feminist Theory and Politics* (4th edition). Oxford: Oxford University Press.

This book, written by an internationally renowned feminist Judith Lorber, looks at various evolving theories of gender inequality. Lorber's own paradigm of 'reform, resistance, rebellion', is the structure of the analysis offered here. The book provides details of the accomplishments associated with feminism over the last 40 years and the challenges that are currently being tackled. The book has a global focus in that it discusses feminism in China, India, South Korea and Japan. There is also a useful overview of feminism's theories on the sources of gender inequality, its politics and its contributions.

Sen, Gita and Östlin, Piroska (eds) (2012) *Gender Equity in Health: The Shifting Frontiers of Evidence and Action*. London: Routledge.

This edited volume brings together experts from a variety of disciplines, who write about three areas: health disparities and inequity due to gender, the specific problems

women face in meeting the highest attainable standards of health, and the policies and actions that can address them. The book clearly demonstrates the importance of intersecting social hierarchies (e.g. gender, class and ethnicity) for understanding health inequalities and associated policy implications. It is an interesting read.

Thompson, Martha E. and Armato, Michael (2011) *Investigating Gender.* Cambridge: Polity Press.

This book explores how gender is related to broad societal structures of oppression in a student-centred approach. The book explores five key themes, such as the social construction of gender differences, gendered inequalities, the intersections of gender with other systems of privilege and oppression, a relational global perspective and, finally, the necessity of working towards social justice. The book also has a focus on international issues and explores these across countries such as China, Kenya, Mexico and Sweden.

5

SOCIAL DIVISIONS AND INEQUALITY: ETHNICITY

Key learning outcomes

By the end of this chapter you should be able to:

- Understand the way in which ethnicity is defined
- Understand the relationship between social inequality and ethnicity
- Understand the different ideological positions associated with explaining the existence of ethnic inequalities

Overview of the chapter

This chapter provides an overview of ethnicity as a contemporary social division, defining ethnicity and exploring its relationship with social inequality. It explores how ethnic divisions are evident within a range of contemporary contexts. This chapter outlines some progress that has been made in terms of reducing inequalities associated with ethnicity, although, despite this, many inequalities remain. These are linked to social inequality, status and power in complex ways. Thus, this chapter explores the complex relationship between ethnicity and social inequality, highlighting the explanations offered in the literature that tell us about why inequalities associated with ethnic classifications remain a problem within contemporary societies across the world.

What is ethnicity?

Both race and ethnicity are concepts that cause much debate. Race is a highly contentious concept that has no basis in science because all humans are virtually identical genetically. Therefore, when terms such as 'race' are used as a way of differentiating between people, such classifications have emerged from social and historical processes. 'Ethnicity' is another term that is loaded with contention. It is usually used to refer to the cultural practices of a group of people. However, in some instances, it is used as 'code' for race. Race and ethnicity are socially constructed identities which vary across time, space and situation (Allen and Chung 2000).

Defining ethnicity

Giddens defines ethnicity as '…the cultural practices and outlooks of a given community of people which sets them apart from others. Members of ethnic groups see themselves as culturally distinct from other groups and are seen by them, in return, as different'. (2009: 633)

Ethnicity is usually used to describe a collective identity and is based on the assumption that a collectivity has its roots in a common ancestry related to heritage, religion, culture, nationality, language and geographical territory. In the contemporary world it is usual to assume that everyone has an ethnic identity. Therefore, ethnicity is often understood as a fixed aspect of our identity. However, the notion of ethnicity as fixed has been challenged recently, with commentators arguing that it is dynamic and fluid, rather than static. Ethnicity is socially constructed, as is the idea of an ethnically homogenous national state. Ethnicity is a social construct specific to a social and historical context (Afkhami 2012). Despite debates about the term, ethnic identities do exist in contemporary societies as social forces and these are fundamentally tied to social inequalities. Ethnicity and perceptions of ethnicity as a dividing line between people are a mechanism of social stratification and relate to inequality of opportunities (Le Grand et al. 2008). Ethnic groups are often minority groups.

Defining minorities

Minorities are a group or category of people who can be distinguished either by their physical or cultural traits or by who are socially disadvantaged. (Macionis and Plummer 2002)

There are majority and minority groups within all societies, and these groups of individuals interact in different ways, as illustrated in Table 5.1.

Table 5.1   Patterns of societal interaction

Type of interaction	Description
Pluralist societies	In pluralist societies racial and ethnic minorities are distinct but have social parity. However, for many commentators the pluralist ideal has not been reached in Europe or indeed elsewhere.
Assimilation	This is the process by which minorities gradually adopt patterns of the dominant culture (it is often associated with a melting pot image). However, as assimilation occurs, some individuals see this as a threat to the identity of their people and culture. Assimilation can be forced. However, it cannot be fully avoided as the biological reproduction by people of different racial groups breaks down racial categories.
Segregation	This refers to the physical and social separation of categories of people. For example, in the USA and South Africa, the lifting of formal laws which required segregation did not lead to integration, and to a large extent blacks and whites are still separated. Inner cities in the USA are often only Hispanic or only black and, while few whites experience segregation, one in five black people spend some of their lives in segregated inner cities.
Genocide	This refers to the systematic annihilation of one category of people by another, with one of the most well-known examples of this occurring in the Second World War when Adolf Hitler attempted to eradicate the Jewish population, in what is now called the Holocaust. Despite a bank of evidence to demonstrate that the Holocaust occurred, there are still some contemporary individuals who deny that it ever happened.

Source: Adapted from Macionis and Plummer (2002)

Table 5.1 shows a range of social interactions that have occurred across societies as a result of ethnic differences. As you will see from the table, many of these interactions are not positive and there are many ongoing ethnic conflicts across the globe. Segregation has been cited as the cause of ethnic conflict. For example, 10 years ago the UK Bradford riots occurred as a result of racial tensions between different ethnic groups, and some media commentary discussed how segregation within Bradford between residents of different ethnic origins had served to increase racial tensions. Bradford was labelled as a 'racial tinderbox' where the city's large Asian community was estranged and at odds with the white working class (Bakare 2011). Often ethnic conflicts are related to religious difference too. For example, China's rule of Tibet is well documented as an approach that limits religious freedom, and in protest there are frequent self-immolations (individuals commit suicide by burning themselves alive in public places) by the Tibetan population. There are many violent conflicts that are occurring, and that were evident in the past, related to identity and ethnicity (Stewart 2010).

Occasionally, ethnic groups establish cultural identity as a significant form of resistance to racism. In the context of the UK, Gilroy (1987) argues that this was often done by African Caribbeans through dance and music. However, in postmodern society many people adopt ethnic identities, such as a black cultural style, as a form of fashion. While this demonstrates changing patterns of ethnicity as well as different levels of perceived status associated with different ethnic categories, it may serve to disenfranchise individual ethnic groups from their own identities.

Identify is related to inequalities in complex ways. Identity implies difference and defining characteristics which are exclusionary for those who do not share them. Le Grand et al. (2008) argue that ethnicity can be understood as a status marker that differentiates between groups and individuals. Thus status is related to ethnic identities, with some groups holding higher status than others. These perceptions of status vary across societies, within as well as between different ethnic groups. This can be tied to further segregation and intolerance through lack of understanding in relation to ethnic differences. Ethnic differences are also strongly related to inequalities, as this chapter will now illustrate.

Ethnic inequalities

Le Grand et al. (2008) argue that ethnicity is an important category of social stratification in contemporary, multi-ethnic societies. Contemporary sociology continues to deal with issues such as ethnic discrimination, racism, ethnic identity, ethnic minority rights, transnational migration and diasporas.

Defining diaspora

Individuals who have been forcefully geographically dispersed (Macionis and Plummer 2008). For example, in colonial times there were many African diaspora as a result of the slave trade. War and conflict often leads to such dispersion too, and there were many diaspora after the Second World War.

Sociologists also continue to explore ethnic inequalities because being an immigrant or belonging to an ethnic minority for many means that they belong to a category of disadvantage even within contemporary societies. Such disadvantage is not based on a particular ethnicity but is related to being defined as different. Definitions of difference related to ethnic groups affect some more than others.

Defining ethnic inequality

'A racial or ethnic minority is a category of people, distinguished by physical or cultural traits, who are socially disadvantaged, as distinct from the dominant minority. In other words, minorities are set apart and subordinated.' (Macionis and Plummer 2008: 332)

Ethnic minorities are characterised by having a distinct identity. Some groups acknowledge this identity as it is highly visible, while others downplay its significance. Minority groupings are also characterised by their experiences of subordination in many areas of their lives (Macionis and Plummer 2008). Thus, ethnic inequalities are well evidenced across the world, as this chapter illustrates. Complete the following Learning Task to explore contemporary patterns of ethnic inequality across the world.

Learning Task 5.1 – exploring inequalities related to ethnicity

Use the internet to access the Institute of Race Relations website at www. irr.org.uk/

1 Click on the News Service Section, which is one of the tabs across the top of the web-page. Now scroll down and see the list of countries on the right-hand side of the screen, under the sub-heading 'Places'.
2 Explore the list of countries and read the news related to racial and ethnic inequalities. There are reports of violence, murders and protests that are all linked to ethnic social divisions. The UK is also included on the list.
3 What does this news tell you about the level of inequalities within the world today?
4 Explore other areas of the website to read more about research in this area. What can you conclude from your reading?

Having completed the Learning Task, you will now be more aware of the nature of contemporary social divisions associated with ethnicity. These inequalities significantly affect the life chances and quality of life of those who experience these inequalities. For instance, in relation to employment opportunities, ethnic minorities often work in particular areas of the economy, and often in jobs that are lower paid and involve shift work, both of which impact on individuals in many ways, for example, in the types of housing that can be afforded, the area in which individuals live, and access to education and health services. Furthermore, unemployment is higher among ethnic minorities, and even if individuals are able to gain educational qualifications, these do not give them the same protection against joblessness as other groups within society. Wilton (2011: 96) demonstrates from his UK survey that on 'virtually all measures of labour market attainment, minority ethnic graduates reported inferior outcomes compared to their white peers'. Thus, despite having high-level qualifications (degrees), ethnic minority graduates were less satisfied with their careers, earned less than their white peers and were more likely to find themselves in non-graduate jobs (Wilton 2011). Ultimately, these findings in relation to employment disadvantage are reported across a range of research studies, and therefore are part of a broader evidence base which is clearly demonstrating social inequalities in this area.

How can we measure ethnic inequalities?

Salway et al. (2011) argue that much social research does not include minority ethnic people and communities and does not engage meaningfully with issues of ethnic diversity and inequality. Furthermore, where research does engage with these issues, there are a wide range of theoretical and methodological approaches. They suggest that more guidance is needed to support researchers in measuring various aspects of ethnicity.

In the UK, a range of official surveys collect information on ethnicity. The findings from these surveys are able to provide information about the circumstances of ethnic minority populations. These data sets also clearly demonstrate that ethnicity as a social category shapes societies (Afkhami 2012). Given that ethnicity constitutes an important element of the social world, it is important to measure it.

However, collecting data on ethnicity itself remains challenging because of the complexities associated with defining ethnic identities, which include the subjective, multifaceted and fluid nature of ethnic identification. Furthermore, ethnic identities, however we define or measure them, also change over time. This means that individuals may record themselves as one ethnic group at one time and another on a subsequent occasion. These changing understandings are influenced by personal, social and political attitudes and developments. For example, 'Black', used to be an unacceptable term at one time, but now it is embraced by many. Indeed, the term 'South Asian' is currently under debate in the UK because some suggest that it does not capture the differences within the populations that it describes. Moreover, new populations or issues may emerge (Afkhami 2012). As Salway et al. (2009: 4) argue: 'Researching ethnic inequalities presents significant conceptual and methodological challenges. Furthermore, there are real concerns that poor research may do more harm than good.'

These issues mean that measuring ethnic differences is a challenging area, and that there are no simple answers to these complex measurement issues. Despite these challenges, measurement does occur and there is a range of research evidence which, depressingly, demonstrates the range and scope of ethnic inequalities.

Ethnicity and inequalities: the evidence

There have been improvements in many societies in relation to the recognition of inequalities as well as some attempts to reduce inequalities via the use of legislation. For example, in the UK, the first Race Relations Act was introduced in 1964. It banned discrimination on the grounds of race, colour and ethnic origin in public places. This was accompanied by the establishment of the Race Relations Board, whose remit was to handle complaints. The Act was subsequently extended in 1968 and 1976 to broaden its scope and the establishment of the Commission for Racial Equality also followed. This legislation, while a positive move in some senses, because it demonstrated the recognition of inequalities in this area, has received widespread criticism for being ineffective. This is demonstrated in the plethora of evidence which shows the widespread nature of ethnic inequalities both in the UK and across the world, historically and within contemporary society. Across the contemporary world, there are many examples of ethnic inequalities, as illustrated in Table 5.2.

These are just some of many examples. There are many historical examples of ethnic cleansing, in which ethnically homogeneous areas are created through the mass removal of other, different ethnic populations. Croatia is a relatively recent example of a country in which ethnic cleansing was used to remove thousands of Serbs. Consequently, a war broke out in 1992 in which the Muslim population were forced into camps and Muslim women were systematically raped (Giddens 2009). These practices have since been condemned, although the work of the European Union Fundamental Rights Agency (2011a) on racism and xenophobia

Table 5.2   Global examples of ethnic inequalities

Country	Example of inequality
South Africa	Apartheid: This was a system of racial segregation enforced through legislation until 1994. It resulted in the rights of the majority black inhabitants being curtailed while white supremacy and Afrikaner minority rule was maintained.
Zimbabwe	White farmers: President Robert Mugabe instigated a land seizure programme in 2000 which involved the reallocation of formerly white-owned farms to officials who often had no knowledge, experience or interest in farming. This policy led to white farmers suffering multiple land invasions and violence, with some farmers being killed.
Rwanda	Rwanda has different ethnic groups, including the Hutus and Tutsis. Civil war broke out in 1994 and consequently Hutu extremists attempted to destroy the entire Tutsi population. Tutsis were killed in large numbers, including entire families. Tutsi women were also systematically and brutally raped. Anyone opposing the campaign was also murdered, including Hutus. Approximately 800,000 men, women and children were killed (United Human Rights Council 2012).

demonstrates that there continues to be a large amount of discrimination across Europe in a range of areas. For example:

- The *Migrants, Minorities and Employment* report (European Union Fundamental Rights Agency 2011a) highlights patterns of inequality between migrants and minority groups in the labour market. It shows that migrant and minority women face significant structural disadvantages in the labour market, citing discrimination as an important factor leading to inequality for migrants and minorities.
- The *EU-MIDIS 5 Data in Focus* report (European Union Fundamental Rights Agency 2011b) illustrates that individuals belonging to 'visible' minorities, such as Roma and people of African origin, are more likely to suffer multiple discrimination. This report suggests that:

  o Those from ethnic minorities are almost five times more likely to experience multiple discrimination when compared to those from the majority of the population.
  o Those who look different from the majority feel discriminated against more often. For example, Roma and people of African origin are more likely to experience discrimination than other groups.
  o Young ethnic minority/immigrant men reported higher levels of discriminatory treatment.

Furthermore, Fekete (2011) uses a range of evidence to demonstrate that there are new patterns of hate across Europe, with attacks against certain ethnic groups being widespread and systematic. She cites the recent example of Anders Behring Breivik, who killed 77 people in Norway in 2011, motivated by nationalist sentiments and anti-Muslim beliefs. She argues, too, that asylum seekers and migrant workers are the targets of rising nationalism. Another area of racism that is increasingly well documented is that of Islamophobia.

Example of contemporary racism – Islamophobia

Muslim cultures are widespread around the world and in some countries, including the UK, there are expanding Muslim communities. This has led to questions being asked in relation to ethnicity, prejudice and tolerance in several countries.

There are some groups of westerners who argue that Islam is a dangerous force, a fundamentalist religion that embodies many prejudices against modern ideas and practices. Many Islamic states are not democratic and have practices related to sexuality and gender that often receive criticism. These attitudes have led to a growing rise in prejudice called Islamophobia. Some

> more liberal commentators argue that Islam is a religion of many guises and that there is a lack of general understanding about it within many communities. Debates continue in this area, with media contributions, political discussions and changing patterns of lifestyles among some Muslims too, who choose to accept more multicultural values.
>
> Adapted from Macionis and Plummer (2008)

These shifting attitudes and identity conflicts have been analysed in a global context, with Stewart (2010) arguing that Islam versus the West, as a division and battleground, has replaced previous ideological divisions, such as the Cold War. For Stewart (2010: 7), such changing patterns demonstrate that 'Today, then, mobilization along group identity lines has become the single most important source of violent conflict'. Contemporary ethnic and identity differences are perceived as socially significant in many contexts.

Clearly, some (but not all) differences between the general population and ethnic groups lead to prejudice and discrimination, as well as differential treatment and resulting inequalities. For some commentators it is these inequalities that lead to conflict (see Stewart 2010). However, it is important to note that there are inequalities between and across ethnic groups. The National Equality Panel argues that 'there is generally as wide – or even wider – variation in the equivalent net incomes within ethnic groups as within the population as a whole' (Hills et al. 2010: 391). In addition, there are many countries that do not hold data in this area, and so it is still difficult to demonstrate the levels of ethnic inequality across all societies. For example, many countries do not record racially motivated crimes. Indeed, there are many countries in which systems disadvantage ethnic groups. For example, the USA is a country which is well documented for having racial biases within its criminal justice system. Complete the following Learning Task to explore this further.

Learning Task 5.2 – exploring racism within the USA

Use the internet to watch the Ted Talk entitled 'Bryan Stevenson: We need to talk about an injustice', which is available at: www.ted.com/talks/bryan_stevenson_we_need_to_talk_about_an_injustice.html

1 Did you have any awareness of these issues and racial divisions before you had listened to and watched this talk?
2 Has the talk changed your views of the ways in which institutions operate within societies? Take some time to reflect on the ways in which institutions and societal systems may serve to disadvantage some groups.

Now that you have completed the Learning Task and read about some of the ethnic inequalities that exist within contemporary countries, it should be no surprise to learn that there is evidence to demonstrate a range of inequalities related to ethnic grouping within the UK. Platt (2011) examined UK patterns of inequality and showed it is important not to view minority groups as singular coherent groups. Inequality within groups also demonstrates that disadvantage is not necessarily common to all members of a group (Platt 2011). UK evidence of ethnic inequality is drawn from a range of areas, as the selected examples below illustrate:

- The 2010/11 British Crime Survey (BCS) showed that the risk of being a victim of personal crime was higher for adults from a mixed background than for other ethnic groups. It was also higher for members of all BME (Black, Minority, Ethnic) groups than for the white group (Ministry of Justice 2011).
- The overall number of racist incidents recorded by the police was 51,187 in 2010/11 (Home Office 2011). While this was less than the previous year, for many it was the tip of the iceberg because many incidents are unreported.
- One in seven adults aged 25–65 from ethnic minorities are not working but want to. This is lower than a decade ago but still much higher than the figures for white people (The Poverty Site 2012).
- The proportion of Black African, Bangladeshi and Black Caribbean working-age households who are workless is much higher than the equivalent proportion for white British households (The Poverty Site 2012).
- Offenders from ethnic minorities are more likely than their white counterparts to be sentenced to prison for certain categories of crimes (Bell et al. 2012).
- Black women are among the most economically disadvantaged in the UK (Macionis and Plummer 2002).

Given technological developments, there are also new ways in which racism is perpetuated throughout the contemporary social world. For example, social networking sites have been used in many countries (the UK, Bulgaria, the Czech Republic, Denmark and Finland are just some examples from a long list) to incite racial hatred and communicate extremism (Fekete 2011). This leaves particular challenges for the policing of this area. These attitudes feed into racism and of course discrimination. Racism and experiences of discrimination can also be detrimental for the health of those at the receiving end. Thus, another significant area in which ethnic inequalities are demonstrated is in relation to health inequalities.

Health inequalities

Research indicates that ethnic minority groups display a greater ill-health burden. Indeed, associations between ethnicity and health status have been recorded since the routine collection of health data began (Davey Smith et al. 2000). Inequalities in health between ethnic groups in the UK have been extensively documented, with studies demonstrating worse health among ethnic minority people when they are compared to white people. There are some exceptions. For example, Chinese people tend to have similar health to the majority white population (ICLS 2010). However, in general, health inequalities are much worse for ethnic minorities:

- Black British people are 30% more likely than white people to describe their health as fair, poor or very poor; while Pakistani and Bangladeshi people, who generally have worse health than all other ethnic groups, are 50% more likely than white people to report fair, poor or very poor health (ICLS 2010).
- 2007 figures show that South Asian men were 50% more likely to have a heart attack or to experience angina than men in the general population. Caribbean men were also 50% more likely to die of a stroke when compared to men within the general population (Parliamentary Office of Science and Technology 2007).

These health inequalities have been explained in relation to socio-economic factors because people from ethnic minority groups are more likely to have lower paid and more insecure jobs, worse housing and greater chances of being in poverty than the white majority population. UK research in this area is sparse, although there has been much more work in the USA in terms of exploring the links between socio-economic position and health outcomes related to ethnicity (Davey Smith et al. 2000). As earlier chapters have shown, poverty and low socio-economic status are strongly related to inequalities. Poverty and inequality are intimately intertwined, while often being described as theoretically separate in the literature. Analyses of poverty related to the spread of incomes shows that poverty tends to be higher when inequality is higher (Platt 2011). Research related to health inequalities and socio-economic position tells us that 'the lower occupational social class of many people from minority ethnic groups cannot account for the overall ethnic differences in mortality' (Davey Smith et al. 2000: 390). Therefore, while socio-economic position (social class) is important in explaining health inequalities, there is more analysis needed when ethnicity is added to class position.

The effects of racism and negative experiences of medical and health services have also been highlighted as part of explanations analysing these poorer health outcomes. Interestingly, although overall use of primary care is similar (or even greater) among people from ethnic minority groups compared to white people, ethnic minority people are more likely than white people to find physical access to their general practitioner (GP) difficult; experience longer waiting times; feel less satisfied with their care; and receive less referrals (ICLS 2010).

Cultural explanations have also been examined and there is much evidence in this area examining health-related behaviours such as patterns of smoking, drinking alcohol, sexual behaviour, concepts of health, kinship patterns and communication. These areas are all complex and there are differential health behaviours according to ethnic group. For example, smoking is generally lower within Black and South Asian groups when compared to the general population. Thus, while some inequalities in health can be explained using cultural differences, there needs to be recognition that considerable variations exist between ethnic groups, and that cultural factors are fluid and constantly refashioned (Davey Smith et al. 2000). Cultural explanations are therefore just one aspect of a very complicated picture/range of understanding about what leads to inequalities in relation to ethnicity.

Racism is a common and defining experience for many ethnic minority people and therefore has also been explored in relation to health inequalities. Racism can affect health in a number of ways (Davey Smith et al. 2000):

1 Racism can indirectly affect health through socio-economic position.
2 Recognition from ethnic minorities of racism can impact on their health (see Wilkinson and Pickett 2009).
3 Experiences of racism and associated discrimination may directly affect health in a negative way.

Again, the complexity of explaining ethnic inequalities is clear. The evidence base in this area is also complex as there are many influences affecting the health outcomes of minority ethnic individuals, presenting measurement challenges for researchers. Indeed, migration and its impact on health is also an area in which research has been carried out (see Zimmerman et al., 2011), and migration remains a political 'concern' which affects perceptions of some minority groups within society. For some theorists, therefore, it feeds stereotypes as well as being associated with racism and discrimination.

Explaining ethnic inequalities

Inequalities associated with ethnicity are for some theorists bounded with all other social inequalities. In their analysis of US society, Allen and Chung (2000) argue that race and ethnic inequalities are tied to all other systems of social hierarchies. They also note that Marx, Weber and Durkheim gave no attention to race in their explorations of social inequalities despite racial divisions being prominent at the time in which they were writing. Other sociologists writing at the same time did not, however, ignore the importance of social divisions based on race and ethnicity. DuBois (1970 [1896], 1973 [1899]) emphasised skin colour and racial identity as key aspects of social inequality. His work focused on social and cultural influences in the construction of difference as well as the interrelationship between ethnicity and other social divisions.

Le Grand et al. (2008) argue that immigrants and ethnic minorities often belong to the most under-privileged socio-economic categories in the societies where they live. This means that explaining their disadvantage is more difficult because it is hard to tell whether their disadvantage arises from being labelled as 'different', in terms of ethnicity, or whether it is related to their social class position.

Despite the complexities associated with ethnicity as a social division, many writers have focused on the role played by prejudice and discrimination in perpetuating inequalities related to ethnic status.

Defining prejudice and stereotypes

Prejudice is defined as the 'opinions or attitudes held by members of one group towards another' (Giddens 2009: 636). Thus, those who are prejudiced hold specific views about a certain group of people, and these views are often linked to stereotypes.

Stereotypes are defined as 'fixed and inflexible characterizations of a group of people' (Giddens 2009: 636). There are many stereotypes related to social inequalities that have no basis in fact and are not supported by evidence. These have been explored in earlier chapters, for example, stereotypes about women being more caring than men, about lower social class groups such as Chavs, and about those in receipt of welfare payments being 'work-shy'.

Stereotypes and associated prejudices link into blame and scapegoating of particular groups of people. Scapegoating is the process by which some groups are blamed for the problems of a society. These groups change over time but many stereotypes are fed by both media reporting and political discourse. This process is very clear within the context of the UK. Complete the following Learning Task to explore some of the existing stereotypes within the UK media.

Learning Task 5.3 – exploring UK stereotypes in media reporting

Use the internet to access the following media reports:

- 'London riots: This is what happens when multiculturalists turn a blind eye to gang culture', available at: http://blogs.telegraph.co.uk/news/damianthompson/100100087/london-riots-this-is-what-happens-when-multiculturalists-turn-a-blind-eye-to-gang-culture/

- 'Ten handy ways to make crimes by non-whites against whites disappear', available at: http://my.telegraph.co.uk/thefulminator/tag/asian-sex-gang/

- 'Eastern European criminals blamed for surge in migrant offences', available at: www.telegraph.co.uk/news/uknews/crime/9475500/Eastern-European-criminals-blamed-for-surge-in-migrant-offences.html

(Continued)

> *(Continued)*
>
> - 'At last, hard evidence that can't be ignored: Immigration is reducing jobs for British workers and David Cameron must act now', available at: www.dailymail.co.uk/debate/article-2084923/Immigration-reducing-jobs-British-workers-David-Cameron-act-now.html
>
> 1 When reading the reports, did you see any stereotypes or broad generalisations applied to specific groups of people who are not necessarily all the same?
> 2 Are you critical of media reporting in general and do you think that other people are? Are people likely to accept media reports at face value and, if this is your view, then how might this relate to the perpetuation of stereotypes associated with ethnic divisions?

In some of these media reports, there is evidence of stereotyping and prejudice. There are many media representations of minority groups, with the media often shifting its reporting to construct stereotypes of different ethnic groups. For example, media reports construct black teenagers as muggers, Asian young men as gang members (Alexander 2000; Salgado–Pottier 2008) and Eastern Europeans as bogus refugees (Morosanu 2007). Thus, while contemporary society overtly discourages discrimination, it does remain deeply embedded within media reports and is representative of a more subtle form of racism related to prejudiced views of specific societal groups. There are a number of explanations of prejudice within the literature, as illustrated in Table 5.3. Thus, there are many explanations for the existence of prejudice which ultimately feeds into discrimination.

Table 5.3   Theories of prejudice

Theory	Explanation
Scapegoat theory	Members of a society choose to blame a particular category of people whose position is often (but not always) marginal for the troubles of society as a whole.
Authoritarian personality theory	Suggests that people develop extreme pride in the dominant culture and exhibit intolerance to most or all minorities.
Cultural theories of prejudice	Argues that people develop a concept of social distance and the closer another group is to your own culture, the more likely you are to be tolerant of them.
Conflict theory	Powerful people provoke racism as a means of playing less powerful groups off against each other, thereby protecting their privilege.
Race consciousness	Some minorities promote race consciousness, a strategy designed to win power and influence from special consideration by claiming to be the victims of white people.

> ### Defining discrimination
>
> Discrimination is defined as any type of action which treats different categories of people unequally (Macionis and Plummer 2002).

There are a variety of types of discrimination. Merton (1949) outlined a scale to illustrate the range of discrimination that existed in the USA during the 1940s. Despite the length of time that has passed since Merton developed this scale, it is clear that these groups of people can still be seen in contemporary society. Merton's (1949) scale is illustrated in Table 5.4.

This scale shows the range of prejudice that exists, and this is directly linked to racism in many instances. Another area in which ethnic minorities often face racism is described using the concept of institutional racism. This concept suggests that racism underpins all of society's structures in a systematic manner, rather than existing in the attitudes and actions of a small number of people (Giddens 2009). Thus, this concept illustrates bias in the attitudes and actions inherent in the operation of societal institutions. The concept is underpinned by unconscious racism: people often claim to be upholding religious or democratic values but they do not reflect on the implications of the attitudes and actions they take. Within this conceptual framework, organisations such as the police and health service are seen to favour certain groups (usually those who do not belong to an ethnic minority. The UK police service has received many criticisms for being

Table 5.4   Robert Merton's scale of discrimination

Type of discrimination	Description of characteristics
Active bigots	Active bigots are both prejudiced and they discriminate. Individuals in this category tend to be extremely disconnected from mainstream values and feel able to act as they desire, irrespective of any existing laws, norms and morals within society.
Timid bigots	Timid bigots are prejudiced but do not actually discriminate. Individuals in this category tend to be afraid of acting on their prejudices, not wanting to be caught or punished.
Fair-weather liberals	A fair-weather liberal is not prejudiced but does tend to discriminate. Individuals in this category tend to be those who go along with the crowd or obey orders. They may feel guilty because they act under pressure, in contrast to their inner values.
All-weather liberals	All-weather liberals are neither prejudiced nor do they discriminate. These people tend to be highly educated, non-traditional and open-minded individuals who often do not remember that others rarely feel the same way they do.

Source: Adapted from Merton (1949)

institutionally racist, for example following the death of Stephen Lawrence in London in 1993. Complete the following Learning Task to explore the concept of institutional racism.

Learning Task 5.4 – exploring institutional racism within the UK police service

Use the internet to visit the following website: www.archive.official-documents.co.uk/document/cm42/4262/4262.htm, where you are able to view the Macpherson Report, the official publication of the findings of the Stephen Lawrence Inquiry.

1 Read the introduction so that you are familiar with the crime and also the conclusion. What does the report say in relation to racism?
2 Now visit www.civitas.org.uk/pdf/cs06.pdf and view the report that discusses whether or not institutional racism exists within the police service. A different analysis is given here.
3 What are your thoughts about institutional racism? Do you have experiences of institutional racism? Use the internet to explore the issue further – there are hundreds of news reports and discussions about the Stephen Lawrence case.

This Learning Task will have helped you to explore the ways in which some institutions operate in unfair and, on occasion, discriminatory ways. Fekete (2011) argues that there are clear, anti-democratic tendencies within state apparatus such as the police and armed forces. For example, in 2010 the English Defence League (EDL) set up an online armed forces division which at one point had 842 members, again linking to institutional racism. Racism is, of course, much broader than just the practices that occur in institutions, and for many sociologists the dynamics of racism are changing, as discussed earlier in this chapter. These changes are associated with migration as well as the failure of policy in this area.

Social policy failures

Later chapters discuss policy in relation to inequalities in more detail, showing how social policy can be a tool for dealing with inequalities. However, for many, policy has not been effective in reducing ethnic divisions. For example, attempts to categorise racial violence as a separate crime have not succeeded in many countries.

Policy discourse in many countries is also problematic in the way in which ethnic differences are viewed. Burnett (2011) argues that in the context of changing patterns of migration across contemporary societies, there are now new patterns of racial violence. He illustrates how governments describe this as 'symptomatic of breakdowns in community cohesion, unsuccessful integration and even a failure of multi-culturalism' (Burnett 2011: 3). However, these explanations do not pay attention to the ways in which state policies support racism, are divisive and allow the space for far-right organisations to capitalise on hostilities. Burnett (2011) argues that racism is explained away within contemporary societies as being caused by recent migration. However, the broader political and social context needs to be examined to explain how racial violence is worsened. For Burnett (2011: 11):

What exists at the moment, throughout the UK is a political consensus, hammered home repeatedly, that immigration is undermining the social fabric of the UK, whilst at the same time an austerity programme is pushing more and more people into poverty, eradicating employment, exacerbating inequalities and eroding public services which migrants are blamed for putting pressure on. This is a recipe for hostilities and violence.

Indeed, migration policy often has a racial dimension, either as one group feels compelled or is forced to leave or as host nations associate problems with a new immigrant group (Macionis and Plummer 2002). Unfortunately, these attitudes and such political discourse can also be seen in a number of other countries and is well supported by media reports documenting the 'problem of migration'. Thus, there is much racism and ethnic antagonism across Europe and the wider world, leading some commentators to argue that racism is on the increase.

New forms of racism have emerged based on the denigration of cultures associated with immigrant Europeans (Macionis and Plummer 2002). Consequently, many countries are adopting a fortress mentality in limiting migration and asylum seeking. For example, leaders such as Angela Merkel (Germany) echo David Cameron's (UK) attitude to multiculturalism (Fekete 2011). These ideological explanations are interesting and, for many, explain the new forms of racism that are occurring, but sociologists have long been attempting to explain ethnic and racial inequalities.

Overview of sociological contributions

In their attempts to explain racial and ethnic inequalities, sociologists have put forward a range of theories, as illustrated in Table 5.5. These explanations are not the only views. The anthropological literature also offers insight here, and some analyses suggest that ethnicity is developed instrumentally and used by groups and leaders to support them in their achievement of political and economic goals. Constructivist theorists (those that see the social world as constructed through processes and understandings) agree with this view but also focus on making and remaking ethnic boundaries and how this occurs. They suggest that differences are emphasised within social constructions, again for political purposes (Stewart 2010).

Table 5.5   An overview of sociological explanations of racial and ethnic inequalities

Type of theory	Discussion
Bias theory	Bias theories blame the members of the majority and focus upon racism and prejudice as the causes of inequalities.
Structural-discrimination theories	This approach, while recognising racism, also accounts for structures within society. Thus, racism is understood as part of broader societal practices and institutional approaches which limit opportunities for those in specific social groupings. This approach is seen as less victim-blaming.
Institutional discrimination	Institutions both define and enforce norms that can be racially distinct, thus institutions within society disadvantage specific groups of people through systems of interrelated practices.
World capitalism	This approach argues that capitalism is a system that has shaped race and racism in many contexts because it is based upon a system of class exploitation in which individuals from certain ethnic groups have been at the lowest class position due to their work roles and colonial history.

Source: Adapted from Long (2012)

Given the range of ethnic inequalities that still exist, as this chapter has shown, and the problematic discourses being used in political circles, the future of ethnic relations is one in which both racism and prejudice are likely to remain within all societies for some time to come. Of course there will be some changes, as the lessons of history demonstrate, and it is likely that some areas will continue to divide on ethnic lines, while others will move towards greater multi-ethnic integration (Macionis and Plummer 2002).

Case Study: How ethnicity intersects with other social divisions

As this chapter and Chapter 4 have demonstrated, there is now a wealth of evidence that explores social stratification beyond the construct of social class. Thus, many forms of contemporary social stratification are non-class-based forms of social division. Indeed, the relationships between social divisions such as gender, ethnicity and social class also need to be explored (Anthias 2001). Anthias (1998) illustrates the importance of understanding the differences within social divisions and categories as well as their complexity. She illustrates the ways in which ethnicity is intersectional, using a number of examples such as:

- Ethnic cultures often have rules about sex difference, gender roles and sexuality within them.
- Gender relations act as boundaries between ethnic groups.

- Members of minority ethnic groups experience a duality of class relations. They experience the external dominant class system as well as the system that is internal within their own group.
- Gender intersects with race too and thus racist rules may be used to increase sexism.

Ultimately, then, gender, race and class are cross-cutting social divisions that meet at certain points and, as a result, produce different and stratified social outcomes. Anthias (1998) concludes that what is needed is not recognition and discussion of different identities, such as those related to ethnicity, but rather collaboration by those experiencing inequalities in their struggle to tackle these issues as this is one way in which attention is afforded to the intersectionality of social divisions.

Summary of key points

- Ethnicity is located within the social stratification system which affects the life chances, economic status and health of different groups of people. Power and powerlessness as well as status are related to ethnic stratification.
- Despite improvements in the laws of some countries, there still is significant evidence of ethnic inequalities across the world. Ethnic position is clearly correlated with a variety of inequalities. A range of theories exist which can be used to explain ethnic inequalities. This chapter has focused in particular on prejudice and discrimination.

List of questions to stimulate debate and reflection

1 Consider ethnic inequalities in your own life. For example, reflect on the experiences of those in your own social networks. What kinds of attitudes do you and your friends hold towards certain groups? Are there any illustrations of discrimination or racist attitudes?
2 What countries do you think are particularly challenged in terms of ethnic inequalities within the world today? In at least one country, can you identify how such inequalities have been challenged?
3 What do you think about the role of the campaigners and social movements in changing ethnic inequalities? What successes can you identify and what challenges remain? Can campaigns such as these tackle ethnic inequalities within the current global context?

Further reading

Castles, Stephen and Miller, Mark J. (2008) *The Age of Migration: International Population Movements in the Modern World London* (4th edition). Basingstoke: Palgrave Macmillan.

This book offers a global perspective on the nature of migration flows, why they take place and their consequences for both states and societies around the world. Chapters provide up-to-date descriptions and comparative analyses of major migration regions across the world. The role of population movements in the formation of ethnic minority groups is explored, as is the impact of growing ethnic diversity on societies. For example, economies, cultures and political institutions are all shaped and affected by changing patterns of ethnicity.

Fenton, Steve (2012) *Ethnicity* (2nd edition). Cambridge and Malden, MA: Polity Press.

This recently revised book discusses an extended range of theorists and illustrations from around the world in relation to the shifting and contested concept of ethnicity. The book discusses increased migration to the USA from Central and South America, ethnic identities and current delineation along ethnic and racial lines. The book explores global issues as well as the emergence of right-wing movements within Europe, reflecting on what these changes mean in relation to ethnicity.

Lamont, Michèle and Mizrachi, Nissim (2012) *Responses to Stigmatization in Comparative Perspective*. London and New York: Routledge.

In this book, commentators from a range of disciplines look at the responses to stigmatisation from the perspectives of ordinary people. Case studies from a variety of countries, such as the USA, Brazil, Canada, France, Israel, South Africa and Sweden, are explored to illustrate how minority groups deal with stigmatisation in their everyday encounters.

6

GLOBALISATION AND THE GLOBAL DIMENSIONS OF INEQUALITY

Key learning outcomes

By the end of this chapter you should be able to:

- Understand the concept of globalisation
- Understand the complex relationship between globalisation and social inequality
- Understand the different ideological positions associated with the concept of globalisation that are used to explain its impact

Overview of the chapter

This chapter contextualises current understandings of inequality within a broader global context, showing that inequality cannot be understood without a global perspective. The chapter explores the key question of how globalisation has affected and altered inequality by discussing the concept of globalisation and exploring its relationship to inequality. The chapter introduces competing opinions about whether globalisation is beneficial for creating a more equal society as well as introducing discussions and evidence suggesting that it actually worsens inequality. The chapter addresses key questions such as how current global economic trends are affecting inequalities as well as discussing lessons from the 2008 'global' recession in relation to inequality. The chapter discusses how globalisation impacts on the nation state in terms of social inequality.

Defining globalisation

Globalisation has been defined in a number of ways within the academic literature, which shows that it has many components, such as social, cultural and economic aspects. Therefore, globalisation is an imprecise term, but for many theorists it is a process driven by technological change and advancements in communications. Global social change is nothing new. Historical records show many changes over periods of time. However, the rapid change that has occurred over the last three decades is said to be unprecedented. In brief, globalisation can be described as the increased social, economic and political interconnectedness of the world.

> ### *Defining globalisation*
>
> Globalisation is 'the fact that we all increasingly live in one world, so that individuals, groups and nations become ever more dependent'. (Giddens 2009: 12)

Holton (2005) suggests that globalisation involves interconnection, the interdependence of activities across boundaries and the development of consciousness and identification of the world as a single place. He argues that globalisation is not a fixed structure, and discusses the role of individual agency within the process. Clearly, understandings of globalisation are complex, and Held and McGrew's (1999) transformational definition demonstrates this. They argue that globalisation can travel in different directions and vary in the forms it takes by place, class and time. The key components for them include:

1 Interconnectedness – the stretching of activities across boundaries, and the widening of networks.
2 Intensification – connections are intensified and have grown in magnitude.
3 Speed – global interactions are faster as a result of improved communications and transport.
4 Impact – the impact of distance events is magnified, with local incidents having global consequences.

These different definitions are by no means the only ones offered. There are four areas of research in the social sciences literature exploring the impact of globalisation, as detailed in Table 6.1.

Table 6.1   Four areas of globalisation research

Approach	Key points	Discussions about inequality	Criticisms
The world-systems approach	Theorists explore the role of individual countries in terms of their changing roles in the international division of labour within a capitalist world system	• Condemns the way in which transnational corporations operate in lower income countries, e.g. using cheap labour	• No specific concept of the global society • It neglects class struggle • It distorts the history of capitalism and does not deal with development adequately • Tends to neglect political and cultural factors
The global culture approach	Theorists suggest that globalisation is driven by the culture of the mass media, which threatens national and local identities because we have all become part of a global village	• Suggests that local cultures are threatened by the dominant global culture expressed within the media	• The approach, by focusing upon culture, risks ignoring the material realities behind cultural interpretations • Ignores those without access to the media • Does not account for cultural resistance • Tends to neglect economic factors
The global polity and society approach	Proponents argue that the concept of a global society has only become believable in the modern age because of science, technology and industry creating a different world	• Suggests that the development collective consciousness can be used to help solve global problems	• The idea of global polity or a global society based upon subjective relationships to globalisation and global consciousness is speculative • The suggestion that global consciousness can be used to tackle social problems is utopian • Difficult to empirically research
The global capitalism approach	Globalisation is driven by globalising capitalism	• Some suggest that capitalism is the solution to inequality, while for others it exacerbates inequality in numerous ways	• There is confusing and contradictory evidence in relation to illustrating the impacts of global capitalism • Does not pay enough attention to global forces other than capitalist ones

Source: Adapted from Sklair (2002)

The central point of discussions about globalisation is that 'many contemporary problems cannot be adequately studied at the level of the nation-states … but need to be seen in terms of transnational processes, beyond the level of particular countries' (Sklair 2002: 27). Often such arguments focus on global forces and global power, suggesting that nation states are becoming less significant when compared to global actors, including transnational corporations. Such corporations drive global capitalism, consumerism and social change. The idea of an interconnected global society has raised several questions about the relationship between globalisation and inequalities, which is explored later in this chapter. Given that many social problems and issues are increasingly conceptualised as 'global', and therefore in need of global solutions, the role of global policy actors is important too. Thus, there are ongoing debates about the intersection of the global with the national in social policy terms, exploring power, politics and process.

So what does all this mean at the level of the individual? Giddens (1994: 5) suggests that the processes of globalisation result in 'the transformation of local, and even personal, contexts of social experience', highlighting the different levels at which globalisation permeates through the social structure. Martell (2010: 2) makes a similar point in saying that the large-scale global processes, including international political power and economics, have an impact on our individual lives because 'the global economy and distribution of wealth affect, for example, our chances of employment alongside our material circumstances generally'. He also pays attention to how globalisation results in cultural impacts and how the role of the global media is changing our lives. The influence of migration and changing food habits are also afforded attention. In Martell's (2010) analysis, globalisation and global politics significantly influence our lives. Now complete the following Learning Task, which will help you to think about how globalisation relates to your own biography.

Learning Task 6.1 – biographical relationships and globalisation

Think about all the ways in which globalisation has affected your life, making a list as you reflect about your own biographical experiences. The questions below will help you to think about this.

1 Think about the way in which the media has made you part of the 'global society', listing examples of your global knowledge. For example, do you remember specific media reports about an event? Which countries are featuring on the news regularly at the moment?
2 Think about how you communicate now and how technology influences this. Do you have friends on Facebook who are from other countries and who you chat to regularly? Who do you follow on Twitter? Are there other ways in which you communicate across geographical divides, for example, via email or Skype?
3 Consider the food you eat. Where does it come from? What types of food do you prefer? Consider where you have travelled and your cultural awareness. What about your musical tastes – are these globally influenced too?
4 How might globalisation have an impact on both your physical and mental health?

Globalisation influences our lives in many diverse ways, as this Learning Task will help you to identify, with many benefits resulting from technological advancements in communication and travel. Has globalisation brought mainly benefits to your life?

These questions are not the only ones that you may consider. Did you think about how your biography may look if you were living in a different context? There are individuals and communities who do not have access to technology in the same way, who are facing financial challenges – what might their view of globalisation be in terms of their biographical experiences?

This Learning Task demonstrates that globalisation impacts on us all in different ways, which is important in exploring the relationship between globalisation and inequality. Before we can begin to do that, we need to understand what globalisation actually adds up to. Martell (2010) offers a concise summary of the concept of globalisation:

1 It is global in distance – it needs to reach all continents and involve long-distance relationships in economic, political and cultural terms.
2 It is globally inclusive in inputs – it is not an unequal process (for example, Westernisation) but rather involves inputs from across continents and many countries within them.
3 It involves interdependency – there is interdependency rather than just interconnectedness. Thus, a decline in trade will affect the country in which the trade is occurring as well as the country receiving the goods.
4 It involves stability and regularity – there are structures and systems that relate to the processes of globalisation, rather than temporary connections.
5 It involves global consciousness – the concept is not just about people doing things globally; individuals also need to have an awareness of the world as one space. There are many critical debates within the literature about this. Commentators argue that globalisation simply involves the elites, who are able to benefit themselves at the expense of others, resulting in greater inequalities.

Globalisation is also influenced by a range of factors such as the rise of information communications technology, economic factors, transnational corporations, the electronic economy and political changes (Giddens 2009). There are many debates within the literature about globalisation, with some writers arguing that it is not occurring. Martell (2010) recognises that the criteria he lists suggest that globalisation is a process moving towards fulfilling these, rather than already encompassing them all. He also suggests that many processes are occurring that perhaps are not globalisation, as sceptics recognise. However, these remain important and therefore should be studied. Similarly, Lee (1998) suggests a number of ways in which globalisation may impact on health, again showing why it is important to study what is happening globally. Lee (1998) asks several important questions in reflecting on the relationship between globalisation and health, including:

- Are patterns of disease changing? For example, within and across countries are diseases spreading differently?
- How is health care being financed globally and is the globalisation of finance influencing health care funding?
- Are more regulations needed to protect health in terms of global trade practices?
- Are there inequalities in global access to health care information?
- In terms of global governance, are the key players adopting a positive role in terms of improving health?
- Finally, are there health issues which need to be dealt with via the global legal system?

Theorising globalisation

While it is clear that the social world in which we live is changing, and that globalisation is a well-discussed topic, within the broader academic literature debates continue in terms of exactly what globalisation is. Given that the concept of globalisation refers to an unpredictable process, it is not surprising that it is understood differently. Held and McGrew (1999) summarise the academic writings about globalisation into three specific theoretical schools of thought: the sceptics, hyperglobalisers and the transformationalists, as summarised in Table 6.2.

Table 6.2 Theorising globalisation: a summary of key arguments

Theory of globalisation	Key aspects
Sceptics	<ul><li>Globalisation is overstated</li><li>Modern globalisation is simply more intense than historical patterns</li><li>The world economy is not truly integrated in terms of trade</li><li>Regionalisation is growing, showing that the globalisation is not as significant as some suggest</li><li>National governments remain important</li></ul>
Hyperglobalisers	<ul><li>Globalisation is real, with clear consequences</li><li>Globalisation has led to a borderless world (Ohmae 1990, 1995)</li><li>Nation-state role is less important within a globalised economy (Albrow 1997)</li></ul>
Transformationalists	<ul><li>Globalisation is the central force behind a range of changes</li><li>While transformations are happening, old patterns still remain in place, e.g. national governance</li><li>Globalisation is an open process that is subject to change</li><li>The world is no longer state-centric, as national governments have to adopt new approaches to cope with the complex conditions associated with globalisation (Rosenau 1997)</li></ul>

Source: Adapted from Held and McGrew (1999)

Such debates will be found throughout this chapter because there is simply no agreement about what globalisation is, how it is changing the world and its relationship to global inequality. Currently, the evidence suggests that the transformationalist view is the most accurate because global processes are having a large impact in many aspects of social life (Giddens 2009), as this chapter demonstrates. Ongoing debates about whether globalisation is positive or negative are also likely to continue.

Globalisation debated: is globalisation positive or negative?

Given the definitional issues associated with the concept and the different theoretical viewpoints highlighted, it should be no surprise to find that there are many competing opinions in terms of the effects that globalisation is having, and whether or not it is positive. Pro-globalisation commentators suggest that it is positive and an important mechanism for addressing inequality. Globalisation is seen to increase growth and wealth and, as a result, decrease poverty (Labonte 2010). Wolf (2004) argues that globalisation is the solution to both poverty and inequality. Similarly, the World Bank holds the position that globalisation is important for poverty reduction, arguing that current poverty is residual, that is that the benefits associated with globalisation have yet to reach those in the poorest parts of the world who remain excluded from economic development. From this perspective, globalisation is potentially important in dealing with inequalities. Indeed, despite the existence of global inequality, as discussed in Chapter 1, overall standards of living have been raised across the world, with many indicators showing improvements (Giddens 2009).

The economic advantages cited by some are not the only advantages discussed in relation to globalisation. Moghadam (2005) discusses the development of the global women's movement, suggesting that the globalisation of politics and international non-governmental organisations has allowed women's movements to grow globally and therefore to expand campaigns for gender equality. Furthermore, Martell (2010) argues that globalisation exposes women to more education and information, empowering them and allowing them to secure more equality. Bhagwati (2004) cites lessened inequality and increased positive global governance as positive outcomes of globalisation. He argues that it is domestic policy rather than globalisation that is particularly damaging. Others focus attention on the cognitive dimensions of globalisation. For example, Scholte (2000) discusses the continued growth of global consciousness as a positive outcome resulting from globalisation. Ideas about the importance of global neighbourhoods and the common global social problems faced by the entire world are positive. However, as Chapter 1 demonstrated, there remain substantial differences between countries and living standards in some places are declining (Giddens 2009).

Anti-globalisation theorists, on the other hand, offer more critical comment and evidence to support their argument that globalisation is negative in numerous ways, including being detrimental in relation to various inequalities. Bhagwati (2004) argues that anti-globalisation sentiments are much more prevalent in the rich countries of the Global North whereas countries in the South see it as a more positive force. In this context, development, which is often cited as beneficial by developers, is seen as a problem by some writers. Stiglitz (2006) argues that development often results in urbanisation, leaving many cities in lower income countries squalid, congested, noisy and with poor sanitation.

There is a vast literature discussing these issues so these are simply summarised in the discussion below in order to provide you with an overview and introduction to the key debates. This will help you to think about the implications of globalisation in relation to social inequality. Here there needs to be a cautionary note. While globalisation is massively debated within the current literature, it is not responsible for all inequality. Atkinson (2003) makes the point that despite rapid globalisation, national taxation and other economic policies still play a role in relation to inequality levels. Thus, in Scandinavian countries such as Sweden, which has a redistributive welfare state, global trends towards increasing inequality can be more effectively managed and, to some degree, prevented when compared to countries such as the UK, which has a more right-wing approach to welfare reform (Giddens 2009). See Chapter 8 for a more in-depth discussion of the relationship between inequalities and social policy. Discussions of globalisation also tend to focus on economics, global politics and the global media, so these will be starting points for discussion within this chapter.

Globalisation and economics

The global economy

Given that the economic model of globalisation is the one analysed most frequently in the academic literature, the global economy is clearly important. There are large-scale global institutions responsible for policies related to the global economy, such as the International Monetary Fund and the World Bank, that have been described as 'the handmaidens of globalization, unfettered trade and capital flows, and the instrument of Wall Street Bankers' Shaxon (2011: 73). Shaxon's (2011) description of the global economy is a pessimistic view in which capital is allowed to flow across borders into off-shore systems that are secret, outside the restriction of usual banking regulations as well as serving to avoid the usual taxation channels. So how does this relate to inequality? Shaxon (2011) argues that since the explosion of the off-shore era in the 1970s, inequality has increased across many countries. His evidence for this is that US wages were lower in 2006 than in 1970 in some industries whereas chief executives' pay has massively increased in general. Furthermore, the number of banking crises and economic disasters has continued to increase. Indeed, they are evidently ongoing at the time of writing, with debates about the economic stability of countries such as Greece being reported in the media (Telegraph 2011) as well as reports about the state of the economy of other European countries including the UK and Italy. Warner (2011) argues that the UK government's fiscal policy requires examination because of the continued economic crisis (see Chapter 8 for further discussion of these issues).

Shaxon (2011) contentiously argues that corruption within the world banking system must be explored in order to understand why some countries are failing and why poverty and inequality is so widespread. Economic corruption on a global scale serves to increase inequality massively. Kar and Cartwright-Smith (2010) examined data from 1970 to 2008 in terms of illicit financial outflows and report findings such as:

• Total illicit financial outflows from Africa were approximately $854 billion according to conservative estimates.
• Less conservative estimates suggest that outflows from Africa may be as high as $1.8 trillion.
• It is the poorest places that report the highest level of outflows. For example, Sub-Saharan African countries experienced the bulk of illicit financial outflows.
• The top five countries with the highest outflow documented in the report were:

    o Nigeria ($89.5 billion)
    o Egypt ($70.5 billion)
    o Algeria ($25.7 billion)
    o Morocco ($25 billion)
    o South Africa ($24.9 billion)

• These illicit outflows were worth more than the development aid entering these countries.

These levels of money illicitly leaving countries result in increased inequality in terms of poverty, wars, debts, violence and lack of real opportunities for individual country members (Shaxon 2011). Furthermore, off-shore banking practices, such as those being described by Shaxon, play a fundamental role in the banking crisis (Henry 2003), again serving to increase inequality for those living in the countries who are not part of the elites, who reap the benefits of off-shore banking and tax avoidance. There are 2,500 tax treaties in the world which ultimately deprive countries of taxation funds. The systems continue to work in this way arguably because rich countries dominate at the continued expense of poorer ones (Shaxon 2011), further exacerbating social inequalities.

Global economic governance simply does not deal with the issues that are causing repeated crises. For example, for many commentators (although not all economists agree about this), the 2008 global economic crisis, which is still causing massive problems for many countries and therefore their inhabitants, was caused by increased levels of debt. While the benefits of economic growth are enjoyed by just a few, the rest of the world is able to solve their problems through acquiring debt (Dorling 2009). Tax havens and illicit financial outflows of capital are a fundamental part of this problem. Rich people are simply able to pay a far lower share of tax, whereas ordinary working people pay a much greater proportion of their income (Shaxon 2011), again exacerbating inequalities. The rich remain able to operate within existing banking systems and are further able to justify the way in which they operate from an ideological viewpoint (Mitchell 2006). As a result of holding positions of power associated with financial wealth, the situation does not change and manages to effectively deflect any challenges. Furthermore, the increased global dominance of right-wing ideology serves to continue to influence the global economy to benefit the rich, irrespective of the impact on global inequality.

As Chapter 1 outlined, the growing dominance of neo-liberalism as an economic ideology has served to increase inequality in many places across the world. Despite this, it underpins economic globalisation and the policies of associated global governance institutions. Privatisation, efficiency, profit making and competitive markets are all components of this approach, despite evidence demonstrating that these do not impact positively on inequalities. Letwin's (1988: xviii) neo-liberal, right-wing approach is clear when he argues that 'privatisation is a policy for all seasons and for many reasons'. His book details the increased privatisation of industries in many countries, starting from the 1970s, even extending to more socialist countries such as Spain. He openly describes how agencies such as the International Monetary Fund, the World Bank and USAID are advocating privatisation in lower income countries because of worldwide interest in the approach. While Letwin debates why governments privatise, he fails to address the effect of such approaches upon the social and political landscapes of the countries whose assets are privatised, instead focusing on economic rationales and justifications that result from the further expansion of capitalism. Complete the following Learning Task to explore your own ideas related to economic globalisation.

Learning Task 6.2 – economic globalisation debate

Look at the following website and read in more depth about globalisation: www.sociology.emory.edu/globalization/. This will help you to complete the following task. Debate whether economic globalisation is good or bad for social inequality.

1 Make a list of points to support both sides of the argument: the reasons why it exacerbates inequalities as well as the reasons why it may reduce inequalities.
2 Which of your lists was the longest?

Finally, think about your own relationship with globalisation. Reflect on how your position in the global world relates to the impact that globalisation has on your own life. If you lived in a different place, perhaps a lower income country, consider how the relationship between globalisation and inequality might differ.

This Learning Task will have challenged you to think about global inequality in relation to economics, and you will have probably listed both benefits and problems when thinking about how globalisation might impact on inequality. Giddens (2009) writes that the benefits of globalisation have been uneven and not enjoyed by all, thus economic globalisation leads to negative experiences for some. Dahlberg (1995) cites the example of a garment worker located in Bangkok who works from 8am until 11pm, six days every week and earns the equivalent of £2 per hour. Indeed, billions of workers who are part of the global labour force face similar conditions, which have led to descriptions of class polarisation as a result of globalisation. Sklair (2002: 126) argues that 'this race to the bottom is yet another consequence of capitalist globalization in which the class polarization crisis is reflected in increased profits for TNCs [transnational corporations] and their local affiliates and near-subsistence wages and insecurity for the workers who get these jobs'. Giddens (2009) goes even further, saying that such workers are the lucky ones because the populations of places that have remained outside the world economy, such as people from North Korea, fare much worse. For many, including Zhu (2000), who discusses the case of workers in China, economic globalisation does not bring better conditions for many workers. However, economic aspects of globalisation are just one element of the concept. Many perspectives discuss globalisation as being driven by multiple causes and being multidimensional and localised in terms of its effects. This discussion is a reaction against economic determinism, in which explanations are associated with just economics (Martell 2010). The type of economics underpinning globalisation is associated with capitalism (Sklair 2002). One aspect of this is the role of large companies in economic development across the globe. Another area of the globalisation literature has focused on the role of such companies as these are an important driver for economic change.

Global trade: the power of transnational corporations

The impact of transnational corporations (TNCs) within the global system is illustrated clearly within the literature, which shows that there are large, powerful corporations dominating the world in a form of capitalist imperialism. This has resulted in groups of people being excluded from participating in the system. Sklair (2002) uses the example of the manufacturing industry to illustrate this, arguing that workers have free occupational choice within their own local economic conditions. Globalisation can alter these local conditions, and not necessarily in terms of always improving them. As globalisation reduces the number of manufacturing jobs in most high-income countries, workers then have to seek alternative employment in other, often less well paid sectors, if indeed any employment opportunities exist. Some employment sectors are now less secure and less well paid, resulting in inequality.

Changing patterns of employment related to globalisation have also resulted in the increased movement of people as individuals migrate in search of employment, both internally within countries and on a broader scale of country-to-country movement (Sklair 2002). This idea of transnational social spaces is important in discussions of globalisation because the capitalist class is organised transnationally. The power of the TNCs is therefore shaping the economy, the workforce and inequality. Research into TNCs is vast, focusing on how they are part of globalisation and the issues associated with them, such as how they are changing gender dynamics and corporate citizenship (Sklair 2002). Sklair (2002: 69) argues that 'if we are to understand capitalist globalization we must understand transnational corporations and their transnational economic practices'.

Indeed, many TNCs have received criticism for their operating practices. Macdonald (2007) argues that neo-liberal globalisation has led to many companies working unethically to increase their profits and, as a result, causing negative health impacts. For example, the drive for economic growth has resulted in increased consumption levels of processed foods and cigarettes (Graham 2010). Pharmaceutical companies have been criticised for their role in increasing global inequalities in the way in which they have tended to operate, excluding access to medicines for those unable to afford them. The use of TRIPs (trade-related aspects of intellectual property rights) by global pharmaceutical companies prevents the production of cheaper generic drugs for several years. Given that approximately 80% of the world's population does not have access to essential medication (Leach et al. 2005), the operation of pharmaceutical TNCs has been heavily criticised by commentators who argue that such companies are simply profit-driven.

On a global scale, pharmaceutical companies and other large TNCs arguably exert large-scale influence because of their economic power, with some being richer than entire lower income countries (Stiglitz 2006). TNCs may also operate in unsafe ways in countries where there are fewer regulatory controls in terms of health and safety, with devastating consequences in some instances. For example, the explosion at the Union Carbide Plant in Bhopal in India during the 1980s killed over 20,000 people and damaged the long-term health of undocumented numbers of people (Stiglitz 2006). Now complete Learning Task 3 to explore the role of TNCs in more depth.

Learning Task 6.3 – the impact of TNCs

A large TNC has established a new factory in a medium-sized city in India. The factory will produce clothing for sale in higher income countries. The company has advocated the positive benefits of its establishment as it will create local jobs in an area which has little employment opportunities. The local inhabitants are generally poor and they are not educated to high standards. The country's legislation is weak in relation to health and safety, and there is some evidence of corruption in government. Furthermore, the company has received media criticism for its employment practices in other low-income countries, featuring in a television documentary which showed that working conditions were poor, employees were pressured to produce quickly (which can become an issue if the welfare of the employee is compromised)and were not well paid, despite the company's large profits.

1 Think about how this company may have an impact on the health and wealth of the local population.
2 List both the advantages and disadvantages of its presence in this locality.
3 Finally, reflect on power, choice, control and ethics, and the overall effect that the establishment of this company may have in relation to inequality. Will this be positive or negative?

This Learning Task will have helped you to explore the complexities associated with how TNCs operate and how their existence impacts on inequality. In some of the literature (see Sklair 2002) there are strong suggestions that the presence of TNCs in lower income countries is both negative and detrimental, with critics arguing that they make profits in such countries by exploiting cheap labour to produce goods that people do not actually need. However, without the presence of these companies, how would people employed by them survive? TNCs may also raise standards of living for those employed by them, providing them with more income than they have had previously, but then exclude others who are not employed, resulting in increased inequality. Whether or not TNCs are good for development, or indeed if development can address inequality, remains open to much debate.

Research into TNCs has also explored the environmental impacts resulting from their activities, which forms part of broader debates about how such companies should be responsible and protect the rights of those that they affect (Sklair 2002). The expansion of TNCs and the attention afforded to them within the academic literature is part of broader academic concerns with consumerism and its implications.

Global consumerism

Global consumerism is discussed as an important driver of globalisation. Western Europe went through a period of rapid social change in relation to lifestyles during the post-war period. People bought new consumer goods for domestic use and cars, which have continued to feed into cycles of demand within contemporary society (Vandenbroucke 1998). Rostow (1978) describes growth in sales of cars and televisions in the USA, Western Europe and Japan, demonstrating mass consumption habits. These patterns of mass consumerism and consumption have continued, especially within high-income countries where many have more disposable income and where purchasing power and possessions are linked to status. The ideology of consumerism is one that permeates many societies and drives economic markets and politics. In recent media and political discussions about the 'credit crunch' and recession, the importance of consumption and consumer confidence is emphasised in plans for economic recovery, and is frequently reported by the media (see Guardian 2011a). For some, mass consumption has been driven by Americanisation (De Grazia 2005), in which not only products are exported but so too are more subtle aspects of the phenomenon, such as the service ethic, the chain store and the big brand goods which can now be seen in many societies. Other writers have focused on the products that have become world famous names. 'Coco-colonisation' and 'Disneyfication' are terms used within the academic literature that are tied to notions of increased American cultural domination. Bhagwati (2004) discusses the worldwide resentment of the United States and argues that these sentiments are an important part of anti-globalisation, which acts as a mechanism to challenge American hegemony. 'McDonaldization' (Ritzer 2008) is also a concept used to describe how many cultures have become similar to fast-food restaurants. There are again challenges to such views. Bhagwati (2004) argues that as humans we have complex self-identities and as a result try to preserve the past. This does not necessarily equate to globalisation being a threat to our cultural identity.

Debates about how consumerism is shifting cultural attitudes continue, but what is important in the context of this chapter is to pay attention to how mass consumption drives the global economy and the inequality that can result. Not everyone is able to consume, so analysing consumption patterns is an indicator of inequality.

Food consumption patterns demonstrate such inequality. The Food and Agriculture Organisation (FAO) (2010) argues that the number of malnourished people in the world is unacceptably high because it is almost at the 1 billion mark, and discusses how the increase in food prices associated with the global economic recession will create additional difficulties in relation to malnutrition and hunger. The FAO report identifies 166 million people as being undernourished across 22 countries experiencing crises. There are, of course, a number of causal factors which lead to malnutrition and hunger, including conflicts, disasters, weak governance, the breakdown of local institutions and crop failures. However, contrast this with the food consumption patterns of higher income countries and this demonstrates clear inequality. The UK population spends more than £10 billion pounds each year on takeaway food such as sandwiches, chips, burgers and curries in an ever-expanding market. This type of consumption is unhealthy, environmentally damaging and exploitative. It is also described as a symptom of broader patterns of hurried lives which demand long working hours and relentless consumerism, resulting in convenience food consumption without consideration of sustainability (Sharpe 2010). A comparison of the massive numbers of those who are malnourished or hungry and the rising numbers of obese people provides a further demonstration of inequality (Tahir 2011). This is worsened by the amount of food that is wasted in the countries of the Global North, who over-purchase and then throw away food on a large scale. Vaughan (2009) argues that eliminating the millions of tonnes of food thrown away annually in countries such as the USA and the UK could lift more than a billion people out of hunger worldwide. This over-purchasing is driven by mass consumerism, which for many serves to increase inequalities in many ways. Consumerism for many writers is tied in to negative consequences, such as increased working hours, more possessions and less life satisfaction. We also consume more than just goods; we consume ideas and therefore the global media is another important aspect of globalisation.

Global media

The global media is an important part of mass consumption patterns for many theorists. Sklair (2002) argues that capitalist globalisation is driven by the cultural ideology of consumption, with television and the internet relentlessly entering into people's lives. He states that 'we can only speculate what Marx would have thought about the fact that in the homes of almost every worker and many peasants there is now a flickering box churning out the words and images of capitalist consumerism day and night' (Sklair 2002: 166). It is true that in capitalist societies, advertisements abound in media settings, such as the television, the internet, billboards and in magazines, usually for consumer goods such as food, drink, cars, personal products and leisure-related goods. Comparatively, Bhagwati (2004: 19) draws attention to the positive influence of the global media and argues that 'no longer can we snore while the other half of humanity suffers plague and pestilence and the continuing misery of extreme poverty. Television has disturbed our sleep...'

While debates abound about how the global media interacts with and changes culture, there are both positive and negative consequences. Inequality is also evident when examining media access: not all have access to the internet or to televisions or the ability to consume the products of the media.

Dorling (2009) describes the media, including the news, as being controlled by a small number of men, such as rich US businessmen, or a select few communist party bosses in countries like China. This level of control allows more advertising and propaganda to be disseminated and to drive the imagined need to consume, which is meaningless, environmentally damaging and detrimental to well-being. He also describes how the media drive forward the culture of celebrity as an advertisement of success as part of broader trends associated with the afflictions of affluence. These viewpoints form part of the notion of globalisation as cultural imperialism, in which the values and beliefs of powerful societies such as America are seen to be imposed on the less powerful in a form of exploitation through the mass media (Sklair 2002). This theoretical analysis has been critically questioned, but the idea of the American dream remains central to global capitalism and it is true that the media is controlled by a select and powerful group. This domination by a powerful and select group is related to inequality, with power and control forming central aspects of the processes of global governance.

Global politics: global governance

In recent years there have been changes in terms of governance, with changing state power, greater interdependence and many global challenges, such as conflict, poverty, environmental degradation, insecurity and ill-health. Many writers have claimed that existing mechanisms for dealing with such issues are in crisis, and there are many calls for transparency and accountability in terms of current governance patterns (R. Wilkinson 2005). Hence, there is a need to critically explore the range of global social actors involved in governance and their roles in relation to inequality. How does global governance work in relation to inequality? Does it serve to reduce social inequalities or is the picture much more negative?

These are key questions that need to be addressed to fully understand the global dynamics and processes that shape social inequalities. Chapter 7 explores these issues in depth, highlighting the range of global social actors, their roles and discussing the relationship between these and inequalities. The role of global governance actors is seen as key to dealing with the effects of globalisation and the many challenges that the world is currently facing. One of the most debated issues is that of the environment, with climate change and sustainability often on policy agendas and in media discussions. Some commentators argue that globalisation has resulted in damage to the environment and that it continues to threaten ecological sustainability.

Ecological unsustainability

There is now an ever increasing body of research about global environmental change, with the media featuring discussions about environmental damage and the sustainability of the planet, and there is substantial evidence to support calls for social change. Many high-profile agencies, such as the World Bank and the World Resources Institute, acknowledge that the present global system is simply not sustainable and have been aware of this for some time (World Resources Institute 2000). The environmental challenges posed as a result of the human impact on the environment are indeed many. Commentators suggest that the push to consume, driven by global capitalism, is a significant problem in relation to environmental degradation. Globalisation is also a large threat to the environment because it results in environmental damage (Feacham 2001) and contributes to climate change. Globalisation increases travel and therefore the associated pollution. In addition, the increased demand and use of energy sources and the growth in consumption of consumer products and associated waste also impact negatively on the environment.

Paul Wilkinson (2005) suggests that new environmental threats have emerged through complex and extended pathways with global reach. Girling (2005) discusses rubbish and its impact on the environment, arguing that in a 'gadget age', where we need power, our consumption of that power damages the environment, for example, through the use of batteries and the consumption of electricity. Modern farming methods are described as 'spray-on', with herbicides and insecticides damaging the environment too. Then there is the issue of what happens to all of the items that people no longer require, such as rubbish, used cars and broken fridges, which all damage the environment in production, use and by being discarded.

Rubbish is fundamentally tied to inequality because many of the world's poor find themselves receiving unwanted cast-offs from richer sections of society. Commentators suggest that this is the result of 'environmental racism'. Bullard (1990, 1993) described how ugly and toxic waste is often found in the USA in areas where the inhabitants are black and poor. India is one clear example of a poorer country that 'recycles' much of the richer world's waste. Gould (2008) wrote about the scandal of recycled rubbish finding its way to India. In comparison, McDougall (2007) argues that the recycling industry is helping people to claw their way out of poverty in such locations. Contradictory evidence and debates again abound.

While the effects of climate change remain debatable, many writers argue that the impact will affect the most vulnerable disproportionately, with climate change effects further increasing inequalities. Sernau (2011: 315) argues that:

> for a time ... the rich can avoid the heat brought on by global warming by buying bigger air conditioners; they can avoid breathing polluted urban air and drinking contaminated water by driving cars with cabin air filters and buying prestigious brands of bottled water. They can hope to import dwindling natural resources ... and export their waste products to locations far away.

The poor, however, are not in a position to be able to make such choices and consequently will experience the issues caused by a lack of sustainable development. Table 6.3 summarises some of the potential impacts of environmental damage and how these relate to inequality.

Table 6.3 shows the variety of effects that are likely to result from environmental degradation, and it is clear from evidence that those who are the most likely to suffer the worst consequences of this are those who are the least powerful within society. Thus, the poorest will pay the most in terms of environmental impacts. This is a further demonstration of another type of inequality that is, for many theorists, exacerbated by globalisation. More positive discussions within the literature argue that increased global awareness of ecological problems is a positive development (Vandenbroucke 1998). However, if this awareness does not translate into action at individual, community, national and global levels, the effects will ultimately be experienced by those in the most disadvantaged social positions. Now complete Learning Task 4 to explore the impact that climate change may have in relation to health inequalities.

Table 6.3   Environmental impacts related to globalisation, consumerism and inequality

Environmental impact	Relationship to inequality
Degradation and worsening pollution	By destroying the environment, basic needs, such as food, shelter and clean air and water, are all under threat (Stone 2009). Degraded environments are associated with health problems and high levels of mortality. WHO figures show that already each year 800,000 people die from causes related to air pollution, 3.5 million from malnutrition and 1.8 million from lack of clean water (WHO 2005b). Those living in poorer conditions are the ones who will experience these effects the most, having no financial capital to deal with problems associated with environmental damage.
Decreasing biodiversity	Increasing species shifts and extinctions may lead to the collapse of food chains (Summerhayes 2010), increasing food prices. Those who are least well-off are also the least protected against the lack of food and associated problems, such as malnutrition.
Environmental disasters	This will lead to populations on the move, resulting in homelessness and overcrowded conditions (Summerhayes 2010), which are detrimental for health and well-being. Again, those who are least well-off are less able to protect themselves against the loss of possessions and livelihoods, further increasing inequality.
Global warming	In 2000, climate change was estimated to have caused over 150,000 deaths worldwide (WHO 2005a) and the future remains bleak because of the time it will take for the full impact of climate change to take effect (Pope 2008).

Learning Task 6.4 – climate change and global health inequalities

Given the list of possible effects related to ecological problems, and the unequal distribution of these effects, take some time to consider the impact that climate change may have in relation to health.

1 Revisit Table 6.3 and think about how these impacts will affect health.
2 The World Health Organization has published a wealth of literature about health and climate change, so visit the WHO website to expand upon your ideas in this area: www.who.int
3 Now make a list of the likely challenges to health that result from global warming.
4 You should also consider the range of problems that health services may face when trying to deal with the plethora of problems caused by climate change. You might wish to start with basic points about challenges to funding and staffing levels and then develop your list from there.
5 Finally, how might health problems related to environmental change lead to further inequalities?

Having completed the final Learning Task of this chapter, did you consider that people may have to move because of environmental challenges? For example, people may have to move away from degraded and polluted areas. Such movement has health-related consequences and is likely to result in higher demands for health services too. Migration is also another key aspect of globalisation, and again can be analysed in relation to inequality.

Migration

Given that the causes of globalisation are so far being discussed in economic terms, it is important to focus on migration because the movement of people is often economic in motivation and there is inequality associated with this. There are many types of migration, as Martell (2010) discusses, including legal, illegal, forced, voluntary, temporary or, indeed, permanent. Much migration is economic because it is about the movement of labour. Thus, people migrate to look for work, often to try to find better economic conditions and to thus improve their lives.

One area where economic migration is documented is the increased mobility of health professionals across borders. This type of migration has been labelled as 'brain drain' because high proportions of nurses and doctors, educated and trained in their home countries, leave to work in locations where pay and conditions are much more favourable, usually in higher income countries, taking their expertise with them. Macdonald (2006) states that the UK National Health Service would not operate without the staff it gains from other countries. Increasing demands for health professionals in the Global North continue to attract economic migrants. In Zimbabwe from 1990 to 2000, 840 out of a total of 1,200 medical graduates left their country. Similarly, in 2001, more than 2,000 nurses from Africa left to work in the UK (Sanders 2005). While this is beneficial for the country the health professionals migrate to, and positive for the migrants themselves, who are able to improve their earnings and standards of living, it worsens health inequalities. Many of the countries that are left without professionals are experiencing serious health problems and need qualified doctors and nurses.

Economic migration can also be problematic for the receiving societies, where existing residents argue that the migrants take their jobs, and there is evidence that migration can lead to wage decreases within receiving societies because increased competition leads to employers cutting wages. There are many complexities here because immigration often solves labour shortages, and it can increase wages by allowing sections of the economy to expand. Therefore it is positive in overall terms (Martell 2010).

There are, of course, negative impacts resulting from the increased movement of people around the globe, such as the increased spread of deadly epidemics. Feacham (2001) argues that threats from emerging and re-emerging infectious diseases are increased by globalisation.

One area in which migration results in inequality is through the consequences of racism and the unfair treatment of migrants, with immigrants often constituting the poorest sections of society in many countries, with fewer opportunities for education and employment, and the experience of discrimination (Martell 2010). It is highly skilled workers who are likely to benefit within the labour markets of the developed world. Most theorists agree that those who are low-skilled are disadvantaged in terms of earnings and employment prospects and that this disadvantage is increasing (Vandenbroucke 1998). Skills differences are therefore an important dimension of inequality, and are often used as an explanatory factor for wage inequality. Thus, inequalities are related to personal history and qualifications (Giddens 1994), which then result in changing lifestyles and levels of status, as illustrated throughout earlier chapters. These personal inequalities are located within a broader framework of global inequality and globalisation.

Global inequality

What is the relationship between globalisation and global inequality? Despite much discussion and debate within the literature, there are different viewpoints about this, and competing empirical evidence. The neoclassical theory predicts greater equality as a result of globalisation because this construction of the world views wealth as the result of the decisions that individuals make, not the result of processes of coercion, theft, colonisation, or social inequality. In neoclassical theory, those who become wealthy do so by hard work. Wealth also is seen to trickle down to those less well-off. However, the endogenous theory suggests that inequality will result. In this theory economic growth is understood to be the result of internal forces not external factors. This is a theory of economic growth in which economic development is explained but given that this can be uneven, inequalities can result. A third theory, the dependency approach, argues that different benefits result from the processes of globalisation. This is a social science approach, rather than an economic theory and suggests that resources flow from poor and underdeveloped states to wealthy states, enriching the latter at the expense of the former.

Economic growth has been prioritised within policy circles as a specific anti-poverty measure in its own right, with negative links between such growth and poverty simply being overlooked. The problem is that trends in income inequality across many countries have been different, thus making it difficult to fully theorise and understand the impact that globalisation is having (Harjes 2007). Disagreements have consequently arisen, where some argue that inequality is driven by skills-based technological change as well as changing job distribution and types of jobs. These changes are said to result from advances in technological developments and outsourcing; therefore globalisation is blamed. Others argue that changing patterns of inequality can be explained by changes within labour market institutions, such as the introduction of minimum wages, which is not related to the processes of globalisation (Harjes 2007). Given these complexities what can be said about globalisation and global inequality?

Has inequality increased or decreased?

Chapter 1 illustrates the complex patterns of inequality that exist within the social world today and demonstrates that inequality has both increased and decreased. There are large gaps between the richest and the poorest countries, and inequality has also increased within many countries. However, some countries have developed economically and joined more advanced economies. For example, Brazil, Russia, India and China have all made notable progress in economic terms, as has South Korea. Measuring inequality remains challenging (see the discussions in earlier chapters) and there is a lack of accurate data in some countries, further exacerbating the problem.

Is globalisation responsible for increased inequality?

There is no clear answer to this question, so the relationship between globalisation and inequality remains a complex puzzle. While, in theory, globalisation can contribute to equality, potentially increasing demands for labour, increasing economic opportunity and development, the reality is more complex and remains unexplained. Many factors need to be explored within processes of social change, which also determine levels of inequality, such as economic influences, political relationships and technological developments. The measurement of all these, as well as inequality itself, poses significant challenges. Bhagwati (2004) also asks whether increased inequality matters, suggesting that this depends on the society in which this is happening.

Why is globalisation disappointing in development and economic terms?

Given that pro-globalisation theorists suggest positive outcomes, why is the reality different? Again, there is no simple or clear answer here, but some suggested explanations include the optical illusion theory, in which people have been living in invisible poverty in rural areas but then move into urban places which makes their poverty more visible. Another theory is that of the endogenous policy explanation, which suggests that globalisation encourages countries to move to more market-based policies, which undermine institutions that had previously mitigated against both poverty and inequality. Economists are constantly in debate about why globalisation is disappointing.

What is the future of global economic inequality?

It is difficult to be optimistic when writing about current levels of inequality. The future looks bleak because of the slow-down in economic growth globally in the aftermath of the 2008 'global' economic crisis. Put simply, many economies are experiencing difficulties. For example, the Russian economy, in moving from social-ism to capitalism, has left many individuals poorer. Indeed, there has been a crisis in the Eurozone, which has been well reported in the UK media, in which the weak-ening of the value of the Euro is threatening economic stability and may result in countries having their credit ratings downgraded (Guardian 2011b). Different effects are also being recorded in EU countries. The UK picture has been one in which unemployment rates have fluctuated, especially as the public sector has seen an increase in job losses and the private sector has not compensated by employing more (as was expected within some policy circles) (Allen 2011). Indeed, in the wake of the global economic crisis, many negative impacts in terms of global inequalities are clear.

Many contemporary challenges remain in relation to inequality. For example, the dramatic increase in the world's population (to 7 billion people; BBC News 2011c) is a clear challenge to inequality because poverty and population growth are inter-related and some of the world's poorest countries are the ones in which population growth is the greatest (Giddens 2009). Such an exponential rise in the world's population (it has doubled in the last 50 years; BBC News 2011c) raises questions such as can the world be fed and adequately housed, have access to water and basic sanitation or will large sections of the population be condemned to a life of poverty and inequality (Giddens 2009)?

The growth of the population also raises questions about the sustainability of the environment, especially if current western patterns of consumption and associated waste continue. The factors underlying population growth are complex and affected by a multitude of factors. Birth rates remain high in many low-income countries because of attitudes to family sizes, which are seen as desirable, lack of access to contraception and religious beliefs opposing contraception. The example of the social 'one child' policy implemented in China to control population levels is rele-vant here. While it has been effective in reducing population growth, it has also worsened inequalities because the traditional preferences for boys has resulted in selective abortions or newly born girls being killed. Other countries also face chal-lenges to population growth, such as India (Giddens 2009).

The key challenges that require global governance interweave with capitalism, as outlined by Harman (2009: 327):

> Climate change, peak oil and global food shortages will add to the overall economic instability of the system expressed in a boom and bust cycle. … We can expect many more clashes within and between states as problems of food security and energy security lead to shifts in surplus values.

Harman (2009) ultimately predicts an increasingly disorderly and potentially violent world, which will of course be a problem in relation to the levels of and experience of social inequalities. Some suggest that it is not a problem for capitalism, though. Klein (2007) discusses the rise of disaster capitalism, in which those in powerful positions profit from natural disasters such as tsunamis and exploit war-torn countries such as Iraq in order to profit. The globalisation of disaster capitalism is also detrimental for social inequalities.

Case Study: Globalisation and health inequalities

There is a large bank of literature that explores the relationship between globalisation and health inequalities. Many argue that our health is increasingly conditioned and determined by global processes and relationships (Yuill et al. 2010).

- Some theorists have identified a globalisation of health trends as a result of the globalisation of unhealthy lifestyles. For example, increased food consumption and inactivity is resulting in a number of health problems across the world. Heart disease, stroke, cancers and other chronic conditions are seen as the result of such lifestyles. The consumption of increased levels of alcohol and risky sexual behaviours are also cited as problematic for global health, a consequence of which are increasing rates of liver disease and sexually transmitted infections (Warwick Booth et al. 2012). So how does this relate to health inequalities? Individuals in some lower income countries are now experiencing what has been labelled as a 'double burden of disease'. The World Health Organization (2012) highlights how many low- and middle-income countries are now facing this double burden of disease, in which they continue to deal with infectious diseases and under-nutrition, while also experiencing a rapid upsurge in non-communicable disease risk factors such as obesity.
- Globalisation has allowed individuals in rich countries to access treatment in poorer countries, while many residents of these countries cannot afford treatment and care. Health tourism is an industry sustained by 617 million individuals and it is growing year on year (Carrera and Bridges 2006). For example, India will potentially receive US$2.2 billion from health tourism by 2012 (Macready 2007). However, while globalisation has facilitated health tourism, Leach et al. (2005) argue that approximately 80% of the world's population lives without access to essential medication.
- Increased migration associated with globalisation has also resulted in a 'brain drain'. Large numbers of doctors and nurses, who are trained and educated in their own lower income countries, leave to work in other countries where pay and conditions are much more favourable, resulting in their important skills being lost to their home countries.

Summary of key points

- There are many debates about the concept of globalisation, including debates about its relationship with social inequality. The evidence is contradictory in terms of the impact that globalisation is having, with many theorists offering different interpretations of how globalisation is happening.
- Globalisation is related to inequality in many complex ways. Global processes intersect with numerous social divisions and inequalities. In some instances, globalisation has resulted in benefits for those in the most disadvantaged positions. However, in many circumstances globalisation has resulted in increased inequalities.
- The future of globalisation and its associated inequalities is open to interpretation and many challenges remain that relate to global inequalities, such as food insecurity, environmental degradation and population growth. Such challenges may result in increased inequality because it is clear that the most vulnerable, living in poverty and in lower income countries, remain most at risk of suffering the adverse consequences which result from these challenges.

List of questions to stimulate debate and reflection

1 Pay attention to the media, watch the news, read newspapers and look at news reports online. You should be able to find regular reports that demonstrate the existence of many aspects of globalisation across the world, in a variety of contexts. Explore these examples. Are they positive or negative in how they relate to inequality?
2 If you were a global policy maker charged with developing global governance for a fairer and more equitable world, what would your priorities for action be and why? How would you try to improve standards of living and to tackle general inequality?
3 Is globalisation good? Can global capitalism and the processes of globalisation associated with it be used to tackle the problems of inequality across the world? Reflect on the discussions and theoretical perspectives provided in this chapter in order to answer these questions.

Further reading

Lemert, Charles, Elliott, Anthony, Chaffee, Daniel and Hus, Eric (2010) *Globalization: A Reader*. London and New York: Routledge.

This book contains a full historical outline of how globalisation has developed as well as acting as a comprehensive guide to all aspects of globalisation. For example, the book discusses key debates about governance, global culture, global economic issues and future challenges. This is a comprehensive collection of edited chapters that is lengthy but detailed.

Martell, Luke (2010) *The Sociology of Globalization*. Cambridge: Polity Press.

This book gives a good overview of sociological analyses of globalisation, examining all aspects of the concept, including cultural, political and economic aspects. The book also touches on power, inequality and conflict throughout, and so is an excellent introduction to the ongoing debates about globalisation within the field of sociology.

Ritzer, George (2010) *Globalization: A Basic Text*. Chichester: Wiley-Blackwell.

This is a book which provides an excellent introduction to the key debates about globalisation. It covers key theories, such as imperialism, Americanisation, neo-liberalism and cultural theory, while focusing on issues such as the media, the environment and inequalities. It is an excellent introductory read.

7
THE GLOBAL SOCIAL POLICY ARENA AND INEQUALITY

Key learning outcomes

By the end of this chapter you should be able to:

- Understand the concept of global governance
- Understand the complex range of global actors, their agendas and ideological positions
- Understand the relationship between global governance and social inequalities

Overview of the chapter

This chapter extends the discussion started in Chapter 6, which focused on globalisation in relation to inequality, and will critically explore the global social policy arena. Global governance and global social policy are important in relation to inequalities, so this chapter will examine the processes of global governance and the relationship between global policy and inequalities in the world, building upon the discussion started in Chapter 6. The chapter examines the importance of global governance and key global economic players which influence current patterns of inequalities. Key transnational players, such as the World Bank and the World Trade Organisation, are reviewed to illustrate and critique their role. Can these institutions be a force for creating a more equal world or is their agenda more complex? The chapter also discusses the key global challenges which policy makers need to tackle, and how these relate to inequalities.

What is global governance?

The forces of globalisation have arguably led to an increased range of global policy actors, shaping social policy, funding and provision. Global governance has grown in recent years, with several organisations becoming more important following the recognition that poverty, social inequality and several other problems are obviously interrelated and require action at the global level. Yeates and Holden (2009) argue that global analyses are ultimately needed to comprehend social policy formulation as well as its results. Scholte (2000) also writes about the growth of global consciousness in facing problems that span the globe. However, in recent years, 'global governance' has become a frequently used expression, as shown by the publication of a journal of the same name. The meaning of the concept of global governance remains diverse, depending on the person employing it or the circumstances under which it is used. Similar to the concept of globalisation, the term does not have a definition which has achieved general consensus.

> ### *Defining global governance*
>
> The Commission on Global Governance (1995: 2) describes global governance as the 'sum of the many ways individuals and institutions, public and private, manage their common affairs'.
>
> According to Griffin (2010: 88), studying global governance is seeking 'to understand and describe the structures, mechanisms and processes through which collective decisions are made in contemporary world politics.'

Chapter 6 has already touched upon the concept of global governance and highlighted some issues associated with it in relation to inequality. Given the complexities that have been highlighted, a key question that is often asked is why do we need global governance?

Why do we need global governance?

The increasing range of global policy actors is seen by some commentators as an absolutely essential development, in order to ensure that policy making is dealing with the current global challenges that the world is facing. George and Wilding (2009: 27) argue that 'a global approach is needed to deal with problems that are global in character' and that more and more issues are global in both their implications and impact. George and Wilding (2009) list ten areas which demonstrate the need for global governance. These include greater global interdependence, support for the idea of human rights and global problems. The box below outlines the key global challenges for contemporary policy makers.

Challenges for global policy makers

- ○ Economic stability and the need for continued growth
- ○ Wealth and poverty – inequalities
- ○ Population growth
- ○ Population movement
- ○ Demographic change, including a 'greying'/ageing population
- ○ Food supplies and inequalities in access
- ○ Energy supplies and inequalities in access
- ○ Environmental challenges – climate change, sustainable development and pollution as well as inequalities in impact
- ○ Technological development – inequalities in access as well as disadvantages such as the development of new weaponry
- ○ Conflict and war
- ○ Terrorism
- ○ Health – infectious diseases, lifestyle diseases, changing patterns of disease and health inequalities
- ○ Crime and drugs

The list in this box is by no means exhaustive. There may be issues that you can think of that are not included. Clark (2001) highlights other problems facilitating the need for global governance, such as ethnic conflicts, failed states and weapons of mass destruction. Chase-Dunn and Lawrence (2011) list their three major challenges as follows:

1 Global inequalities
2 Ecological degradation
3 A failed system of global governance.

The key point is this, there are a number of global social problems that have emerged in recent years and, as a result, there is a greater need for global social policies to tackle these issues (George and Wilding 2009). Consequently, new patterns of governance have had to be established to cope with these new challenges. Linked into notions of global consciousness, there has also been the emergence of ideas about global citizenship and global human rights (McCarthy 1997), with key players in the global governance field discussing such concepts. Now complete the following Learning Task to explore the complexities associated with defining global priorities.

Learning Task 7.1 – exploring global priority setting using an economic perspective

Use the internet to view a short talk featuring Bjorn Lomberg, who was involved in the Copenhagen Consensus in 2004. This can be found at: www.ted.com/talks/bjorn_lomborg_sets_global_priorities.html

Now think about the points raised in relation to the setting of global priorities and reflect on the discussion.

1 Do you agree with the viewpoints put forward by Bjorn Lomberg?
2 What is your opinion of the policy to tackle global issues? Should it be economically influenced?
3 Do you feel that global priority setting is flawed in any way?
4 Do you think that the priorities highlighted here have been tackled effectively given that this footage is now seven years old?

Given the many problems already identified in Chapter 6, which talks about the relationship between globalisation and inequalities, strong and fair global governance is one mechanism through which equity can be built. The United Nations Development Programme (1999) argues that a form of globalisation related to global citizenship and sustainability can be achieved. In this vision, human rights are respected, poverty reduction is a key priority and there is a concern for equity. As there is strong evidence that globalisation has increased inequality, insecurity and injustice (Scholte 2000), such changes, if they can be achieved, should be welcomed.

Townsend (1999) uses evidence of the increasing polarisation between the rich and the poor to call for the invention of an international welfare state, which would implement and monitor international agreements targeting poverty reduction. His vision also includes the mobilisation of new alliances across countries with the purpose of promoting new ways of dealing with inequality: for example, changes in international taxation, regulation of transnational corporations and new guarantees of human rights by recognising the importance of universal social insurance. See Chapter 9 for a full discussion of the potential solutions to current inequalities. Again, this is a positive vision of the role of global governance, but one which, given the extent of social inequality in the world, is clearly needed to tackle 'the prospect of even greater self-destruction, experienced as an accompanying feature of social polarisation' (Townsend 1999: 88).

Furthermore, states also need global social policy because it is crucial in both securing and maintaining state legitimacy and authority. There are many complexities associated with globalisation (see Chapter 6), thus the state, if acting alone, will not be able to fulfil its responsibilities in developing economic policy, environmental policy, and policy to secure the welfare of its citizens (George and Wilding 2009).

However, given the economic issues that many countries in the world are facing following the prolonged financial crisis which began in 2008, there are many debates about how effective current global policy is. Indeed, current global concerns have centred very much on economic stability, economic growth and development, and other important issues have taken less precedence. Now complete the next Learning Task to think about how policy can potentially be made to work at a global level.

Learning Task 7.2 – tackling the issue of climate change globally

The Kyoto Protocol is an international agreement linked to the United Nations Framework Convention on Climate Change. It includes targets for 37 industrialised countries and the European Community for reducing greenhouse gas (GHG) emissions, for example, an average 5% reduction against 1990 levels over the five-year period 2008-2012 (United Nations 2012). However, some countries, such as the USA, have not ratified the treaty, and many countries have not met the targets. How can we ensure that global policy is more effective?

Verdung (1988) argues that if you look hard enough, policy instruments can be reduced to three simple mechanisms:

1 Carrots – meaning incentives and rewards such as remuneration.
2 Sticks – meaning regulation and punishment.
3 Sermons – meaning advice, guidance and information provision.

Think about all three of these approaches in relation to reducing carbon emissions on a global level. If you were a policy maker tasked with creating policy to reduce carbon emissions, think about the above policy mechanisms and answer the following questions:

1 How might carrots work to reduce carbon emissions?
2 How might sticks work to reduce carbon emissions?
3 How might sermons work to reduce carbon emissions?
4 What would be the limitations of all of these approaches if they were to be implemented?

In completing this Learning Task you should now have realised how complex policy making is. Did you end this task with more questions than you could answer? This is a challenge for all policy makers and those working at the global level are faced with other issues too, including the competing priorities of organisations involved in formulating and delivering policy at the global level.

Key global policy makers

Despite the plethora of global actors, the reality of genuine global politics has been called into question by Beck (1999), who argues that there are unique political structures in each country, region and even community. This means that historical and cultural influences meet with global forces to result in different effects in various parts of the world (Chirot 1991). There are also questions of ethnic solidarity and ethnic strife which threaten global-level politics (Sklair 2002). Nevertheless, despite these complexities, the range of global actors is immense, as Table 7.1 summarises.

Table 7.1 gives some indication of the variety of organisations operating under the rubric of global governance. Many of these institutions have made the alleviation of poverty their goal in the post-war era (for example, the United Nations) and therefore are central to current debates about inequalities. Rosenau (1997) argues that global governance is not just about the role of the UN, but comprises a much more complex set of relationships. Table 7.1 indicates that there are indeed many global players and, unsurprisingly, given the numbers of people in the world facing deprivation and the sheer range of challenges that have been identified in this chapter, the work of these organisations has been heavily scrutinised.

Of particular concern in recent years has been the current global economic crisis, which has raised concerns that any recent progress made by the global policy makers will now be at risk. There may be many more people pushed into poverty as a result of the crisis; the Department for International Development (DIFD 2009) estimate that at least 90 million people are at such a risk. Wilkinson and Clapp (2010: 7) argue that:

> What is especially troubling is that the higher numbers experiencing poverty, hunger and deprivation remain despite the fact that the cost of addressing these conditions for the world's poor is miniscule compared to the amounts of money being allocated to bailout major banks in industrialized countries.

They go on to argue that there has been little analysis of the ways in which global institutions and policy makers are attempting to address poverty and inequality and how their strategies are working. This begs the question of whether or not they are effective? Despite this gap in the literature, there has been much debate about the work of global organisations, and their associated policies, detailing both the positive and the negative aspects of their work.

Table 7.1   Summary of key global actors

Organisation	Description	Impact upon inequality
The United Nations	An international organisation committed to maintaining international peace and security, developing friendly relations among nations and promoting social progress, better living standards and human rights.	• Critics argue that the UN has failed in many ways to achieve its aims, e.g. it did not authorise action to stop the massacre of a million people in Rwanda in 1994. It has also been described as ineffective in dealing with tragedies in Somalia and the former Yugoslavia (R. Wilkinson 2005). Therefore, it has not reduced inequalities through the promotion of peace.
The World Bank	Provides low-interest loans to low-income countries, imposing policy conditions for repayment. It aims to reduce poverty by investing in people.	• Imposition of user charges on health services has had detrimental effects for those who are the most economically disadvantaged. • Reducing investment in public services as part of loan conditions (Stiglitz 2006) is again likely to disproportionately affect the economically worst off. • Some projects have caused environmental damage (Abbasi 1999), affecting those unable to move away from the impact (the economically poor). • Increases poorer countries' reliance upon external sources of incomes, which, for some commentators, worsens inequalities.
The World Trade Organisation	Established in 1995, its role is to regulate trade.	• Many negative consequences in terms of inequality, resulting from privatisation of public services. • The erosion of workers' rights, increased inequalities and unaffordable health care for many (Yuill et al. 2010).
International Monetary Fund	The IMF has had a role in shaping the global economy since the 1940s, aiming to encourage economic growth and stability. It also works with lower income countries to stabilise their economies and reduce poverty.	• Public sector reform via structural adjustment policies requires countries to reduce investment in public services, therefore increasing inequality. • Critics argue that the IMF exacerbates financial crises, has not reduced global poverty and simply extends economic liberalism, thus deepening inequality (Wilkinson 1995).
The World Health Organization	Established in 1948 as the UN's specialist agency for health, with the mandate of attaining the highest possible level of health for all people.	• Vertical programmes, such as mass immunisation, have resulted in improved health for many. • Eradication programmes, such as small-pox, malaria and cholera, have had varied success but have led to some health improvements. • Focus upon primary health care has had variable effects, depending upon how it has been implemented, but where it has been implemented fully there have been clearly reported health benefits. • 2010 World Health Report focused upon improving health care access across the world, although large health inequalities remain.

Organisation	Description	Impact upon inequality
Non-governmental organisations	A variety of remits depending upon their focus, e.g. disaster relief, poverty alleviation.	• Varied interpretations of effects, some positive for inequality, others less so. • Private military companies are prominent in new areas of conflict with debated effects (Wilkinson 1995). • Several development programmes have led to a decline in health of some populations (Wilkinson 1995).
NATO (North Alliance Treaty Organisation)	It is an international organisation that brings together the armies of various countries, including the UK and the USA. Formed in 1949, its remit is focused upon security and responding to urgent military situations.	• It is seen as dominated by western influences and American military power. • Previous military action has been questioned on the grounds of legitimacy. • Military action is argued by peace protestors to create inequalities. This is supported by Klein's (2007) arguments linked to disaster capitalism.
G20	Formed in 1999, this is a group of finance ministers from 20 countries who meet to discuss international finance and trade issues.	• Oxfam (2012) argues that the G20 focuses too much upon economic growth and pays little attention to the ways in which inequalities are perpetuated. • Oxfam (2012) also argue that the G20's commitment to shared and sustainable growth is a long way from being realised.
Illicit actors	Engaged in a variety of illegal activities, such as people trafficking, the sex industry and drug trafficking.	• Organised criminal gangs, terrorist networks and hidden markets are all likely to impact upon social inequality in a variety of negative ways.

Positive global governance

The Millennium Development Goals

The work of global actors has been positive in the identification of issues which need global attention and global policy solutions. The Millennium Development Goals (MDGs), which were defined by the UN member states, are an example of the positive role that global governance can achieve. In 2000, a set of targets were adopted in an attempt to deal with poverty and inequalities, to improve health, to develop a cleaner and more sustainable environment and to promote a fairer world. These goals are summarised in Table 7.2.

These goals have been described as a positive outcome to have emerged from increased global governance because they are framed within the context of human rights and comprise an important tool for achieving these targets in an equitable, just and sustainable way. However, despite increasing policy attention given to human rights within global policy making and programming, many argue that in practice these concepts remain

Table 7.2   Summary of the Millennium Development Goals (MDGs)

Goal	Description
MDG 1	Target – to halve the proportion of the world's poor that live on less than $1 per day. In addition, to halve the number of people who suffer from hunger.
MDG 2	Target – to achieve universal primary education for both boys and girls.
MDG 3	Target – to promote gender equality and strengthen the rights of women, especially educationally.
MDG 4	Target – to reduce child mortality by two-thirds and increase the immunisation of young children.
MDG 5	Target – to reduce maternal mortality by three-quarters through improvements in medical care for women during both pregnancy and childbirth.
MDG 6	Target – to halt and possibly begin to reverse the spread of AIDs, malaria and tuberculosis as well as other major diseases.
MDG 7	Target – to halve the number of people unable to access or afford safe drinking water and basic sanitation, and to improve the living conditions of slum dwellers.
MDG 8	Target – to develop global partnerships to improve debt relief initiatives and access to technology, and to enable access to essential drugs at affordable prices for lower income countries fighting infectious diseases.

Source: United Nations Development Programme (2012)

separate (United Nations Development Programme 2010). Additionally, the targets associated with these goals are unlikely to be met by 2015. Some progress indicators demonstrate improvements, and therefore travel in the right direction, but it is still unlikely that they will be fully achieved. For example, at the global level, the maternal mortality ratio fell by 34% from 1990 to 2008, with the largest changes seen in Asia and North Africa, but this is still insufficient to meet the MDG target (Wilmoth et al. 2010).

There are also issues with the money needed to support the achievement of these goals. Oxfam (2010) argues that donors are giving far less than is needed to meet the goals and, given the economic difficulties being experienced by many high-income countries at the time of writing, additional funding seems unlikely to be available. The goals themselves are also open to interpretation and are in many ways vaguely conceptualised. For example, extreme poverty can be defined in numerous ways, and how should the 'promotion' of women's rights be measured? The goals have also been threatened in that the resistance of higher income countries has delayed their implementation. Furthermore, there are many locally contingent factors that compound the goals being achieved, such as wars, corruption and transnational corporations, which all serve to impede progress (Macdonald 2007).

However, this critical perspective is not held by all. Some commentators argue that great progress has been made, when measured against these targets, in many countries. For example, reductions in incidences of HIV/AIDS and maternal mortality rates have been successfully achieved. Complete the following Learning Task to explore the Millennium Development Goals in more depth.

Learning Task 7.3 – exploring the Millennium Development Goals

Use the internet to view a short talk given by Hans Rosling about the evidence of progress towards meeting the Millennium Development Goals. This can be found at: www.ted.com/talks/hans_rosling_the_good_news_ of_the_decade.html. After watching the presentation of statistical data about progress regarding the Millennium Development Goals, answer the following questions:

1 What is your view about the goals as a policy tool?
2 Can global governance be a force for good?
3 What else do you think is needed to ensure that inequalities can be reduced?

Political commitment to achieving these goals remains under scrutiny and, despite some progress, there are still many writers who remain cynical about the commitment of global actors to addressing the causes of inequalities. Certainly, the patterns of inequality discussed in Chapter 1 do not support the notion that progress towards achieving greater equality has been made.

The focus on health

Global policy-making organisations are also increasingly recognising the interrelationship of social problems and 'wicked issues'. Thus policy making is now beginning to take account of this. For example, The World Health Organization's 2008 report, *Closing the Gap in a Generation: Health Equity through Action on the Social Determinants of Health* (Commission on the Social Determinants of Health 2008), outlines the need to tackle social inequality as part of the cause of health inequalities, identifying that the causes of inequality and poor health are found in both social and economic factors. The report makes three cross-cutting recommendations:

1 Improve daily living conditions.
2 Tackle the unequal distribution of power, money and resources.
3 Measure and understand the problem and assess the impact of any action taken.

There have also been moves to create healthy public policy on a global scale. Healthy public policy is policy that has a clear and explicit concern for health (Warwick-Booth et al. 2012). There are several examples already in existence, such as the Framework Convention on Tobacco Control (Labonte 2010), which is the world's first global public health treaty. Negotiated by the World Health Organization (WHO) in 2005, it aims to support an internationally co-ordinated response to combating the use of tobacco. Another notable example of a global healthy public policy is the Kyoto Protocol on greenhouse gas emissions (Labonte 2010). This protocol aims to reduce the levels of emissions on a country basis in order to reduce the effects of climate change and potentially mitigate against the many health effects that are likely to ensue with changing temperatures across the globe. However, its effects are again debated.

The creation of some public-private partnerships has also resulted in significant benefits in relation to health inequalities. For example, the Clinton Foundation's HIV/AIDS initiative has been able to negotiate price reductions for some anti-retroviral drugs for a number of sufferers within specific countries. Bull (2010) argues that this success is beyond what other organisations, such as the UN, could have achieved, and it is primarily because of Clinton's power as an ex-President of the USA and his personal networks.

The work of non-governmental organisations

The increasing proliferation of non-governmental organisations (NGOs) and social movements (discussed in Chapter 6) has led to changes in global governance. They have had a particularly significant impact where pressure is mobilised, sustained and linked to negative publicity (Griffin 2010). For Griffin (2010), this means that forms of global governance can be subject to change and that neo-liberal dominance does not always have to be the only way forward in policy development. Bexell et al. (2010) similarly argue that the increasing number of global actors can serve to democratise global governance through expanding participation via the inclusion of these different actors and the creation of pathways for more direct citizen involvement. Particularly in Africa, NGOs rival governments in terms of providing services, and when many economic sectors in Africa were declining, they were seen as more capable of delivering development (Fowler 1998).

NGOs have also been viewed as a positive alternative to the major drivers of policy, such as the International Monetary Fund (IMF) and World Bank, whose forced structural adjustment programmes had served to increase inequalities in many countries (Brautigam 2000). Bhagwati (2004) also argues that while a few NGOs focus on global issues, many have diverse but positive objectives, such as outlawing bigamy and changing inheritance laws to enable women to inherit. Therefore they can be positive in relation to tackling inequalities.

Despite this positive recognition of the complex interrelationship between numerous areas of social inequality, questions remain about the effectiveness of global goals and targets as well as the influence held by the organisations involved in policy making at the global level. For many critics, global policy making is simply not tackling inequalities. There have been criticisms levelled at several policies for failing to be radical enough in attempting to tackle health inequalities (Crinson 2009). Thus, despite some progress, there are increasing calls from various agencies and social movements for further and more radical changes in several areas of global governance, such as those related to health inequalities, and particularly those related to social inequalities.

Negative global governance

Policy directions

There have been many questions raised about the ideological underpinnings of the organisations responsible for global governance such as the World Bank (Macdonald 2007). Neo-liberalism is argued by many to be at the centre stage of global governance, with international institutions facilitating supply and demand and increasing free trade (Scholte 2005) without consideration of the impact of such policy. Thus, there are many claims that institutions such as the IMF and the World Bank have in fact increased inequality (Stiglitz 2002). Bayne (2010) discusses the 'four devils' of globalisation that need to be tackled through a more sustainable global governance system and are related to neo-liberalism and trade:

1 Loss of jobs.
2 Crime and internal disorder.
3 Financial panic.
4 The danger of poor countries being left behind.

Clearly, if these challenges can be addressed in an effective way, this would result in positive outcomes for the reduction of social inequalities. However, the global forums that exist to deal with international challenges such as these are seen as clearly limited by many. For example, the G8 grouping (eight of the worlds wealthiest countries including the UK, France, Germany, the US and Japan) has been described as being unrepresentative, lacking legitimacy, and ineffective (Gnath and Reimers 2009). The G8 whilst still functioning, has recently broadened its membership and in some instances meets as the G20, a wider group of nations, including the fast-developing economic countries projected to be the future leaders of the world economy, such as Brazil, India and China. For some, this demonstrates the need for reform, with global governance being necessary but currently ineffective in terms of meeting current challenges and changing issues in the twenty-first century. The range of countries being represented at the global level and the numerous organisations governing global level policy and processes, also means that there can be barriers between institutions and power imbalances which hinder meaningful progress.

Current policy directions remain tied to neo-liberal principles and thus are problematic in relation to inequalities. Murphy (2000) argues that contemporary global governance is simply a response to global capitalism. For some theorists (Sklair 2002), these organisations simply represent the transnational capitalist class at work. This has been echoed in the many public protests during high-profile meetings of the World Trade Organisation, the World Bank, the G8 and the European Union. The public have expressed dissatisfaction about the transparency of the work of these organisations and their response to campaigns about international debt relief, poverty reduction, environmental issues such as threats to endangered species and human rights issues such as the use of child soldiers, to name just a few examples (R.Wilkinson, 2005). Ollilia (2005) similarly argues that global policy making is clearly aligned with industrial and trade policies, often to the detriment of global health. There are many other writers who make the same points, such as Cammack (1999), who explores what he suggests are undemocratic global forces shaping the world order. Thus, the ideological underpinnings of some organisations have been critically questioned (Macdonald 2007). Bush (2007) argues that the representation of capitalist interests is actually depicted as positive for poorer countries, and that no alternatives are seen.

Development and aid

Current global institutions focus on development as the answer to addressing inequalities. The dominance of US influence in development approaches is another well-documented area within the literature about global governance (Greig et al. 2007). This has led to neo-liberal development in which the focus on economic growth has overshadowed concerns with inequalities. Assessing the effectiveness of development is another complicated area, particularly as the top-down creators of developmental projects, such as the World Bank, the IMF and aid NGOs, have different visions of the outcomes that they wish to achieve, compared to those in receipt of the projects. Greig et al. (2007) argue that development has been defined and organised by the West as a means of retaining power and a hold over those who are poorer. This can be seen in the way that institutions such as the IMF attach conditionality to poorer countries. Many forums now argue that development is in crisis because neo-liberal approaches have resulted in further inequalities and have been socially damaging. They conclude that humanity does possess the means to challenge inequalities but that current development mechanisms remain problematic.

The aid industry has also received criticism, with commentators questioning whether aid works to tackle inequalities effectively. Moyo (2009) argues that global policy makers live in a culture of aid in which giving to the poor is simply seen as the correct thing to do. She marshals evidence to demonstrate that aid has helped make poor people worse off and that it inhibits economic growth, but that it remains a central lynchpin of development policy within the global arena. She says:

The notion that aid can alleviate systemic poverty, and has done so, is a myth. Millions in Africa are poorer today because of aid; misery and poverty have not ended but have increased. Aid has been, and continues to be, an unmitigated political, economic, and humanitarian disaster for most parts of the developing world. (Moyo 2009: xix)

Moyo (2009) focuses on African countries in particular to show that the aid-based development model currently adhered to by key global players such as the IMF and the World Bank funds an industry, has been linked to corruption and its policies often do not actually reach the poor as intended. She proposes a new policy approach in which reliance upon aid is gradually reduced, other sources of income are tapped and internal governance systems are strengthened (see Chapter 9). Complete the following Learning Task to develop your own understandings in this area.

Learning Task 7.4 – is aid effective?

Use the internet to view the short clip: 'Is Aid Killing Africa? Dambisa Moyo talks about Dead Aid on ABC', which is available on YouTube at: www.youtube.com/watch?v=HIPvlQOCfAQ. Now answer the following questions:

1 Reflect on the footage you have seen. What are your thoughts now? Do Moyo's arguments challenge your own opinions? Have you learned something new from this?
2 Read the comments that people have posted beneath the film. What is this telling you about the opinions held by others?
3 Now take time to think about the future. Are there alternatives to aid?

Similarly, other criticisms of aid are evident within the literature. Bush (2007) argues that the UK Make Poverty History campaign failed because it was a single-issue campaign that focused on reducing debt in Africa. It did not deal with how the debt had emerged and, more crucially, how such debt will continue to emerge within the existing world order. The perpetuation of inequalities within current frameworks of governance are currently ignored with regard to economics and so too with other areas, such as gender inequalities.

Gender inequality

Chapter 4 discusses gender inequality and, given the evidence that exists about this, it is clear that it remains a key challenge for contemporary policy makers. Kilgour (2007) argues that there is a wealth of data, greater awareness and many recommendations about gender inequality and that global policy actors such as the UN and the World Bank agree that it is an issue which needs addressing. Despite this and the many goals that have been set to eliminate gender inequality, there has been a disappointing lack of progress. Griffin (2010) argues that the official discourses of many intergovernmental organisations are devoid of discussions about gender. Women are mentioned when linked to economic productivity. Thus gender equity has been framed in a language of women's economic participation in markets, and markets working for women (see World Bank 2004).

In addition, gender inequities are seen as problematic because they restrict economic development and growth, which ignores the informal labour that women contribute in support of the formal labour market. For Griffin (2010: 101), this is problematic because 'simply adding women to structures constituted as masculine does not, however, tackle the gendered underpinnings of reigning paradigms'. Kilgour (2007 also argues that such equality remains elusive as a goal because the current global governance regime incorporates large transnational companies that are more powerful than states. Held and McGrew (2002: 5) recognises this too when he states that 'the most fundamental forces and processes which determine the nature of life chances within and across political communities are now beyond the reach of individual nation states'. Consequently, private actors also need to be incorporated into current global governance systems and processes. Women need to be participating in global policy making too because if the processes of policy making themselves are skewed, then so too is the policy that is developed. Kilgour (2007) argues that those making policy related to women's inequality need to develop an understanding of structural underpinnings of the issue: the world is gendered and it is this that creates different life chances for both men and women. For her, all issues need to be addressed with a gender lens.

Governance of those governing

The accountability of many transnational organisations has also been questioned, with Bexell et al. (2010) describing the lack of accountability as a democratic pitfall. They go on to argue that international institutions, partnerships and individual global actors all demonstrate unbalanced participation from stakeholders. Ultimately there are many trade-offs that occur in the processes of global governance, such as inclusiveness versus accountability, deliberation versus transparency and representation versus participation. Bexell et al. (2010: 97) suggest that there is need for a discussion about the 'relationship between global democracy, other standards of legitimacy and the role of values such as equity and justice in global governance'. Leadership in the context of global governance is a difficult area and the question remains as to whether globalisation itself is being governed?

NGOs have also been scrutinised within the literature. Are they really a 'magic bullet' for resource-poor countries in terms of development and governance problems (Vivian 1994)? The exponential growth in NGOs has led commentators to suggest that now they also hold too much influence in terms of policy making, especially where they are based in the Global North but work in the Global South (Manji 2000).

Increasing exclusion

Seckinelgin (2010) argues that international organisations remain detached from the very groups at which that they target policy and, furthermore, that their operating mechanisms serve to structurally exclude the people that they are targeting. In addition, 'considerations of inequality of access to political decision-making remain absent at the international level' (Seckinelgin 2010: 206). Chatterjee (2004) also states that people are unable to address the inequality experienced in their daily lives because of the existence of structural exclusion from the policy-making process, which instead remains focused on the development of technical solutions rather than dealing with the struggles that people face in getting access to resources.

Despite this identification of the existence of exclusion, recognised for many years by international actors themselves in their policy documents, such as the Department for International Development 'poverty reduction strategies often fail to reach socially excluded groups' (DFID 2005: 5), and questionable assumptions remain. Do all marginalised groups wish to be included in the political mainstream? Is the solution to the problem of exclusion, top-down decision making about demands and needs? Seckinelgin (2010) poses these questions and argues that poverty in lower income countries is also related to a number of structural international processes that both produce and maintain it. Ultimately, 'policies might try to include people by technically changing the delivery mechanism or establishing procedures for participation of the excluded, but they do not necessarily engage with the structural causes of exclusion that may exist in the system' (Seckinelgin 2010: 212). Given that these structures operate in such a way, persistent inequality is the outcome. Chase-Dunn and Lawrence (2011) argue that existing global institutions exhibit a democratic deficit. Thus, those institutions in power are simply not democratic. Furthermore, they contend that the United States continues to be dominant in military terms, which prevents any challenges by contending states.

Global ecological problems

As earlier discussions in this chapter and in Chapter 6 indicate ecological problems are now a global challenge. Chase-Dunn and Lawrence (2011) argue that rising costs of energy prices, energy-extensive consumption and other scarce resources are likely to lead to wars. They argue that 'The war in Iraq is both an instance of imperial over-reach … and also a resource war because the US neoconservatives thought that they could prolong US hegemony by controlling the global oil supply' (Chase-Dunn and Lawrence 2011: 141). In this challenging context, global environmental governance is clearly necessary for ensuring sustainable development and protecting the environment. Climate change is recognised as a significant problem in the context of environmental governance, posing difficult challenges for policy makers and political systems (World Bank 2009b). Sarkar (2011) argues that some of the most powerful groups in society have benefited so much from existing arrangements that changing the status quo to tackle the effects of climate change is a significant problem, and thus is highly resisted. Furthermore, current energy efficiency measures and policy approaches remain ineffective.

Global economic issues

Rorden Wilkinson (2005) argues that the literature has yet to capture the full extent of what is happening and, more problematically, that there is an absence of discussion which explores alternatives to global governance in its current form. An area where this is evident is in relation to the governance of global finance, which is of course central to inequalities. The 2008 'global' financial crisis has resulted in increased inequality and the need to understand the governance of global finance. Current governance of global finance is based on the Bretton Woods institutions (the World Bank and the IMF) and the World Trade Organisation (WTO), which celebrates open markets and thus perpetuates poverty as well as supporting market-based initiatives in response to poverty relief (Therien 1999). Despite widespread recognition of this, and the continuous cycles of boom and bust experienced in the contemporary world in what Harman (2009) describes as zombie capitalism, the global governance of finance is not changing. Chapter 8 explores the issues with policy making in relation to global financial problems in more depth. The current focus of many nations and global institutions is on generating economic growth. Bush (2007), however, argues that economic growth does not lead to less poverty. As a result of global financial inequalities, there has been a surge in increasing resistance to current governance, the focus on generating more economic growth and the associated negative impacts for many of the world's poor.

Global resistance

The role played by many global actors, such as the World Bank and the IMF, as well as the perceived dominance of America in world economic matters has increasingly resulted in different forms of global resistance. There were anti-IMF riots during the 1980s as a consequence of policies leading to rises in food prices and transportation costs, hitting cities in the Global South particularly hard. Clearly, the institutions of global governance have faced rebellion over a number of years (Chase-Dunn and Lawrence 2011). The most recent anti-capitalist protests have made interesting media headlines across Europe, with protestors still occupying some public space in the UK at the time of writing. The protestors have also been involved in marches in places such as New York, London, Frankfurt, Madrid, Rome, Sydney and Hong Kong, with organisers aiming to initiate global change against capitalism and austerity measures (Gabbatt 2011).

The protests have raised questions about the current global economic system, yet there is no clear consensus about the way forward. Wolf (2011) argues that the failure of the current economic system has led to greater inequality in the form of increased nationalism, chauvinism and racism because of increasing frustrations. Blame is laid in different places, according to where people locate themselves ideologically. Thus, is it the government, is it the application of macro-economic tools or is it entirely the fault of capitalism? Debates continue, as does global resistance. For example, there have been calls for an international labour movement as commentators recognise the need for communication between workers across borders. Sernau (2011) argues that falling wage levels in the industrial sectors of high-income countries are bringing such workers closer to their fellow workers in middle-income countries including those in Latin America. There have also been many successful consumer activism campaigns in relation to poor working conditions in lower income countries. In 1999, US students boycotted Reebok sports shoes as a result of the conditions in Reebok's Indonesian factories (Sernau 2011).

There is also a continuous campaign to boycott Nestlé internationally. This campaign remains active across 20 countries because the company has more reported violations of the WHO Code on the international marketing of formula milk than any other manufacturer. Despite the existence of the code for the marketing of breast-milk substitutes, created by the World Health Organization during the 1980s, there are many reported violations of the rules, for example, free samples being provided in hospitals in poorer countries such as Thailand, South Africa and Bangladesh (Macdonald 2006). The promotion of formula milk, particularly in low-income countries, has well-documented negative impacts on health, leading to higher death rates, malnutrition and higher morbidity (Labbock and Nazro 1995). Consequently, campaigners have created an annual international 'boycott Nestlé week'. Consumer activists have also targeted the use of forced child labour in factories producing goods for companies such as Nike, Dunlop and Adidas (Sernau 2011).

Klein (2001) cites many similar examples of global protest, including the notable example of the Global Street Party in 1999, in which people gathered in many cities to draw attention to sweatshop conditions, the need for fair trade and debt forgiveness for lower income countries. The global media report these protests and the way in which they are policed and how protesters are arrested. For example, BBC News (2011b) reported on the arrests made in Los Angeles when protestors defied an eviction deadline. The plethora of social movements which serve to draw attention to various issues and campaign for change is vast. Other notable examples of global resistance include the recent globalisation of the women's movement and the environmental justice movement, which is concerned with the interrelationship between environmental problems and inequalities (Sernau 2011).

How does global governance relate to inequality?

Policy can be used as a mechanism to tackle inequality by changing the economic circumstances in which individuals live. There is a large bank of evidence that shows how income levels are strongly correlated to other aspects of inequality (see earlier chapters). Those living in the most unequal of societies face more mental illness (including drug and alcohol addiction), lower life expectancy and higher infant mortality, obesity and teenage pregnancy rates (Wilkinson and Pickett 2009). Policy is important here because it can act as a mechanism to try to redistribute income or it can further extend inequality by widening income gaps between the poorest and the richest sections of the world. Fiscal policy (that is, policy concerned with money) and general economics can be used in such circumstances to try to redress inequalities. Policy can be designed to support those on lower incomes, for example to redistribute income by applying progressive taxation rates. Wilkinson and Pickett (2009) argue that income distribution provides policy makers with a way of improving the well-being of whole populations. They state that national policy to tackle inequalities (such as that used by the UK New Labour Government, 1997-2010) has failed, suggesting that this is because rather than reducing inequality, most policies aimed at dealing with such problems attempt to break the link between deprivation and associated problems instead of tackling the root of the cause. This demonstrates that policy has limitations in terms of what it can achieve (see Chapter 8).

Global policy making, too, has not reduced inequalities in many areas and, as this chapter shows, it may increase it. For example, the operation of organisations such as the IMF and the WTO has led to underdevelopment because of the dependence on foreign investment. Structural adjustment programmes (SAPs) implemented by the IMF have also increased inequalities in many countries. The WTO, despite discussing free trade, presides over trade rules which disadvantage some countries and thus furthers inequalities (Chase-Dunn and Lawrence 2011). Murphy (2000) argues that global governance is also inefficient and has thus far been incapable of shifting resources from the world's wealthy to the world's poor. This is as a result of organisations such as the IMF and WTO promoting unregulated globalisation, which is ultimately contributing to the growing numbers of the world's poor (see Chapter 6).

Berry (2010) also presents a depressing picture in arguing that industrial countries have done a poor job of fostering the necessary changes that could have alleviated poverty and reduced inequalities. He identifies inadequate support in some areas as well as bad choices being made in terms of the issues on which to focus. Berry (2010: 64) concludes:

> Most blatant and inexcusable has been the unwillingness to curtail the pernicious effects of the arms trade, bribery of local officials, the sometimes socially ill-advised exploitation of natural resources, and other obviously damaging impacts of industrial country activities.

Sadly, his list does not end there, and he again focuses on ideological bias and an overall lack of coherence in tackling inequality and poverty on a global scale, blaming the institutions acting within the global arena itself in suggesting that they are inadequate. Momani (2010) makes similar points in her analysis of the role of the IMF in tackling poverty and inequality, suggesting that the organisation lacks the expertise to deal with the needs of lower income countries and therefore it has been ineffective in dealing with inequalities. Rather, its policies have exacerbated these. The World Bank's policies, too, have been analysed as increasing poverty and contributing to inequality. Given that the Bank represents nearly 30% of all official development aid, the need for reform has again been identified (Weaver 2010), with the institution seen as irrelevant, illegitimate and ineffective (Birdsall and Subramanian 2007). Weaver (2010) argues that despite demands for reform from member states, and the Bank's public claims that it will change, reform remains elusive. Consequently, inequalities are not being tackled effectively.

Bull (2010) argues that the increasing concentration of wealth in the world is such that it is having large-scale implications within the field of global governance. Private actors are now involved in global governance through elite public-private partnerships and this is often not beneficial for the poor. Thus, current forms of global governance are unlikely to deal with inequality in an effective way because '[a]lthough the global power elite has shown a concern for the pressing issues related to poverty and environmental challenges, it is not likely to support a system that aims to address the power inequalities on which their own power is premised' (Bull 2010: 228).

Case Study: Climate change, global governance and complex risk factors

There are many wicked problems facing the institutions of global governance, including that of climate change. The risk parameters of climate change are social, economic and political as well as the obvious environmental impacts (Deere-Birkbeck 2009). Climate change is fundamentally related to social inequalities because the risks of climate change are not equally distributed, and this leaves unanswered questions about how unequal players in the global governance system can be responsible for the impacts when they have played less of a role in generating them, and indeed have less capacity and power to act in response. Governments and global players have constantly deferred action in this area. Despite climate change being identified as a risk in 1992, governments and global players are still debating concrete commitments well over 15 years later (Deere-Birkbeck 2009). Furthermore, those in lower income countries remain most at risk from the effects of climate change, while being least able to respond to those risks. There have been calls for more collaborative approaches within global governance to address such risks, as well as improvement in areas of weak performance, such as co-ordination, monitoring, information sharing and capacity building (Deere-Birkbeck 2009). There also needs to be meaningful engagement of all relevant stakeholders in developing policy responses in this area and, given the problems identified with current governance mechanisms in this chapter, significant change is needed. In 2000, climate change was estimated to have caused over 150,000 deaths worldwide (World Health Organization 2005a) and its health-related impact is likely to continue because the climate takes time to respond to change (Pope 2008). Therefore, the most vulnerable remain at a higher risk as a result of contemporary inequalities.

Summary of key points

- Global governance has expanded in recent years, with a large number of global actors working on a range of areas and problems. There is a general consensus that there are many global challenges which need to be tackled, including inequalities.
- The work of global institutions and policy makers is well debated in the literature. There have been some successes and targets are often set. However, the neo-liberalist framework underpinning the work of some of these organisations does not result in positive outcomes for the poorest people in many instances.
- Increasingly, amid criticisms of global governance, there are calls for the transformation of existing approaches to dealing with contemporary challenges. This is particularly pertinent in relation to tackling global inequalities.

List of questions to stimulate debate and reflection

1 In terms of reducing the poverty and inequality across the world, what do you think is necessary and how might this be achieved? Do you think that global governance can be positive and help lower income countries?
2 Do you think that most people in higher income countries have a good understanding of the issues associated with global inequalities and the work with which the institutions of global governance are engaged?
3 What are your views on global resistance? Can global resistance be an effective tool to raise awareness and tackle contemporary injustices such as global inequality and ineffective global governance?

Further reading

McNeill, Desmond and St Clair, Asunción Lera (2009) *Global Poverty, Ethics and Human Rights: The Role of Multilateral Organisations*. London: Routledge.

This book analyses two major multilateral development organisations – the World Bank and the UNDP – and some of their initiatives to tackle poverty. The authors draw attention to the gap in rhetoric and practice within current attempts to deal with inequalities such as poverty.

Wilkinson, Rorden and Clapp, Jennifer (eds) (2010) *Global Governance, Poverty and Inequality*. London: Routledge.

This is an edited book that features many interesting debates about the role of global policy makers and institutions in relation to poverty and inequality. The book is well written and user friendly, with short chapters that detail the key issues in global governance. It is an interesting reading and provides a great overview of the issues related to global governance and the problems there are with tackling inequalities.

Wilkinson, Rorden and Hulme, David (eds) (2012) *The Millennium Development Goals and Beyond: Global Development after 2015*. London: Routledge.

The effectiveness of the MDGs is constantly debated, and this is the focus for this edited collection of chapters. The book focuses on what the goals have achieved and what still remains to be done. The book has a broad scope, covering a large range of issues and ultimately discussing how the goals are related to global poverty.

8

SOCIAL POLICY AND ITS RELATIONSHIP TO INEQUALITY: FACILITATOR OR POTENTIAL SOLUTION?

Key learning outcomes

By the end of this chapter you should be able to:

- Understand the concept of social policy
- Understand the relationship between social inequality and social policy both nationally and globally
- Understand that social policy can shape inequality negatively and that it can also be used as a tool to attempt to tackle it

---

Overview of the chapter

This chapter introduces readers to the role that social policy can play in either increasing or attempting to tackle social inequality. The chapter critically explores specific examples of social policy at both the global and national level to assess their impact on levels of inequality within society. Under the New Labour government in the UK specific policies were implemented to tackle inequality and reduce national poverty. Were these policies and interventions successful? What can the UK's efforts tell the rest of the world about how social policy can be used to address inequalities? What about policy in relation to finance and economics, given the current focus on these areas by both national governments and key global players? Is finance fair? The chapter considers current policy strategies in a range of contexts to assess their impact on inequalities.

Introduction to social policy

Social policy can be described as a field of activity decided upon and implemented by the government, a course of action and indeed a web of decisions rather than a single decision (Hill 1997). Policy usually is a stance towards a particular topic and involves a cluster of related decisions and actions, often dealt with in a consistent fashion (Harrison and Macdonald 2008). Social policy is often concerned with tackling social problems and bringing about change, yet it can work in a number of opposable and generalised ways. For example, policy can:

- keep things as they are (maintaining the status quo) or try to change things
- give privilege or advantage to certain groups or try to treat people equally
- promote equality or extend inequality
- promote certain, specific values or accommodate a range of diverse values
- change individuals (or groups) or change environments.

Hence, policy can impact on social inequality in a variety of ways. The policy-making process in which policy paths are determined is also complex and dynamic, and is itself subject to a range of influences from various groups and stakeholders who have an interest in directing policy. Policy is thus made on a number of levels and involves a range of policy actors seeking to influence the process. The roles of policy actors vary within the process. For example, the media and interest groups often serve effectively to raise issues and put policy problems on the agenda, but they have no role in implementation once policy is created. Interestingly, certain issues become important in policy terms and make it on to the policy agenda, with analyses of power often exploring how this works in relation to social inequalities. The media has often played a role in the UK in framing specific policy issues as being important. Now complete the following Learning Task to think about how the media operates in relation to the construction of inequalities.

Learning Task 8.1 – the media and constructions of inequality

View the following media reports:

- 'People would rather go on the sick here than take a low-paid job', *The Sun,* October 13th 2009, available at: www.thesun.co.uk/sol/homepage/features/2677798/The-Sun-examines-the-blackspots-of-broken-Britain-Day-1-Merthyr-Tydfil-in-Mid-Glamorgan.html

(Continued)

(Continued)

- 'Iain Duncan Smith: poverty is not solved by just more money', *The Daily Telegraph* June 14th 2012, available at: www.telegraph.co.uk/news/politics/9331036/Iain-Duncan-Smith-poverty-is-not-solved-by-just-more-money.html

- 'Get a job, Iain Duncan Smith tells parents on the dole', *The Daily Telegraph*, June 13th 2012 available at: www.telegraph.co.uk/news/politics/9330574/Get-a-job-Iain-Duncan-Smith-tells-parents-on-the-dole.html

1 Now consider what these reports are saying about social inequality. How is it being represented in the media?
2 Do you think that media reports are fair and unbiased?
3 Increasingly, the media is beginning to focus not only on those who are poor, but also on the rich and their practices. Explore some of the media coverage on this issue and compare the reporting of the rich to the reports you have already looked at. Use the following report as a starting point: 'Is anyone benefiting from the wealth of the super rich?' *BBC News*, January 24th, 2012, which is available at: www.bbc.co.uk/news/business-16690607

There are some interesting texts that explore this area in more detail. You may wish to read:
    Pascale, Celine-Marie (2012) *Social Inequality and the Politics of Representation: A Global Landscape*. London and New York: Sage.

Robinson et al. (2009) argue that poverty is under-reported and inadequately reported in the UK media. They argue that the media tends to focus on sensationalist stories at the expense of everyday experiences. Thus criticisms of media reports often focus on the way in which poverty is stereotyped and how it labels those experiencing it. It is not just the media who play a part in influencing the policy agenda. Powerful corporations influence the process, with interest groups often working with politicians and government officials to negotiate and lobby as a mechanism to serve their private corporate interests.

This has been particularly reported in the USA (Crinson 2009). Such powerful corporate interests are often not beneficial for levels of equality. Since the 1970s corporations have attempted to influence the political sphere. They influence the process by providing contributions and donations to political campaigns in the USA, and by forming interest groups which are then used to lobby the policy process. These groups and their associated campaigns are well funded, well co-ordinated and influential. Given that many governments do not regulate lobbying, this has led to a range of criticisms in the literature. Furthermore, this means that the wealthy have a greater voice than the poor, with different genders, ages and ethnicities being represented within the policy-making process, but the voice of the poor remains hidden. Chang

(2010) argues that the way in which the policy process operates has been a key driver of income inequality in the last two decades. These influences within the policy process also raise questions about how power operates in policy making.

Power clearly plays a part in the policy–making process, although how power operates within the policy arena is subject to much debate. Table 8.1 explores

Table 8.1   Power within the policy-making process

Theory of power	Key aspects of the theory	How this relates to social inequalities
Pluralist	• Policy is understood to emerge from the interaction of different parties at all stages of development and implementation.	• Competing interests are evident within the process; however, some are not represented, i.e. the poor.
Rationalist	• Policy makers have a good understanding of the problems relevant to the policy-making process. • They choose different options and make clear, rational decisions in relation to policy.	• Policy makers are able to create policy to respond to inequalities in a rational manner. • While there are some countries that have developed policy to tackle inequalities, there are ongoing debates about its effectiveness and which approach is most effective. • This approach does not take account of ideological influences and needs to recognise differential power balances within the process.
Incrementalist	• Policy makers do not start with a blank sheet. • They do not have perfect knowledge about the issues. • They respond by making small and incremental changes.	• Often policy is incrementally changed. However, if policy is failing to tackle inequalities, then small changes are unlikely to alter the direction of policy or to make it more effective.
Institutionalism	• Policy is created by government institutions. • There is a close relationship between policy making as a process and such institutions because policies are implemented by them.	• Government institutions are involved in the process, but they can be influenced by powerful voices and interests. Therefore, policy is not always beneficial for addressing inequalities.
Policy communities	• Policy is made within specific communities via networks such as those that exist between public and private actors.	• Policy communities and networks can be seen as trying to influence the process in relation to specific issues, i.e. different networks view the right to abortion for women in competing ways and seek to influence policy change in line with their views.
Elitist view	• Policy choices are dominated by the upper social classes, the ruling elite. • They use the process to keep power and play a dominant role in society.	• This approach is well illustrated throughout this chapter in relation to UK and US policy since the 1970s, which has very effectively supported the interests of the elite, i.e. those holding wealth.

how power operates within the policy-making process and what this means for inequalities.

Clearly, there are a range of views of the policy process, as Table 8.1 demonstrates. Which view do you most agree with? There are also many policy sectors that are related to social inequality, and one of the most debated is that of welfare.

Welfare policy

Esping-Anderson (1990) argues that there are different types of welfare system around the world, each based on different ideologies and principles. This is important because the organisation of welfare systems fundamentally shapes who has access to the services that are provided, and relates closely to the existence of social inequalities. Welfare states are a mechanism for meeting the basic needs of the population, and these are a crucial area of social policy research. The provision of welfare benefits and public services are closely related to wealth and inequality, with benefit provision being able to reduce inequality (Orton 2008). There are many complex debates based around the provision of welfare and public services.

Important debates in policy related to welfare

○ What constitutes a basic human need? Need is often debated and is open to interpretation (see Chapter 1).
○ How can welfare states ensure that all members of society have access to basic human needs and entitlements?
○ How should welfare be funded? Should it be through taxation? Should the private sector be involved in funding? Should there be a mixture of provision, via the 'mixed economy' of care?
○ How should welfare services be delivered and who should deliver them? Should it be the state? Should it be families? What about the role of the market in this process?
○ What should welfare states do in relation to inequalities? Can welfare services address inequalities?

In the UK, the Beveridge Report (1942) provided the basis of several key policies in post-war Britain, enacted through several Acts of Parliament, including:

- The Education Act 1944
- The Family Allowances Act 1945
- The National Health Service Act 1946
- The National Insurance Act 1946.

Together, these Acts established a number of welfare benefits and enabled mass edu-cation and health care free at the point of consumption for the UK population. The UK welfare system has evolved massively since then, but its principles and provision have fundamentally remained the same. This tends to occur in most countries that have mechanisms of welfare provision (Hudson et al. 2008), where some level of policy inheritance occurs despite changes in government. This is called 'path dependency' (Pierson 2004) and shows that policy mechanisms can shape political interests as well as being influenced by them (Hudson et al. 2008). Thus, the British welfare state has endured for many years.

Blakemore and Griggs (2007) highlighted a number of problems with the UK welfare system in relation to inequalities. They argue that poverty persisted because benefits for some groups were set too low. However, social welfare and benefits provided by the state are not the only contemporary approaches to welfare. There is also occupational welfare provision, such as benefits associated with jobs, and fiscal welfare such as taxation (Orton 2008), which is discussed later in this chapter. There are also questions about who benefits the most from welfare provision. The UK media often constructs the beneficiaries of the welfare state as those who are not able to find employment, while the idea that those who are better off benefit from welfare systems remains hidden. The issue of the better-off benefiting from welfare systems remains hidden because this is a complex area (Orton 2008).

One area where those who are in better social positions benefit from welfare provision is in the relation to health care. The 'inverse care law' is a well-researched area of the British National Health Service. This service is universal and free to all at the point of consumption (aside from some areas that have minor fees, such as dentistry). However, those on lower incomes use health services less frequently relative to their needs and often have less voice in influencing services once they have been accessed (Dixon et al. 2003). This is one area in which those higher up the social scale benefit from welfare provision.

A further area in which differential gains have been recorded is that of education because those on higher incomes can afford to buy homes in the catchment areas of better performing schools. Furthermore, parents who are better off can afford to pay for private tutors and extra-curricular activities which increase inequalities as educational advantage is linked to uptake of higher education and access to better paid jobs.

Since the Coalition government's Spending Review of October 2010 (BBC News 2010), the British welfare system is currently facing huge cuts in its funding. This has led to many debates about the future of welfare provision of the UK and the basis upon which the current UK Coalition government is making cuts. Cuts in welfare provision are also unlikely to lead to positive outcomes regarding inequalities such as poverty. These cuts to public services are seen by some as more than a response to the UK's financial debt; they are viewed as being part of the government's plans to shrink the welfare state and reduce the role of the public sector in service provision. In this respect, it is an ideological standpoint. Ideology is important in relation to the politics of welfare as the dominant ideological viewpoint of a government will impact on their approaches to welfare provision and, therefore, social inequalities. Welfare provision is different in many contexts, and in some cases this is linked to ideology. For example:

- Cuba has long held a socialist approach to social policy. Equity across society has been emphasised as well as universal access. Full responsibility rests on government to fund and deliver social entitlements. Cuba has a universal and free health, education and welfare system. Cuba has achieved good social outcomes by spending money on the provision of services, although maintaining high levels of spending remains challenging.
- The USA has a more neo-liberal approach to policy and welfare provision, with welfare provided mostly by private providers. Some welfare provision was removed under the Bush administration (George W. Bush), such as the aid to families with dependent children programme. President Obama has also failed to significantly reform welfare provision despite his objectives to do so. He has faced fierce opposition, for example in terms of health reform, but nevertheless succeeded in passing the Affordable Health Care Act in 2010, in an attempt to reduce health inequalities.
- The Nordic model is another model of welfare implemented in countries such as Norway, Sweden, Denmark, Iceland and Finland. This approach to the provision of welfare is underpinned by social democratic principles and provides a comprehensive government-funded welfare system. There are good unemployment benefits and equality of provision is key to the model. Provision is funded by progressive taxation, that is, higher taxation of the greatest earners of the nation. The Nordic countries' provision of welfare has resulted in the lowest income inequalities within the world. People also experience more job security and a range of better social outcomes, such as increased life expectancy (Wilkinson and Pickett 2009).
- In Africa, there are a range of social welfare programmes in existence but these were often developed to benefit white workers during the 1960s. Thus, these schemes often exclude many people and leave those who are the most vulnerable without access to welfare provision. There have been some attempts to reform the provision of welfare across Africa but much work remains to be done on a system that was built on unequal principles. For many, welfare is often provided by local communities and family members in the absence of adequate state support.

Approaches to welfare and inequalities in all of these countries are influenced by ideology and related political values.

How do ideological and political values impact on inequalities?

Values are commonly found in social policy and of course in politics too. Each of us holds our own ideological viewpoints, which influence our attitudes to social inequalities and our beliefs about how best to tackle them (if, indeed, we believe that they should be dealt with at all). Table 8.2 outlines several different ideological perspectives and discusses how they relate to inequalities. These descriptions are simplified but the key point here is that ideology underpins policy as well as beliefs about the provision of welfare and approaches to addressing social inequalities.

Ideological beliefs are just one component of the policy process, influencing the way in which policy is constructed. As this chapter has also shown, there are other influencing factors, all of which have an impact on understandings of social

Table 8.2   Ideological positions and their implications for social inequalities

Ideological school of thought	General key points	What does this mean for inequalities?
Conservatism	• Traditional order of society to be continued. • Sees inequalities as inevitable. • Sees the role of the state as minimal and is concerned with welfare dependency. • Values the private sector in service provision.	• Historical rejection of the UK Black Report (Townsend and Davidson 1982) which detailed health inequalities in the UK. • Often reduces public expenditure, which is not positive for tackling inequalities. • Expands the private sector in service provision on the basis of increased efficiency. • Policies often increase inequalities.
Liberalism	• Is concerned with freedom of choice. • Individuals are seen as important and are expected to behave responsibly. • Neo-liberalism is a global economic approach in which state and public spending are scaled back in favour of privatisation.	• Some liberals use state intervention to reduce the effects of the market which is positive in relation to inequalities. • In comparison, Neo-liberalism advocates reductions in spending on health and increased privatisation. • Neo-liberalism shifts responsibility on to individuals. • Neo-liberal policy approaches are associated with increased inequalities.
Socialism	• This is a broad school of ideology which was originally associated with Marxism. • Contemporary socialism has involved governments attempting to change the state and increasing state intervention in the provision of services.	• Expansion of services, including the provision of welfare. • Concerned with equality in provision (the UK NHS is socialist in its underpinnings).
Nationalism	• This is a belief system rather than an ideology. • It sees nations as self-governing, e.g. Scotland. • It sees shared national identity as being important.	• The effects upon inequalities will depend upon the overall political context in which nationalism is employed. • Some nationalist approaches have been damaging for inequalities because of reductions in public spending.

(Continued)

Table 8.2   (Continued)

Ideological school of thought	General key points	What does this mean for inequalities?
Feminism	• There are a number of different feminisms, with all raising the importance of gender inequalities. • Liberal feminists use the legal sphere to overcome inequalities.	• Feminists have drawn attention to inequalities in a range of areas, such as voting rights, educational opportunities, health care provision and the domestic sphere. They are concerned with achieving gender equality and thus play a positive role in relation to dealing with gender inequalities.
Environmentalism	• Term applies to a broad range of ideas focused upon concerns for the environment. • Advocates sustainability and policies that are not harmful to the environment.	• Encourages sustainable development to reduce inequalities. • Encourages reduction in carbon usage and ecological footprints, which, if enacted, will reduce the impact of environmental damage on the most vulnerable (i.e. the most unequal).

inequalities and the way in which policy is constructed to deal with them – if policy is used as a tool to tackle inequalities. Now complete the following Learning Task and explore your own ideological beliefs.

Learning Task 8.2 – ideological beliefs about inequalities

What is your ideological standpoint in relation to social inequalities? Read through the following statements. Do you agree or disagree with each statement? Then think about what this tells you about your political values, referring back to Table 8.2, which summarises key ideologies.

- People are responsible for their own social position in the world.

- People have the same opportunities, but some use them to achieve greater success than others.

- People who can afford to pay for private services such as health care and education should not have to contribute to the funding of public services.

- All welfare services should be in public control.

- The state should intervene in lots of areas of social life, for example by using legislation to influence moral choices such as the termination of pregnancies and the number of children that women can have.

- Welfare services should be free for all consumers irrespective of whether they have contributed to paying for the care in any way.

- Health care is a fundamental human right for all and should not be based on ability to pay.

Now you have reflected upon these questions, what has this exercise told you about your own ideological beliefs in relation to social inequalities. Think about what this would mean if you were a policy maker. Would you attempt to create policy to deal with inequalities or would your policies maintain the status quo?

Having completed the Learning Task, you will be more familiar with your own ideological viewpoint. This will influence your attitude towards fiscal policy and its uses in relation to inequalities.

Fiscal policy

Policy can be used as a mechanism for changing people's social position by generally tackling the economic circumstances in which they live (Wilkinson and Pickett 2009). Policy is important because it can act as mechanism to redistribute income or it can further extend inequality by widening income gaps between the poorest and the richest sections of society. Fiscal policy, that is, policy concerned with money and general economics, can be used to resolve social inequalities. For example, policy can be designed to support those on lower incomes via progressive taxation rates. Other policies can also be implemented in an attempt to deal with inequalities.

New Labour's policy and UK inequalities

Fiscal policy changes:

○ Introduction of Working Tax Credits (2003), which is the provision of additional financial benefit for those on lower incomes who work (means tested).
○ Introduction of Child Tax Credits (2003), to provide additional income for those on lower incomes with dependent children (means tested).
○ The Child Trust Fund was created as a long-term tax-free savings and investment account for children. The government gave every eligible child a voucher to start their fund (although the payments have been significantly reduced from 2011). (Direct Gov 2010)

(Continued)

(Continued)

New Labour's policy to tackle health inequalities:

○ *Saving Lives: Our Healthier Nation* (Department of Health 1999) – White Paper showing a commitment to narrowing the health gap.
○ *The NHS Plan* (Department of Health 2000) – included targets to reduce inequalities in health by 10% (measured by infant mortality rates and life expectancy at birth).
○ *Tackling Health Inequalities: A Programme for Action* (Department of Health 2003) – delivery mechanisms for inequality reduction outlined at a local level, involving local authorities, primary care trusts and the Sure Start Programme (a dedicated service aimed at working with families).
○ The Programme for Action remained in place until 2010 but there were very few additional statements made and tackling inequalities slipped off the political agenda (Crinson 2009). Furthermore, this approach to dealing with health inequalities was dropped because, despite the targets that were set, no additional funding was provided by the government to help address the identified issues.

Despite these policy approaches, evidence showed that gaps in inequalities actually widened during New Labour's term of office, although the numbers of children living in poverty decreased (Department of Health 2005). Despite these attempts to effect social change via both fiscal policy and specific policy aiming to address health inequalities, evidence suggests that these policy interventions have had little effect. Thomas et al. (2010) show that despite government interventions health inequalities did not reduce, and that in some cases they may have actually widened because inequalities measured by mortality rates are influenced by complex and long-term processes. Consequently, changes in fiscal and social policy are unable to tackle inequalities. Wilkinson and Pickett (2009) similarly argue that social policy has failed to tackle inequalities because most policies aim to break the link between deprivation and associated problems instead of addressing the root of the cause. This demonstrates that policy has limitations in terms of what it can achieve. Furthermore, there are several policy areas that are related to social inequalities, because of their complexity.

Learning Task 8.3 – policy sectors and inequalities

1 List as many UK government departments as you can. If you are finding this difficult, go to the Direct Gov website and use the directory at: www. direct.gov.uk/en/Dl1/Directories/A-ZOfCentralGovernment/index. htm. Then list the policy focus of these different departments and some examples of policies.

2 Think about how these policies may impact on inequalities. For example, think about education policy and the changes to tuition fees in higher education. You may also consider employment policy and welfare provision.

3 Now think more globally. Choose a country of interest and explore social policies that relate to inequalities using the internet to search for information. As a starting point you may wish to visit:

- www.bbc.co.uk/news/world-asia-pacific-11404623 – a BBC news report discussing China's one child policy.

- http://news.bbc.co.uk/1/hi/programmes/hardtalk/9732940.stm – a BBC news report on Denmark's welfare system, which is very comprehensive and is currently not being changed.

- www.guardian.co.uk/news/gallery/2007/jul/17/internationalnews#/?picture=330207745&index=0 – a *Guardian* report (including a slide show) about health care in Cuba and health inequalities.

The UK's Coalition government is developing policy in relation to inequalities. However, it is already encountering criticism for reforming the NHS in line with neo-liberal principles because this is likely to impact negatively on inequalities, especially given the current economic climate.

The impact of the 2008 recession

The latest recession has been explained in a number of ways: it has been blamed upon excessive profit making, financial risk taking and a lack of supervision from those who should have been regulating the financial institutions (Lansley 2011). While Lansley (2011) acknowledges the reckless behaviour of the banking system, he argues that it is the growth of inequality itself which is the main cause of the crisis. However, this view is far from being widely accepted. If this view is accepted, then inequality played a significant part in the financial crash, and the crash is likely to generate further social inequalities. Moreover, it is those who are at the lowest end of the socio-economic scale who will feel the impact the most.

Whitfield and Dearden (2012) argue that those living on persistent low incomes are the casualties of the economic boom because they had not benefitted from economic growth and are the group feeling the impact of the bust more than others. This is because of their position in society and the new financial changes being made within the policy arena. Thus, although the changing economic landscape since 2007 is having an impact globally, in the UK it is particularly affecting those who are reliant upon credit to meet their day-to-day needs (Whitfield and Dearden 2012). Furthermore, the recession has added to job insecurity and instability for many individuals, with the financial consequences of labour market instability clearly documented in the literature. Media reports are frequently focusing on the challenges that are being faced by many households across the world as a result of the financial crisis, but what of social policy in these circumstances: is policy able to tackle inequalities related to the financial crisis? What about policy to deal with those who are experiencing debt, given that much has been made by the media about the role played by debt in the financial crisis in the UK?

Debt advice

Debt advice has been a widely used policy tool for dealing with over-indebtedness in many European countries (European Consumer Debt Network 2007). Some studies have shown that such advice can be helpful in the short term. However, the advice simply serves to manage problems rather than tackle the underlying causes (Stamp 2012).

Stamp's (2012) study in Ireland found that person-focused debt advice alleviates financial difficulties but does not resolve them. He cites three reasons for this. First, the clients using such services and those in debt often have fewer resources than the general population. Second, the causes of their financial problems are related to their socio-economic circumstances and are linked to external circumstances, rather than poor money management skills. Finally, those experiencing debt are not able to access legal mechanisms in order to address their problems. Thus, those who are financially excluded are not having their needs met via current policy approaches. This is because policy in such circumstances is failing to tackle the causes of the problem in the first instance. Those who are experiencing financial difficulties as a form of social inequality are not able to address their situation with the support of current policy approaches. Furthermore, there is a lack of understanding about the reasons why those living on low incomes use credit and are more prone to becoming indebted. Policy makers therefore need to 'recognise that addressing particular issues in isolation is unlikely to improve people's circumstances or prospects for the longer term' (Whitfield and Dearden 2012: 89).

However, debt is not just a problem for those at the bottom of the social ladder. In the years prior to the economic recession, the use of credit within the UK had become common. Those in higher earning brackets were also using credit. For example, rising property prices meant that many people could release equity in their homes, and first-time buyers were permitted to borrow several multiples of their own incomes in order to buy a property (Whitfield and Dearden 2011). Whitfield and Dearden (2011) identify the need for the development of financial literacy for all at an individual level and discuss the need for regulation within the financial sector. Other writers have pointed to the lack of adequate policy related to homeownership within the UK context. Wallace (2012) argues that changing patterns of employment and household composition do not match the current mortgage model, which is based on 25 years of stable employment. Thus, policy responses do not meet the circumstances of many borrowers' lives, and the welfare system does not recognise the need for support for those who own their own homes.

When household finances are under pressure, the question remains as to what the role of social policy is in these circumstances. UK governments (Labour and Conservative) have encouraged people to save, invest in pension provision and buy their own homes, leading to changes in the way that assets are viewed in UK society (Lowe et al. 2012). Despite such policies, assets remain unequally distributed (Appleyard 2012). And despite these inequalities, UK policy continues to focus on individual asset accumulation without tackling financial exclusion.

Policy to encourage people to take up work

Since 1997 there has been a focus in UK policy circles on getting people to take up work, stay in work and to 'make work pay', with a range of policies developed in this area to encourage people into work. This active labour market approach is one that can be found across Europe and a raft of social policy initiatives is evident in this area. In order to address both worklessness and social exclusion, work experience, training and skills development became important in 'enabling' people back into work (for example, Social Exclusion Unit 2002; Department for Work and Pensions 2008).

The UK Coalition government has continued in a similar manner by introducing a single welfare to work programme entitled, the 'Work Programme' (Department for Work and Pensions 2010). This is run by private contractors whose levels of payment will depend on their success rates, measured by getting the workless into jobs and keeping them there for over a year. This is also accompanied by further welfare reform to ensure that work pays (Newman 2011). The *Welfare to Work* (Department for Work and Pensions 2010b) White Paper emphasises the importance of work in arguing that, for those on benefits, the returns from work can be low, therefore the government aims to 'reintroduce the culture of work in households where it may have been absent for generations' (Department for Work and Pensions 2010a: 3). This will be achieved through Universal Credit, which aims to improve financial incentives for those who find more work. The unemployed will be faced with increasing conditions and sanctions to motivate them into finding work. The question remains as to how effective these policies are in getting people into employment and in addressing social inequalities related to unemployment, lack of income and social exclusion. There are a range of criticisms of this approach:

- Activation schemes can be seen as part of an increasing trend to govern citizens by calling upon a range of actors to promote employability among specific target groups (Berkel and Borghi 2008).
- The schemes focus on employability via the development of skills, without recognising the multiple barriers to work faced by the long-term unemployed (McQuaid and Lindsay 2002).

- These schemes fail to understand what employability actually means. Employability is thus used as a buzzword rather than being properly understood in policy discourse (Philpott 1999).
- These schemes also indicate that employment has its own course, largely explained by individual 'failures' such as skills gaps rather than any broader structural or economic factors (Lindsay 2010).
- The schemes do not recognise that employment alone is not always enough to offer a sustainable route out of poverty, especially if broader labour market issues, such as supply and demand, are not dealt with (Afridi 2011).
- Despite emphasising skills as economically valuable, the schemes do not identify the actual skills that individuals will need (Lewis 2011).

In summary, for many commentators, these activation policies tend to be based on a number of assumptions that are incorrect, such as the fact that high out-of-work benefits deter people from looking for work, that sanctions are required to encourage people into work, and that active labour market policies reduce unemployment (Newman 2011). Brown et al. (2001) argue that the main assumption of such approaches is that investment in human capital will create demand. This is debatable because skills do not automatically translate into productivity within the labour market, which is limited by the type of work available. Therefore, 'upskilling the workers does not automatically upskill the work' (Lewis 2011: 551). As a result, employability enhancement schemes are not as positive as policy makers indicate. A UK report (Crawford et al. 2011) has also given attention to the way in which social policy is linked to social mobility.

Increasing social mobility through policy

Crawford et al.'s (2011) report for the UK department of Business, Innovation and Skills reviewed evidence on social mobility. The report focused on key policy areas relevant to social mobility, such as employment law, education and skills development and higher education. The authors offer evidence of social policy effects in all of these areas in relation to social mobility, as follows:

- Employment: the minimum wage has reduced wage inequality in the UK, although the report does not indicate how significant these reductions are. The national minimum wage sets minimum hourly rates that employers must pay their workers.
- Further education: further education is one way in which young people from deprived backgrounds can be upskilled, and fiscal policy, such as the introduction of the Educational Maintenance Allowance (a payment for those on lower incomes to encourage participation in education), did increase participation, though not necessarily attainment. However, Educational Maintenance Allowance is now closed within England.

The report concludes that if policy is to improve social mobility by improving skills levels, then previous policy mistakes must be avoided: the acquisition of skills is not an end goal in itself. Attaining skills does not necessarily result in employment, as already discussed. Indeed, UK media reports have focused on the lack of employment opportunities for those who are highly educated, such as university graduates, who, despite holding such qualifications, find themselves in poorly paid and low-status jobs, if they can find employment at all (Burns 2012). Carlson (2011) highlights similar trends in Canada. Thus, policy to upskill and educate individuals does not necessarily mean that individuals can find work, or indeed earn well.

Another area in which social policy has been used in an attempt to address inequalities in the UK is that of poverty. However, the UK is not the only state to adopt an approach to tackling poverty, as the next section highlights.

Poverty and state approaches: social policy

There has been policy focused on poverty for many years in many countries, including the UK, although its effectiveness is always under scrutiny, given the inequality evident in many societies. Poverty is highly politicised and there are a variety of viewpoints about it (see the discussion of ideology earlier in this chapter). State responses to poverty can involve dealing with health, education, neighbourhoods and housing. Welfare, too, is an area that is linked to levels of inequalities, as discussed earlier in this chapter.

- UK poverty reduction policy – in 1999 Tony Blair promised to end child poverty. His government set a range of targets by which to measure progress. Indeed, evidence suggests that following a raft of policy in this area, in which work was encouraged, made to pay and the tax and benefits system were amended, there was significant progress made in this area (Ridge and Wright 2008). However, this still did not meet the original targets set and progress slowed.
- Poverty reduction policy in Malaysia – policies since 1970 have focused on economic development and growth as the mechanism by which to reduce poverty. Some analyses show large reductions in poverty. The rapid expansion of employment opportunities and a state-level emphasis on evenly distributing the benefits of growth have been credited with significant improvements in poverty levels (Abhayarante 2003).
- Poverty reduction strategies in India – policies have again emphasised growth as a means of reducing poverty, and have met with some success, according to overall figures. However, Bhaduri (2007: 552) argues that, as a consequence of development policy, there are two Indias: 'The India that shines with its fancy apartments and houses in rich neighbourhoods, corporate houses of breathtaking

size, glittering shopping malls. ... And then there is the other India. The India of helpless peasants committing suicide ... tribals dispossessed of their forest land and livelihood, and children too small to walk properly, yet begging on the streets of shining cities.' This image does not provide a positive picture for present-day policy and social inequalities in India remain.

- Global policy – in 2005, millions of people in over 70 countries asked world leaders to put an end to poverty. There were protest marches, fund-raising initiatives such as Live 8, and a focus on social policy change with world leaders from the richest countries discussing the removal of debts from poor countries as well as changing policy to ensure that trade would become fairer. Despite numerous pledges, and some removal of debt (for example, Zambia had its debt cancelled), trade has not significantly changed. Furthermore, the increased aid pledged at the same time has not been realised (see Chapter 7 for a more detailed discussion of global policy approaches to social inequalities).

Complete the final Learning Task of this chapter to explore poverty and social policy in the context of the United States.

Learning Task 8.4 – exploring poverty and social policy in other contexts

Use the internet to view the following lecture: 'Poverty in the United States: Some Policy Observations', which is available at: www.youtube.com/watch?v=lNgQe0tZo_g. Make notes while you watch the clip.

1 How is policy linked to poverty in the American context?
2 Is policy an effective tool for dealing with poverty in America?

America, like the UK, is a very unequal society and in recent analyses of policy within both contexts, there has been discussion of the way in which social policy is being used under a capitalist framework and how this is having a detrimental effect on social inequalities, despite some policies which attempt to tackle inequalities in minor ways. Certainly in the UK context, a plateau has been reached in terms of the impact that social policy is having in relation to employment, work and welfare, and thus social inequalities, because despite policy concerns with social exclusion, society is simply structured around market relations (Orton 2011). This issue of economic growth and development as the pathway to reducing inequalities (see the World Development Report *Reshaping Economic Geography* (World Bank 2009b) is strongly supported by social policies, and has consequently received criticism within the literature (see Chapters 6 and 7).

Policy, capitalism and inequality

Lansley (2011) highlights how the UK has become increasingly unequal over the last 30 years (see Chapter 1 for other figures demonstrating changing patterns of inequality within countries). His explanation for this increased inequality is one that focuses on the growth of the rich and the size of their wealth. This trend is also seen in the United States. Lansley (2011) identifies social policy as a key influencing factor in the rises of inequality within both the UK and the USA, and argues that it is fiscal policy in particular that requires change in order to address contemporary inequalities.

Patterns of increasing polarisation of wealth are demonstrated in the increasing pay rises of those at the top (which are well-documented in the UK media, as bankers' bonuses have come under much scrutiny). It is interesting, too, that after the collapse of communism in many Eastern European nations, within-country inequalities have risen as state industries are sold off and a market economy has been introduced. The introduction of privatisation in countries such as Mexico has also been accompanied by the polarisation of wealth. Economic growth, hailed as the policy solution to poverty and development issues (see Chapter 7), is linked to increasing inequalities across the world. For example, countries in Latin America and Asia are now replicating the UK and the USA with in-country polarisation patterns of wealth and inequality. However, policy makers remain wedded to the notion of economic growth as the way forward and continue to develop policies that support this.

Clearly, the evidence about the existence of inequalities is damning (see Chapter 1). What remains more problematic are understandings of how to tackle it, and the way in which policy can be used as part of the solution. Inequality is seen, by some, as necessary; it is the result of effective market performance rewarding those with talent. Lansley (2011) argues that fiscal policy is constantly creating cycles of boom and bust, with vast gaps in income and uneven sharing of wealth resulting in economic collapses. This, he argues, is likely to continue because, despite the recent global financial crisis, social policy continues to travel in the same direction.

Historically, policy has been used as a tool to manage capitalism in many countries of the world. However, during the 1980s, fundamental shifts occurred in the construction and implementation of policy which are still being felt today, as they have resulted in significant rises in inequality levels (Lansley 2011). The policy changes that have resulted in these significant changes are identified by Lansley (2011) as follows:

- The war on the unions and labour power, successfully won by Thatcher and Regan. Union power has been significantly weakened and, as a result, wages have been affected. There has been a crisis of pay in many countries, including America, the UK and Canada, with uneven wage patterns being the norm.
- Policy has been used to shift economies in some countries to a more aggressive market-based model. The UK and America have travelled this road and seen the largest falls in wage-share and increased gaps in pay-productivity, that is, growing inequalities.

- There has been a shift in macro-economic policies which moved away from maintaining employment to fighting inflation.

  o The result has been significant increases in the numbers of unemployed, which have resisted change. Unemployment, for example in the UK, has affected some areas more than others, with entire communities affected and social conditions dramatically changed. Decaying communities can be seen in many areas, with high levels of unemployment and young people without economic purpose in life.
  o Policy to encourage Britain to move away from the manufacturing basis of the economy to a more service sector and financially based economy have led to the growth of poor quality and insecure work. While some of these increases in vulnerable employment and associated increased inequalities can be explained by globalisation (see Chapter 6), they are also deeply related to policy shifts within countries that have moved to more market-based economies.
  o The increase in service sector work has resulted in a polarised workforce. Service sectors jobs are low paid and require limited skills and training. Comparatively, there are high-paying, more secure jobs that require higher levels of education and training. Polarisation of jobs means polarisation of income and greater inequalities. There has been a rise in downward occupational mobility and social mobility.

Economic and social policy can ensure that living standards increase and that life chances are improved. The development of the British welfare state and subsequent improvements for the British population can be used as an example to support this point. However, policy changes in the UK since the 1980s have resulted in increased inequalities. New Labour, elected in 1997, did not attempt to change the direction of policy overall, despite some small policy changes that they implemented in order to tackle inequality, as identified earlier in this chapter. However, their overall approach to finance and lack of financial regulation resulted in greater inequalities. The UK Coalition government is focused on welfare retrenchment and cutting back public spending, which is likely to increase inequalities further. Despite some discussion from the Coalition government about increased financial regulation, there have been no significant policy changes since they gained power.

Fiscal policy and financial regulation

Earlier chapters have touched on the importance of finance in relation to levels of inequality, identifying Shaxon's (2011) work on tax havens and illicit financial outflows as being detrimental to many countries. Indeed, Shaxon identified the lack of financial regulation in this area as a key problem. Much media attention has been given to the financial sector and taxation rates as a result of the recent economic crisis, and this area of social policy is one clearly linked to inequality levels.

In the UK in the 1980s, the taxation system was shifted from progressive to regressive taxation policies; current tax burdens fall more heavily on lower income groups. Indeed, there are loopholes in the law which allow higher earners to pay proportionally less tax and tax havens have been left untouched (Lansley 2011). Progressive taxation can work to ensure more equal societies are created. A progressive approach to taxation takes a larger share of income from those who earn more. Comparatively, regressive taxation approaches do the opposite in that they take more from those on lower incomes and less from those on higher incomes. Government approaches to taxation directly impact on inequality and wealth (Orton 2008).

Orton (2008) argues that while government policies aim to tackle poverty, wealth in itself is not seen as a significant issue. He argues that taxation is a policy mechanism that can be used to tackle inequality but that in some instances it actually serves to increase it. For example:

- Within the UK, tax avoidance (that is, the use of regulation to minimise the amount of tax that individuals have to pay) is perfectly legal.
- Tax reliefs on pensions benefit the better off as the more you can afford to accumulate, the more the pension provider contributes.

Thus, while there is considerable scope for governments to tackle inequality via fiscal policy, UK government decisions about taxation since the 1980s have encouraged the accumulation of wealth and allowed a small number of people to accumulate riches. The wealthy are also benefitting from the provision of universal public services in what Orton (2008) labels 'the hidden welfare state'. This serves to limit the success of other policies in which the government is explicitly attempting to tackle inequalities. Ultimately, then, social policy is ineffective in many areas because it is failing to tackle the capitalist system itself.

Case Study: Economics for a finite planet?

Jackson (2011) argues that the world is failing in the task to live well and hold society together in the face of complex economic challenges and widespread inequality. He asks: 'What can prosperity possibly look like in a finite world, with limited resources and a population expected to exceed 9 billion people within decades?' (2011: 3). It is an interesting question and one that is much debated in relation to the disparities in wealth and income across the world. Policy makers suggest that we need more economic growth as this is the mechanism by which we can achieve societal improvements, better quality of life and benefits for all. Does such economic growth address the needs of the bottom billion identified in this chapter? Jackson

(2011) suggests that prosperity is not necessarily related to income and wealth, and economic growth will not reduce poverty. His argument is supported by the increased inequalities experienced in recent years across the globe despite large-scale economic growth and good times. Now that most of the world is facing economic difficulties, resolutions to inequality appear limited, with nations focused once again on achieving economic growth. Jackson (2011) argues that the economy is broken and that the world is facing too many environmental challenges to continue with business as usual. He advocates for job protection, the creation of new jobs and a shift in policy to focus on justice and happiness. His argument is centred on the idea that consumerism is a significant problem as it is linked to wealth. Thus, we need an ecologically sound economic model, a different kind of capitalism and fairer societal processes that are more able to address inequalities. Other commentators make similar arguments (see Chapter 9), but often those in power hold the economic wealth and are keen to protect it and their prestige. Thus, many challenges remain.

Summary of key points

- Social policy as a discipline is crucial in helping us to understand how the social and economic environment in which we live influences inequalities through the mechanisms of health and welfare systems.
- Social policy is related to levels of inequalities in a variety of ways and is underpinned by complex ideological values and beliefs.
- Fiscal policy is an area of social policy that has been identified as being significantly related to contemporary levels of social inequalities and to the growth on in-country inequalities.

List of questions to stimulate debate and reflection

1 Do you agree with the statement that social inequalities are political? Think about the involvement of politicians in shaping welfare provision and examine media reports discussing inequalities to help you to form a conclusion.

2 Think about your own ideological values, which you began to explore in this chapter. What would these mean if you were a policy maker tasked with dealing with social inequalities? Reflect on the likely consequences of your ideological approach for specific societal groups such as those who are more vulnerable.

3 Have you ever given consideration to fiscal policy and issues such as taxation? Do you agree with progressive taxation and would you be happy to be progressively taxed if you acquire a good job with a high salary after working hard to gain qualifications and achieving a good education?

Further reading

Ben-Ami, Daniel (2010) *Ferraris for All: In Defence of Economic Progress*. Bristol: Policy Press.

The growth of the economy and the spread of prosperity are increasingly seen as problematic rather than positive. This book argues that society as a whole benefits from greater affluence. This book therefore calls for social policy to develop more prosperity, suggesting that action is needed to encourage more growth. The book is well written and provocative.

Lansley, Stuart (2011) *The Cost of Inequality: Three Decades of the Super-rich and the Economy*. London: Gibson Square.

This book focuses on economics in relation to inequality, and the way in which social policy currently operates to perpetuate economic inequality within countries such as Britain and the USA. It provides a history of social policy changes that explain the recent financial crisis and critically questions the current model of fiscal policy.

Rowlingson, Karen and Mckay, Stephen D. (2011) *Wealth and the Wealthy: Exploring and Tackling Inequalities between Rich and Poor*. Bristol: Policy Press.

In recent years wealth and the wealthy have begun to receive more attention in the academic literature, with this book adding to the field. The book provides a clear overview of all of the areas related to wealth, addressing a range of questions such as: What is wealth? Who has got it? Where might we draw a 'wealth line'? Who lies above it? The key area of the book that is relevant to this chapter is the section that asks what might policy do about wealth and the wealthy? The book is critical in the analysis of policy in this area, examining 'asset-based' welfare and taxation.

9

SOLUTIONS TO INEQUALITY: HOW DO WE CREATE A MORE EQUAL GLOBAL SOCIETY?

Key learning outcomes

By the end of this chapter you should be able to:

- Understand the challenges that remain in relation to contemporary inequalities
- Understand the many different solutions that are offered as a means to change current patterns of inequalities and contemporary challenges related to these
- Understand the different ideological positions associated with the array of solutions presented within the current literature

Overview of the chapter

This chapter brings together all of the previous discussions about social inequality to consider the question of how a more equal global society can be created. So is globalisation part of the solution? Can we effect better social policy both nationally and globally to change inequalities? This chapter critically debates whether equality is actually possible within a capitalist framework, as well as the implications of a more equal global society economically. Is this attainable? Indeed, the crucial question of whether more equality is even desired by the key global powers is examined, given that the likely impact of a more equal world may disadvantage some currently powerful nation states. The chapter explores a range of potential solutions for inequality, the ideological positions underpinning the proposed solutions and ends with an exploration of what the future holds in relation to likely patterns of social inequality.

What is the challenge?

In 1942 Beveridge wrote a report on the future of the welfare state in the UK. His report identified that there were five 'giants' threatening the UK population (see Chapter 8):

- Want – people did not have sufficient income
- Idleness – unemployment, because there were not enough jobs
- Squalor   poverty and poor housing conditions
- Ignorance – gaps in educational provision
- Disease   poor health made worse by a lack of affordable and accessible medical care.

These five giants underpin the modern welfare system, which is based on five pillars of social security (related to want), employment, housing, education and health (Hudson et al. 2008). They are also clear indicators of historical social inequalities. They beg the question of what are the giants that we are currently facing? It can be argued that whilst social policy historically aimed to tackle these five giants, that some of these still remain an issue despite action in this area. For example, poverty remains a persistent issue, although there have been improvements in educational provision and the availability of medical care. Many nations are still facing these giants and, furthermore, contemporary challenges have moved beyond the level of the nation state. Sachs (2005: 24) argues that 'our generation's challenge is to help the poorest of the poor to escape the misery of extreme poverty'. As you read this, you may agree with this challenge, but the statement does not suggest that the ultimate goal is equality for all, and the mechanism by which this can be achieved, for Sachs (2005), is that of economic development, which has been problematised earlier in this book (see Chapter 7). Sentamu (2011) offers a more radical vision of the giants that need attention, highlighting income inequality and rising unemployment, especially that experienced by young people, because these problems are harmful for both individuals and society. Throughout this book, the range of inequalities that are evident across the contemporary globe have been outlined and discussed in depth. Thus there are:

- Income inequalities such as poverty
- Inequalities related to social divisions such as age, gender, social class, social status, ethnicity and area-based differences
- Inequalities related to globalisation and migration
- A number of global challenges such as the food supply, climate change and the sustainability of the planet
- Health inequalities
- Inequalities related to the provision of services and social policies
- Security and the need for peace.

This list is only a brief overview and there are many other challenges linked to social inequalities, as this book has already discussed. Complete the first Learning Task of this chapter, which will help you to see that these challenges are interrelated and also that attention needs to be paid to the larger picture.

Learning Task 9.1 – exploring the great disruption

Use the internet to access YouTube at: www.youtube.com/watch?v=tsXID 1kSuf4 and listen to the talk: 'The Great Disruption: How Humankind Can Thrive in the 21st Century'.

1 Take some notes while listening. Is this perspective realistic? Do you agree with the nature of the problems identified in this short talk?
2 Given that this was filmed in 2008, can you see any significant changes in policies and economic approaches now that several years have passed?

Clearly, the list of challenges facing the world is long and complex, as Learning Task 1 illustrates. Furthermore, the range of explanations that are used to understand the vast scope of social inequalities is itself complex and contradictory. There are numerous ideological views that underpin understandings of the ways in which inequalities arise and continue. Therefore, it should be of no surprise now to learn that the debates about how to tackle these issues are again complex. This chapter will now explore some of the many perceived solutions.

Is technology the answer?

Rather than focusing on politics, Berry (2010) suggests that a shift is needed in relation to technological change and transfer in order to tackle inequality and poverty. For example:

- Research and development can be used to raise the productivity of farmers in lower income countries, with this being particularly needed in Sub-Saharan Africa.
- Patent practices in their current form also need to be changed so as to allow better environmentally-related technology to be moved around the world more quickly.

He also argues that addressing several problematic areas will not cost industrial countries and therefore that the fostering of war needs to be stopped. Sachs (2005: 50) also makes a case for the practical solutions that can be given to lower income countries, saying: 'Even the geographical obstacles can be overcome with new technologies, such as those that control malaria or allow for large crop yields in marginal production areas.' Sachs (2005) recognises the complexity of finding solutions for the inequalities experienced by all in suggesting that there is no single remedy. He, like Berry (2010), draws attention to the need to change policies seen in recent wars on terror as they fail to account for the deeper causes of global instability. Technological development, however, also feeds into weaponry, defence systems and war efforts, which create large profits and support a significant industry.

While technology may offer some solutions in relation to inequalities, it remains the case that it is driven by powerful commercial interests and the need to grow companies and profits, which is ultimately incompatible with what is required to achieve a more equitable world. Jackson (2011) argues that we are too keen to believe in technological miracles and, as such, hold false beliefs that technology can provide the answers, because a perceived strength of capitalism is its ability to support technological development. However, the reality is that consumerism depends upon innovation and novelty, which are not necessarily the same as protecting long-term social goals or the environment. However, perhaps lower income countries can be protected through laws and social policy approaches?

Is social policy the answer?

Chapter 8 reviewed social policy as a mechanism for tackling inequalities, demonstrating its numerous effects across inequalities, but not all of these were successful. Thus, for some theorists, social policy can be a large part of the answer, although current approaches will need to be significantly changed for policy to work as an effective tool. Lansley (2011: 288) argues that 'What is required is a set of interlocking measures that tackle the root causes of instability – the unequal distribution of the gains from economic progress and the higher concentrations of income, wealth and power'. Complete the following Learning Task to explore the problems of current neo-liberal policy, which are evident across the globe as the dominant social policy approach.

Learning Task 9.2 – poverty and neo-liberalism

Use the internet to access YouTube and listen to Susan George discussing the problems with neo-liberal economic approaches: www.youtube.com/watch?v=_viNHVzadeM

1 George holds the view that there are unequal gains from economic progress between the Global North and Global South. Are you aware of these issues?
2 Revisit Chapters 6 and 7 to remind yourself of the global context of these issues. Reflect particularly on the concept of globalisation.
3 What are your own views regarding privatisation and neo-liberalism? Where do you position yourself ideologically?

Globalisation, for many commentators, is underpinned by such neo-liberal ideology and thus is open to much criticism and debate regarding its effects on inequalities. Chapter 6 explores this in depth and shows that there is no consensus about whether globalisation is part of the problem or indeed a significant part of the solution.

Given that these issues are well discussed and evidenced, many authors have identified the need for change in this area. Lansley (2011) is one such writer. Therefore, from his perspective there needs to be:

1 A new approach to work: inequality can be tackled through work if work is guaranteed, decent wages are provided and there are limits to the financial rewards given to those at the top (see Chapter 8 for more about policy in this area).
2 Inequality needs to be dealt with on a global scale, so there needs to be a financial strategy to ensure that countries are less vulnerable to instability and that a fairer capitalist system is used (see Chapter 7 for debates about global social policy). A new economic and business model is required, as described here:

   a Current shareholder value requires reform so that a different value system can be used in which tighter control is exercised, and the wider implications of financial and corporate behaviour are recognised.
   b Labour power (that is, the workers) need to be given more voice and allowed to work in a more flexible way, such as in the Scandinavian model where there is more workforce protection, collective labour power but also stringent welfare benefit provision.
   c There needs to be tougher policies on taxation as many systems take more from the poor than the rich. Progressive rather than regressive taxation is

essential. Tax avoidance should also be tackled more aggressively, with a global 'tough stance' needed to tackle tax havens.

d Reform of the current banking system is also required, for example, separating the retail and investment aspects of banking to create more transparency, limiting bonuses via regulation and increasing taxation of the banks. Lansley (2011) suggests the creation of a global transactions tax to be applied to all financial deals.

3 There also needs to be some work at the national level. For example, individual countries can create policies to support fairer wage shares and to reform their own financial governance systems.

Lansley's (2011) focus is very much on the financial component of current social policy and, given the current economic trends, it is clear that attention is needed within this area. Similarly, Stiglitz (2012) suggests the need for reform of the financial sector in his analysis of the USA, as illustrated in Table 9.1.

Table 9.1   Reform of the financial sector to reduce inequalities: USA

Area of reform	Discussion of what is needed
Curbing the financial sector	Inequalities have risen because of the excesses of the financial sector. Thus, action is needed in a number of areas, such as reducing risk taking, making banks more transparent, changing lending practices and closing off-shore banking provision.
Stronger competition laws	There are many sectors in which competition is too weak because large and dominant companies work to effectively reduce competition (markets are not as efficient as politicians suggest). Thus, laws in this area need to be changed.
Improving corporate governance	There is too much power held by those in senior corporate positions and consequently they work to benefit themselves. Laws therefore need to be implemented in order to allow shareholders to have more influence.
Reform of bankruptcy laws	Currently the rules favour those who are at the top of the scale. Again, laws need reform in this area to ensure that there are fairer lending practices. Currently, bankruptcy law has led to a bloated financial sector which has resulted in greater exploitation of those who are poor, ultimately leading to greater inequality.
End government giveaways/ reform tax	Governments currently give away a range of benefits to companies via the existing tax system. This often serves to increase inequalities and therefore changes are needed in this area.
Legal reform	The current legal system does not provide justice for all; those who are the richest are advantaged by current legislation. More accountability is needed.

Source: Adapted from Stiglitz (2012)

Stiglitz (2012) argues that changes in all of these areas will not only improve the economy, but they will also increase equality. His focus is particularly on the USA, although many of these ideas are equally applicable in other countries, including those across Europe. He also suggests the need for broader changes such as:

1 Improving access to education
2 Helping ordinary citizens to save
3 Health care for all
4 Tempering globalisation
5 Restoring employment
6 Increasing the power of the workforce.

He concludes that time is running out and argues that the need for reform is more urgent than ever because trends in social inequalities are worsening. However, while the financial governance of policy is the main focus of Stiglitz's (2012) analysis, social policy is a broad field and there are other areas that require examination too in order to effectively deal with inequalities.

George (2010) focuses on a broader range of social policy areas and offers the following suggestions that will lead to the creation of a fairer society:

- The Green New Deal: individual solutions to dealing with climate change, such as changing lifestyles and light bulbs, will not meet the challenge ahead. Activists and climate change experts need to work with governments to formulate projects and schemes which bring sectors together. What is needed is the support for the development of an eco-friendly industry, alternative energy provision and green developments in all areas. China is investing massively in both wind and solar power and other countries can use the same approach. This will not be easy, but it is essential that coalitions are built that can deliver policy solutions to the environmental challenges that we are facing.
- Put the banks under citizen control: the banks need to be nationalised so that they are governed by people and used to serve society. Credit should still be available, but it should be used for the public good – thus the banks could lend to people and businesses with a green focus. Supporting the green economy in this way would also lead to the creation of jobs. Banks should also lend to social enterprises – companies that are run in a fair way in which workers are allowed to participate and the distribution of profits is also more equitable. Social enterprises can be formed in close geographical proximity and then use each other's wastes and inputs to save energy and further contribute to the green agenda.
- Tell politicians how we feel: we must communicate how we feel to those in political circles. The unfairness and inequality that results from their decisions has to be known. The media can also be used as a tool to support this process.
- No corporate bailouts: companies can be saved but this needs to be done with restrictions so that companies have to operate within a greener framework.

Companies can be encouraged to produce socially useful products by tapping into the creativity of workers in this area.

- Debt of the South: many countries that are in debt can have their social hardships reduced through the cancellation of their debt. Debt could be cancelled when lower income countries comply with certain conditions (but not the conditions that are currently stipulated in relation to reducing public services). The new conditions should again be tied to the environment, encouraging countries to undertake reforestation and conservation projects. These measures would not exclude investment in other services, such as health care, but they are important. Lower income countries would be an ideal starting point in which to reduce emissions at the same time as both poverty and inequality.

- Reform the tax system: similar to the earlier arguments presented in this chapter, George (2010) calls for tax system reform, globally and nationally. The tax system simply needs to be made fairer. This is often referred to as the Tobin Tax and is a more progressive taxation approach. This process can be started through the establishment of a coalition of willing countries, and can then be extended and used to push for changes at the international level. The tax system needs to account for emissions, and therefore a carbon tax is necessary. Tax havens also require international attention to ensure that revenue is not lost from countries. Tax havens contribute to inequality and poverty across the world and therefore need to be made illegal or controlled. Shaxon (2011) similarly identifies the need for changes in relation to tax havens and the financial sector. He also argues that the most important change that is required is one in which cultural shifts are achieved.

George (2010) offers a much more detailed analysis in her discussion, but these are the core suggestions for change that she proposes. She argues that material growth cannot continue forever, but that other kinds of growth can, such as friendship, love and learning. To achieve this, we need to trust each other and to distance ourselves from the 'grab what I can' mentality that is often dominant within our consumer societies. As individuals, we also need to recognise that the environmental threats we are facing are not distant. She ends by saying that the world is crying out for a grand narrative in which we can create a fairer and greener world. This will ultimately lead to a promising, although not perfect, future.

For some commentators the issues associated with war creation, as a result of vested interests, can be tackled by social policy and legislation. For example, banning arms sales and developing a Charter for Natural Resource Revenues is suggested by Collier (2008) as a useful starting point. Effecting these measures would halt one-sided negotiations which currently monopolise lower income countries and result in natural resource exploitation. Legislation could also be used to deal with inequalities created as a result of commercial interests. Transnational corporations that engage in socially destructive practices should be penalised, for example those that sell cigarettes, unhealthy food and dispose of radioactive materials. Thus, health could also be improved via policy tools. Given the range of health inequalities illustrated in earlier chapters, and their link to broader structural inequality, the need for action in this area has been clear for many years.

Labonte (2010: 240) also suggests the need to tackle health inequalities through a number of achievable healthy public policies for the future. Healthy public policies are not limited to health care; rather, they recognise the importance of all policy areas in relation to health. Thus, policies that can improve health include:

- Changes to current global taxation rules so that wealth is redistributed, because more equal societies have far better health outcomes across the globe (Wilkinson and Pickett 2009).
- Radical reform of current global policy-making organisations such as the World Bank and the World Trade Organisation. This reform would serve to increase public spending on education, health care, water/sanitation and other interventions which not only promote equality which is good for health, but would also improve health through such service provision.
- Finally, he suggests the cancellation of poor countries' debts and the implementation of fairer trade to allow the economies of poor countries to develop.

The key underpinning argument suggested by Labonte (2010) is that a new global governance system is required which is more ethical and rights-based. This echoes the work of others writing about health, such as Marmot (2010), who over many years has concluded that there is simply the need for fairness within health policy, and if this was present, then health would improve (Simons 2012). The need for fairness is also identified by others in relation to policy-making processes. Berry (2010) suggests that the current global decision-making process needs attention to allow for the interests of lower income countries.

Reform of global governance

Momani (2010) focuses on the International Monetary Fund and the need for reform of its organisational practices. She highlights that while the organisation has paid attention to its critics in recent years, it has simply increased its rhetoric about reducing poverty and involving countries in its policies. She argues that the IMF needs

> substantive changes to the way things are done, and this requires bottom–up reform of the organization's staffing resources. Without any serious challenge to the IMF's organizational dynamics ... things will remain 'business as usual' and the rhetoric reality gap will continue to widen.

Weaver (2010) focuses on the World Bank as an institution in need of reform. She argues that this opens up the more central question of how all global governance institutions and systems might be redesigned to be more effective at tackling poverty and inequality. She identifies the need for lower income countries to be represented and heard within the context of World Bank policy making. She too focuses on staff within the organisation, suggesting that changing the staff can act as a mechanism to alter the way in which the Bank thinks about development, as well as serving to increase its transparency. However, despite her calls for change, there is recognition that previous reorganisations have failed, and that demolishing the Bank in the current context of crises is not an option. She ends her analysis by arguing that we need a realistic vision of the Bank, otherwise it will never live up to its ideals. Ultimately, this does not seem to be a positive analysis for the future of social inequalities.

Sachs (2005), too, recognises the need for change within global governance systems, suggesting that the poor need to govern themselves and be empowered to do so through the development of new strategies. Given the complexities highlighted in Chapter 7 regarding global governance, this seems an unlikely approach to be adopted. Reform is also problematic. However, despite the failures associated with reforming the current institutions of global governance, there are other changes happening that may have an impact on the current operations of global governance.

Both China and India are gaining global economic power, and their involvement in policy making and related institutions is likely to reshape both global policy and society. The dominance of the West is under threat (Sachs 2005). However, this does not mean that inequalities will be dealt with in a different way: China and India are focused on economic growth and do not offer alternative policy approaches in relation to tackling inequalities. Would alternative views of poverty help here?

An alternative view of poverty

Bush (2007) argues that there is a need to address a range of issues because of the way in which current debates about poverty and income distribution are being framed within a neo-liberal economic framework. Issues which need consideration are as follows:

1   There is a preoccupation in the literature with education and skills improvement as mechanisms to reduce poverty. This can be seen in the African Commission, and in many national policy contexts (see Chapter 8 for a discussion of the UK approach). For Bush (2007), education and skills development need to be linked to a purpose and extended to include gendered elements, as women are often overlooked in current analyses.

2 The literature on tackling inequalities focuses on changing the organisation of markets which currently exclude some countries from their institutions and relations. Thus, countries such as several African states should be included into the world economy with the view that economic inclusion will tackle poverty. Economic inclusion and growth do not simply result in less inequality because markets are mechanisms for exerting both authority and power.

3 Current ideological approaches need to be changed. Inequalities are not currently viewed in a holistic way and their creation is not understood. Put simply, the creation of wealth produces poverty.

4 Current research into inequalities is also fundamentally flawed. Again, the dominance of neo-liberalism is the issue here, with economists using quantitative techniques to investigate inequalities which are ultimately very complicated, both socially and politically.

5 There is also the need to change the focus on to politics. The political conditions that are needed to improve income distribution and reduce inequalities are often ignored.

Strategies to tackle poverty

It has been suggested that social capital is related to poverty and one way in which poverty can be tackled is through ensuring that the poor have access to the types of capital that enable development. Sachs (2005) suggests that those experiencing poverty lack six types of capital:

1 Human capital – nutrition, health and skills to allow people to be economically productive.

2 Business capital – machinery, facilities, services and industry.

3 Infrastructure – water, sanitation and roads that feed into business activity.

4 Natural capital – land, soil and adequate eco-systems to service humans.

5 Public institutional capital – the law, adequate justice systems and services that underpin peace.

6 Knowledge capital – this is the scientific and technological capability that increases productivity.

He suggests targeted interventions by donors to address these capital deficits. He outlines nine steps to achieve the goal of ending absolute poverty. These are outlined in Table 9.2 alongside some challenges to his suggestions.

Sachs' suggestions have been heavily criticised as part of a wider critique of current approaches to dealing with poverty and inequalities. This questioning is also true regarding both development and economic growth, which have been seen as useful tools within policy circles (see Chapter 8). Complete the following Learning Task to explore this further.

Learning Task 9.3 – making poverty history

Use the internet to view the Make Poverty History website, which is available at: www.makepovertyhistory.org/takeaction/. On the left-hand side of the page, go to 'films to watch' and click on it. Watch the short film where Bono is talking about campaigns to tackle poverty and answer the following questions:

1 How much money does Bono say that donors have given to recent campaigns?
2 This was filmed in 2005. Significant amounts of time have passed and there have been more campaigns and fundraising activities since then, but what has happened in relation to poverty? Is poverty history?
3 Given the issues with tackling poverty, and the persistence of it as a problem, what are your thoughts about campaigns, fundraising and current approaches?

Table 9.2   Steps to achieve an end to poverty?

Sach's (2005) steps to end absolute poverty	Some issues for consideration
1 Commit to ending poverty	There have been many commitments to this already in a range of political settings but this has not produced significant changes in this area.
2 Adopt a plan of action	There have also been many plans of action, but these too have failed in a variety of contexts.
3 Raise the voice of the poor	This is often suggested in policy circles (see Chapter 7), but as yet the mechanisms by which to achieve this are not working effectively.
4 Redeem the role of the USA in the world	For many critics, this would result in greater inequalities and therefore the role of the USA needs careful consideration. Ultimately, this may not be possible in the wake of the development of other economic powerhouses, e.g. China.
5 Rescue the IMF and World Bank	These institutions are problematic (see Chapter 7, and calls for reform are also included in this chapter). However, their remit has to be recognised as having some limitations even if they can be successfully reformed.
6 Strengthen the UN	Again, the UN has received criticism from a variety of commentators. What can it realistically achieve even if it is stronger?
7 Harness global science	Technology can be used to address poverty and other global problems, such as climate change. However, for this to be successful it has to be taking place within a broader context of change (see George 2010).
8 Promote sustainable development	Development has been problematised throughout this book; it has limits and, for many, to be successful it needs to occur within a broader context of change.
9 Make a personal commitment	While individual action can in part help to address poverty and inequalities, there also needs to be action at the political and structural level in order to achieve greater equality.

As earlier chapters illustrated, there have been attempts to tackle the problem of poverty and some attempts to deal with a number of social inequalities, but these challenges remain. A further potential solution that is often suggested is the need for development, particularly in low-income countries and deprived areas.

What about more development and growth?

So far this chapter has concentrated on the need for change in several areas, particularly calling into question current approaches. Ben-Ami (2010) argues that there are good reasons to critically examine the mainstream views around economic growth and inequality. However, he argues that many statistics are flawed, and that includes those used to support evidence against economic growth. He argues that growth is actually the answer to poverty, and highlights flaws in the World Banks statistics. He uses China as an example of a country where economic growth has been accompanied by reductions in poverty. Therefore, in questioning the current evidence base and the tools of measurement being used (which are complex, as earlier chapters have illustrated), he concludes that it is possible for the poor to benefit from growth, even if inequality is widening. Ultimately, then, Ben-Ami (2010: 215) argues that: 'It is clear to most experts that it [economic growth] plays a central role in reducing poverty, even if the rate of the trend and the impact on inequality is less clear.' For Ben-Ami, attacking growth is commonplace and this is problematic not only because, in his view, growth is positive, but also because it affects the way in which development is being delivered. Development is no longer about industrialisation and modernisation; rather it is about those in the poorest countries achieving the most basic of entitlements. This actually represents a lowering of horizons for these countries and the people who live in them. Consequently, development needs to be broader in its aims and conceptualisation, hence the title of his book – *Ferraris for All*.

Equality is a positive goal when it is aiming to increase the living standards of the entire population, but this needs to be done in a way that does not extensively interfere with lower income countries and the personal lives of individuals across the world. How this can be achieved is, however, left unsaid, although, for Ben-Ami (2010), economic growth is a good starting point in creating greater equality. Other commentators offer alternative suggestions.

Creating greater equality

Dorling (2012) argues that we can achieve greater equality by depriving the rich of their advantages. In order to achieve this he suggests that there needs to be a deeper understanding of the benefits that greater equality will bring, such as more social cohesion, more trust within societies and generally nicer communities with lower crime rates. More importantly perhaps, he outlines how equality is better for the functioning of markets.

Markets fail when there is greater inequality and the more inequality there is, the less efficient markets become in terms of how they operate. Dorling (2012: 147) provides examples to show how markets are usually less efficient in unequal societies, suggesting that: 'In Britain more people own cars than they can drive at any one time as compared to the number of adults with young children who lack a car but would usually find life much easier with one.' Furthermore, the push to accumulate, already described as an illness by James (2007), actually leads many individuals into having more possessions but far less leisure time to use them. Markets that create inequality, the evidence suggests, are not good for our well-being, but greater equality is. However, winning the argument for greater equality is not quite so simple. For example, in suggesting that basic income levels are guaranteed across all populations, the rich would be more than angry! James (2007) argues that although greater equality can be created through such measures, this vision is not everyone's dream; in fact, for many it is simply a nightmare. This ultimately relates to the ideological views held by people who are advantaged by current markets.

Similarly, Rowlingson and McKay (2012) want more attention to be paid to the wealthiest members of society. They call for a major review of those who are wealthy, arguing that there has not been enough thinking about what this wealth means and how it impacts on others. They suggest that social policy changes are also needed, and therefore argue that states need to become involved in order to reduce the current gaps between the rich and the poor. Ultimately, this will mean interfering in the market, although markets are not perfect, as some seem to suggest. They recognise that a variety of capitalisms can exist and that there are policy options that can support change for greater equality in the form of closing the gap between the rich and the poor. To achieve this change, however, will require a shift within current neo-liberal ideology and related understandings of the ways in which market mechanisms operate.

Ideological change?

Sentamu (2011) suggests that we need a culture shift in order to tackle the inequalities that exist within the world today. He writes about the very comfortable position in which many of us living in high-income countries find ourselves, for example, having access to bathrooms with running water, experiencing central heating and having more than enough to eat, which sound very positive. However, this vision of paradise is not quite what it seems, and many societies face complex issues such as crime rates, violence, rising rates of mental illness and personal debt. These social failings are of course linked to social inequalities (Wilkinson and Pickett 2009). The recent economic crisis and the consequences for inequality have also led many to argue the need for a different ideological vision. Nevertheless, the current policy framework means that the costs of economic difficulties are being shouldered by those who are at the bottom of the ladder and thus are socially vulnerable (Sentamu 2011).

Dorling (2012) argues along the same lines, saying that the many people who suggest that we have to tolerate current inequalities because this will lead to a better future for everyone, are in fact those who are richer and more advantaged. Thus, those who perpetrate injustice do so using ideological tools to effectively hide social inequalities. These tools are illustrated in Table 9.3.

Table 9.3   The tools used to perpetrate injustice within contemporary societies

Tool/tactic	Explanation
Covering up of injustice	Poverty is for those who are losers; those who have failed exams and not achieved at school. Ultimately, those who do not do well against contemporary measures of success are hidden away from the rich in poorer areas.
Devaluation	Disadvantaged groups are stigmatised and prejudice is thus increased in relation to certain groups (see earlier chapters for numerous examples).
Reinterpretation	Injustice is either explained away or it is justified through a range of arguments; it is constructed as inevitable, e.g. as the result of processes such as globalisation.
Inequality is officially approved	Societal systems, such as welfare provision, are constructed as fair, although these systems are often biased and this bias remains hidden.
Intimidation is used	Those who challenge inequality are at risk; you are attacked in some way that shows that you are unrealistic or too political.

Source: Adapted from Dorling (2012)

For Dorling (2012), this ideology can be changed because he argues that it is just a few who wish to perpetuate inequalities, and many are therefore likely to want to be part of the solution. Complete the following Learning Task to hear more about the persistence of social inequality.

Learning Task 9.4 – examining why social inequality persists

Use the internet to access YouTube and listen to Danny Dorling explaining why social inequality persists at: www.youtube.com/watch?v=MBzYYeAolAA

1 What ideologies does Dorling identify in his explanation of social inequalities?
2 Are his arguments convincing and do you agree with his points?

Now that you have completed the Learning Task, it is worth noting that Dorling is certainly not alone in his views about the persistence of inequalities due to flawed economics. Jackson (2011) argues along similar lines, saying that we need to work for change and use economics in the context of a finite planet (see Chapter 8). Thus, we need to express change in the way that we live, in what we purchase, in our modes of travel, in the way we invest money, and in what we do in our spare time. There are several ways in which we can achieve such change, as the need for change to current economic approaches is clear; they are based on distorted social logic (current approaches rely upon understandings that are flawed because neo-liberal economic approaches are not working in the way they should, yet policy-makers continue to rely upon them) . What is required is therefore a fairer social logic in which ecological limits (the capacity of the environment to support human life) are also recognised.

George (2010) highlights how fear is the discipline of capitalist society and, as such, is used as a mechanism to perpetuate the status quo. She highlights how people are afraid. They are:

> afraid things will get worse, afraid, if they have a job, that they will lose it and, if they have none, that they will never find one, afraid that their children will be worse off than they are. In some countries they fear losing their health care, retirement or unemployment benefits. Many ... are living day to day, month to month, afraid they may become homeless at any time. (George 2010: 194)

She also highlights that people are angry because of the inequalities that are evident across society – at the bankers and their bonuses despite the economic crisis. Currently, it is the ordinary people of the world who are paying for the crisis, which is a clear injustice and another dimension of the contemporary dynamics of social inequalities. This fear is used to sustain our inertia and to maintain powerlessness while the dominant ideology prevails.

All of these analyses of the ideological aspects of the perpetuation of current inequalities, and the earlier discussions in this chapter, assume that the economic model of recent years has failed. It has failed in its own terms, but it has also failed people and the planet (NEF 2010). Change is possible but, again, ideology has to shift to recognise both social and environmental value in the policy-making process, the importance of redistribution and markets that can account for social and environmental costs and benefits. Thus, the need for a 'Great Transition' is identified. We may individually have to give up some things, but these are not the things that are important (NEF 2010). What does this mean for the future of social inequalities? Will there be a more equal world?

The future of social inequality

Despite the array of solutions that have been suggested in this chapter, some commentators argue that solutions are simply not on the horizon. Lansley (2011: 275) says:

'Despite the evidence of the economic limit to inequality, little or no domestic or global action is being taken to cap and reverse the rises in the concentration of income and wealth in the last two decades.' It is hard to disagree with Lansley's analysis when he highlights that, despite the recent large-scale economic crisis and the need to rescue the global banking system, the economic approach used for the last three decades remains in place. Although there has been the heavy media coverage and political debate about the role of the banks in many high-income countries, there has been no challenge to the dominant ideology which supports the role of the market. Thus, there are no policy drives to effect change in this area, there has been no radical shake-up of the ways in which banks operate, and the banks are generally perceived as still being too large to fail.

Given the lack of changes, the massive financial rewards still being handed out to those at the top of the financial system and the continued lack of transparency in many areas, Lansley (2011) concludes that the seeds of the next financial crisis have already been sown. This is, of course, an indicator of future social inequality; financial crises and recessions lead to greater inequalities, especially as the current gaps between the rich and the poor are not being tackled. Shaxon (2011: 289) identifies the need for financial reform but concludes that without it '[a] tiny few will have their boots washed in champagne while the rest of us struggle for our lives in conditions of steeping inequality'.

Furthermore, Ben-Ami (2010) argues that the prospects for achieving universal prosperity are limited because of the environmental concerns and challenges experienced by many. Jackson (2011: 187) argues this point too:

> In a world of 9 billion people all aspiring to western lifestyles, the carbon intensity of every dollar of output must be at least 130 times lower in 2050 than it is today. By the end of the century economic activity will need to be taking carbon out of the atmosphere not adding to it.

Indeed, progress and growth are also represented as being detrimental for individuals (James 2007). Thus, many current approaches present the need for restraint. However, this 'need for restraint' simply serves to perpetuate existing power divisions in the world and again perpetuate inequalities.

Clearly, the social problems that the world is facing are clear; they are numerous and complex. Life is not fair for many people, as this book has constantly demonstrated. The social structures that we are born into have a great influence on our lives, block opportunities and lead to discrimination (Crone 2011). Changes to the social structure are needed to solve our current social problems. This chapter has presented an array of proposed changes. Ultimately, whether you believe social inequalities can be tackled depends upon your perspective. Lansley (2011) is pessimistic about future inequality, as is Ben-Ami (2010), whereas Dorling (2012) offers a more positive conclusion, saying that many people wish to change the world. George (2010) argues that it will take years to get action and that for this reason we must start now. New Economics Foundation (NEF 2010) argue that it can still turn out right, suggesting that we can live within the natural limits of the world but that in order for this to happen we need to revalue the environment and the social components of our world. Thus, we have to change what we have already been taking for granted for many years. Crone (2011: 242) is also positive in his analysis when he says:

> Most of us want to solve our social problems and live in a society (and world) that is humane and just. Knowing that we have already made progress in ameliorating a number of our social problems ... I cannot help but conclude that now, more than ever before in history, we can and should have hope that we will someday solve our social problems.

Obviously, time will tell!

Case Study: New measures of success?

For many years the measure of success for many individuals and countries has been related to economic growth and profit. However, in the contemporary world, this approach is now being questioned. More attention is now being directed towards people's happiness and well-being, and many commentators are questioning the relationship between economic growth, happiness and mental well-being. Layard (2011) illustrates that over time in rich societies any increases in income are not accompanied by associated increases in happiness. Relative income is actually more important; income inequality results in less happiness. Economic growth, as we currently know it, is therefore not positive for our levels of happiness or our well-being.

Happiness and well-being are, of course, complex issues and Layard (2011) discusses how they are related to other determinants, such as trust. He shows that trusting societies are more equal and also happier in general. He also discusses the importance of work in relation to happiness: the quality of the work that we do is important in providing us with satisfaction and happiness. Layard (2011: 4) concludes: '...the time is ready for radical cultural change, away from a culture of selfishness and materialism, which fails to satisfy, towards one where we care more for each other's happiness – and make that the guiding raisin d'être for our lives.'

Happier societies should therefore be the focus of policy making, and changes that support this development would be helpful in addressing inequalities too.

Summary of key points

- The scope of inequalities across the social world is huge, as this book has demonstrated throughout. This chapter has provided a broad range of suggestions for tackling the problem of social inequality.

- Ideological position and values are related to the way in which inequality is constructed and understood. These values also underpin contemporary solutions and calls for action.
- Some analysts argue that the future is positive in terms of social inequalities, while others remain pessimistic. It will be our future generations who will assess the actions that we take and the effectiveness of our approaches.

List of questions to stimulate debate and reflection

1 Think about the approaches to solving social inequalities discussed in this chapter. Do you agree with a particular approach? In your view, what do you think is needed to create a more equal and a more sustainable society?
2 What is your own ideological position? You should have reflected on this throughout earlier chapters and now should be able to recognise how this influences your thinking about the solutions to social inequalities. Can we solve social inequalities within a capitalist framework?
3 If you were a policy maker with an interest in solving social problems, which areas would you tackle first? What social problems are more amenable to a solution using the mechanisms of social policy? You should also consider the barriers that you would potentially face in attempting to create greater equality.

Further reading

Crone, James A. (2011) *How Can We Solve Our Social Problems?* (2nd edition). Los Angeles: Sage.

This book contains chapters discussing an array of contemporary problems, such as poverty, gender inequality, racial/ethnic inequality, health care provision, crime and unequal education. It offers sociological insight and analysis throughout and is an interesting read in relation to the range of contemporary social inequalities.

Dorling, Daniel (2012) *The No-nonsense Guide to Equality*. Oxford: New Internationalist.

This is a short introduction to the concept of equality and an easy read. Using a wide range of evidence, Dorling shows why inequality is the key issue of the contemporary world and explains the need for greater equality. Alternative routes are demonstrated and the key ways in which greater equality can be achieved are outlined.

George, Susan (2010) *Whose Crisis, Whose Future? Towards a Greener, Fairer, Richer World.* Cambridge and Malden, MA: Polity Press.

This book looks at the scope of the current crisis across the world, exploring poverty, financial markets, climate change and the lack of power that many of us experience within the contemporary social world. The author offers her insight about why we are experiencing this range of problems when the world is actually wealthier than ever before, and explores what we need to do in the future to create a fairer and more equal place to live.

REFERENCES

Abbasi, Kamran (1999) 'The World Bank and world health: Changing sides'. *British Medical Journal*, 318: 865–9.

Abbott, David (2001) 'The death of class?' *Sociology Review*, November.

Abhayarante, Anoma (2003) *Poverty Reduction Strategies in Malaysia 1970–2000: Some Strategies*. Sri Lanka: University of Peradeniya.

Afkhami, R. (2012) *Ethnicity: Introductory User Guide*. ESDS Government, available online at www.esds.ac.uk/government/docs/ethnicityintro.pdf (accessed 1.10.2012).

Afridi, Asif (2011) *Social Networks: Their Role in Addressing Poverty*. York: Joseph Rowntree Foundation.

Agarwal, Bina (1994) *A Field of One's Own: Gender and Land Rights in South Asia*. Cambridge: Cambridge University Press.

Agarwal, Bina (2010) *Gender and Green Governance: The Political Economy of Women's Presence Within and Beyond Community Forestry*. Oxford: Oxford University Press.

Albrecht, Gary L. and Devlieger, Patrick J. (1999) 'The disability paradox: high quality of life against all odds'. *Social Science and Medicine*, 48: 977–88.

Albrow, Martin (1997) *The Global Age: State, Society and Society Beyond Modernity*. Stanford, CA: Stanford University Press.

Alesina, Alnerto and Perotti, Robert (1996) 'Income distribution, political instability, and investment'. *European Economic Review*, 40: 1203–28.

Alexander, Claire E. (2000) *The Asian Gang: Ethnicity, Identity, Masculinity*. Oxford: Berg.

Allen, Katie (2011) 'UK unemployment hits 17-year high'. The *Guardian*, www.guardian.co.uk/business/2011/dec/14/uk-unemployment-hits-17-year-high (accessed 19.12.2011).

Allen, Walter R. and Chung, Angie Y. (2000) '"Your Blues ain't like my Blues": race, ethnicity, and social inequality in America'. *Contemporary Sociology*, 29 (6): 796–805.

Anthias, Fiona (1998) 'Rethinking social divisions: some notes towards a theoretical framework'. *The Sociological Review*, 46 (3): 505–35.

Anthias, Fiona (2001) 'The concept of social division and theorising social stratification: looking at ethnicity and class'. *Sociology*, 35 (4): 835–54.

Appleyard, Lindsey (2012) 'Review article: household finances under pressure: what is the role of social policy'. *Social Policy and Society*, 11 (1): 131–40.

Atkinson, Anthony B. (2003) *Income Inequality in OCED Countries: Data and Explanations*. CESifo Working Paper No. 881. Hamburg: Centre for Economic Studies/Institute for Economic Research.

Atkinson, Rowland and Kintrea, Keith (2004) 'Opportunities and despair, it's all there: practitioner experiences and explanations of area effects and life chances'. *Sociology*, 38 (3): 437–55.

Bachrach, Peter and Baratz, Morton S. (1962) 'Decisions and non-decisions: an analytical framework'. *American Political Science Review*, 57: 947–52.

Baistow, Karen (1994) 'Liberation and regulation? Some paradoxes of empowerment'. *Critical Social Policy*, 42 (143): 34–46.

Bakare, Lanre (2011) 'A decade after the riots, Bradford is still uneasy about race relations'. The *Guardian*, www.guardian.co.uk/commentisfree/2011/jul/07/bradford-riots-race-relations (accessed 11.10.2012).

Barnes, Colin (2003) *Disability Studies: What's the Point?* Lancaster: University of Lancaster.

Barry, Kathleen (1983) 'Feminist theory: the meaning of women's liberation', in Haber, Barbara (ed.) *The Women's Annual 1982–1983*, Boston: G.K. Hall, pp. 35-78.

Barry, Brian (1998) *Social Exclusion, Social Isolation and the Distribution of Income*. CASE Paper 12. London: Centre for the Analysis of Social Exclusion.

Bauman, Zygmunt (2004) *Wasted Lives: Modernity and its Outcasts*. Cambridge and Malden, MA: Polity Press.

Bauman, Zygmunt (2011) *Collateral Damage: Social Inequalities in a Global Age*. Cambridge: Polity Press.

Bayne, Nicolas (2010) 'The G8 and the globalization challenge', in *Academic Symposium G8 2000: New Directions in Global Governance? G8's Okinawa Summit*, www.g8.utoronto.ca/scholar/bayne2000 (accessed 16.4.2012).

BBC News (2007) 'Social sites reveal class divide', 25 June, http://news.bbc.co.uk/1/hi/6236628.stm (accessed 16.8.2012).

BBC News (2010) 'Q&A: Government Spending Review' www.bbc.co.uk/news/business-10810962 (accessed 1.3.2013).

BBC News (2011a) 'Saudi woman to be lashed for defying driving ban', 27 September, www.bbc.co.uk/news/world-middle-east-15079620 (accessed 3.10.2011).

BBC News (2011b) 'Occupy Los Angeles arrests made after eviction deadline', www.bbc.co.uk/news/world-us-canada-15914092 (accessed 19.12.2011).

BBC News (2011c) 'The world at seven billion', www.bbc.co.uk/news/world-15391515 (accessed 19.12.2011).

BBC News (2012) 'Uganda pro-gay groups face ban by ethics minister Lokodo', www.bbc.co.uk/news/world-africa-18531948 (accessed 12.9.2012).

Bebbington, Paul (1996) 'The origins of sex differences in depressive disorder: bridging the gap'. *International Review of Psychiatry*, 8: 295–332.

Beck, Ulrich (1999) *World Risk Society*. Cambridge: Polity Press.

Bell, James, Bowcott, Owen and Rogers, Simon (2011) 'Race variation in jail sentences: study suggests Minorities more likely to be jailed for certain crimes, Differences remain the subject of contention'. The *Guardian*, www.guardian.co.uk/law/2011/nov/25/ethnic-variations-jail-sentences-study (accessed 8.10.2012).

Ben-Ami, Daniel (2010) *Ferraris for All: In Defence of Economic Progress*. Bristol: Policy Press.

Berger, Peter and Luckman, Thomas (1966) *The Social Construction of Reality*. London: Penguin.

Berkel, Rik van and Borghi, Vando (2008) 'Introduction: the governance of activation'. *Social Policy and Society*, 7 (3): 331–40.

Berry, Albert (2010) 'What type of global governance would best lower world poverty and inequality', in Wilkinson, Rorden and Clapp, Jennifer (eds), *Global Governance, Poverty and Inequality*. London: Routledge, pp. 46–67.

Beveridge, William H.B. (1942) *Social Insurance and Allied Services: The Beveridge Report*. London: HMSO.

Bexell, Magdelena, Tallberg, Jonas and Uhlin, Anders (2010) 'Democracy in global governance: the promises and pitfalls of transnational actors'. *Global Governance*, 16: 81–101.

Bhaduri, Amit (2007) 'Development or developmental terrorism?' *Economic and Political Weekly*, 42 (7): 552–3.

Bhagwati, Jagdish (2004) *In Defense of Globalization*. Oxford: Oxford University Press.

Bhopal, Raj (2008) *Concepts of Epidemiology: Integrating the Ideas, Theories, Principles and Methods of Epidemiology* (2nd edition). Oxford: Oxford University Press.

Biddle, Lucy, Brode, Anita, Brookes, Sara T. and Gunnel, David (2008) 'Suicide rates in young men in England and Wales in the 21st century: time trend study'. *British Medical Journal*, 336: 539–42.

Birdsall, Nancy and Subramanian, Arvind (2007) *From World Bank to World Development Cooperative*. Centre for Global Development Essay, October. Washington, DC: Centre for Global Development. Available at www.cgdev.org/content/publications/detail/14625/ (accessed 15.8.2012).

Blakemore, Ken and Griggs, Edwin (2007) *Social Policy: An Introduction* (3rd edition). Maidenhead: Open University Press.

Blanden, Jo (2009) *How Much Can We Learn from International Comparisons of Intergenerational Mobility?* London: Centre for the Economics of Education.

Blanden, Jo, Goodman, Alissa, Gregg, Paul and Machin, Stephen (2004) 'Essays on intergenerational mobility and its variance over time, place and family structure', in Corak, Miles (ed.), *Generational Income Mobility in North America and Europe*. Cambridge: Cambridge University Press.

Bloomwood, David (2011) 'Beyond bad man theory: theorising men's privilege and marginalisation'. Seminar, Leeds Metropolitan University, 28 September.

Boswell, Terry E. and Dixon, William J. (1993) 'Marx's theory of rebellion: a cross-national analysis of class exploitation, economic development and violent revolt'. *American Sociological Review*, 58 (5): 681–702.

Bottero, Wendy (2011) *Placing People in the Past: Family History and Understandings of Inequality*. CRESC Working Paper 104. Milton Keynes: Open University.

Bourdieu, Pierre (1984) *Distinction: A Social Critique of the Judgement of Taste*. Cambridge, MA: Harvard University Press.

Boyden, Stephen (2004) *The Biology of Civilisation: Understanding Human Culture as a Force in Nature*. Sydney: University of New South Wales Press.

Brautigam, Deborah (2000) *Aid Dependence and Governance*. Expert Group on Development Issues, Sweden.

Breen, Richard and Goldthorpe, John H. (1999) 'Class inequality and meritocracy: a critique for Saunders and an alternative analysis'. *The British Journal of Sociology*, 50 (1): 1–27.

Brown, Phillip, Green, Andy and Lauder, Hugh (2001) *High Skills: Globalization, Competitiveness and Skill Formation*. Oxford: Oxford University Press.

Brundtland, Gro Harlem (2003) 'Global health and international security'. *Global Governance*, 9: 417–23.

Bull, Benedicte (2010) 'The global elite and multilateral governance', in Wilkinson, Rorden and Clapp, Jennifer (eds), *Global Governance, Poverty and Inequality*. London: Routledge, pp. 209–34.

Bullard, Robert D. (1990) *Dumping in Dixie: Race, Class and Environmental Quality*. Boulder, CO: Westview Press.

Bullard, Robert D. (1993) *Confronting Environmental Racism: Voices from the Grassroots*. Boston, MA: South End Press.

Burnett, Jon (2011) *The New Geographies of Racism: Peterborough*. London: Institute of Race Relations.

Burns, Judith (2012) 'Number of graduates in basic jobs doubles in five years'. *BBC News*, www.bbc.co.uk/news/education-18627327 (accessed 22.8.2012).

Busfield, Joan (2000) *Health and Healthcare in Modern Britain*. Oxford: Oxford University Press.

Bush, Ray (2007) *Poverty and Neoliberalism: Persistence and Reproduction in the Global South*. London: Pluto Press.

Butler, Judith (1990) *Gender Trouble: Feminism and the Subversion of Identity*. New York: Routledge.

Butler, Judith (1993) *Bodies That Matter: On the Discursive Limits of 'Sex'*. New York: Routledge.

Butler, Judith (1997) *Excitable Speech: A Politics of the Performative*. London: Routledge.

Butler, Judith (2004) *Undoing Gender*. New York: Routledge.

Butler, Judith (2005) *Giving an Account of Oneself*. New York: Fordham University Press.

Butler, Judith and Weed, Elizabeth (eds) (2011) *The Question of Gender: Joan W. Scott's Critical Feminism*. Bloomington, IN: Indiana University Press.

Cammack, Paul (1999) 'The mother of all governments: the World Bank's matrix for global governance', in Wilkinson, Rorden and Hughes, Stephen (eds), *Global Governance: Critical Perspectives*. London: Routledge.

Campbell, David E. and Putman, Robert E. (2011) 'America's Grace: how a tolerant nation bridges its religious divides'. *Political Science Quarterly*, 126 (4): 611–40.

Carlson, Kathryn B. (2011) 'Today's graduates: too few jobs, not enough pay'. *National Post*, 11 June, http://news.nationalpost.com/2011/06/11/todays-graduates-too-few-jobs-not-enough-pay/ (accessed 22.8.2012).

Carrera, P.M. and Bridges, J.F.P. (2006) 'Globalization and healthcare: understanding health and medical tourism'. *Expert Review of Pharmacoeconomics and Outcomes Research*, 6 (4): 447–54.

Cattell, Vicky (2004) 'Having a laugh and mucking in together: using social capital to explore dynamics between structure and agency in the context of declining and regenerated neighbourhoods'. *Sociology*, 38 (5): 945–63.

Chang, Ha Joon (2010) *23 Things They Don't Tell You about Capitalism*. London: Allen Lane.

Chapple, Simon, Forster, Michael and Martin, John P. (2009) 'Inequality and well-being in OECD countries: what do we know?' Paper presented at the OECD World Forum in Busan, Korea, 27–30 October.

Chase-Dunn, Christopher and Lawrence, Kirk S. (2011) 'The next three futures. Part One: Looming crises of global inequality, ecological degradation, and a failed system of global governance'. *Global Society*, 25: 137–53.

Chatterjee, Partha (2004) *The Politics of the Governed: Reflections on Popular Politics in Most of the World*. New Delhi: Permanent Black.

Chirot, Daniel (1991) *Crisis of Leninism and the Decline of the Left*. Seattle, WA: University of Washington Press.

Chodorow, Nancy (1978) *The Reproduction of Mothering: Psychoanalysis and the Sociology of Gender*. Berkeley, CA: University of California Press.

Clark, Ian (2001) 'Globalization and the post-cold war order', in Baylis, J. and Smith, S. (eds), *The Globalization of World Politics: An Introduction to International Relations* (2nd edition). Oxford and New York: Oxford University Press.

Coleman, James S. (1998) 'Social capital in the creation of human capital'. *American Journal of Sociology*, 94 (Suppl.): 95–120.

Collier, Paul (2008) *The Bottom Billion: Why the Poorest Countries are Failing and What Can Be Done about It*. Oxford: Oxford University Press.

Collins, Patricia H. (1990) *Black Feminist Thought: Knowledge, Consciousness, and the Politics of Empowerment*. New York: Routledge.

Collins, Patricia H. (2004) *Black Sexual Politics*. New York: Routledge.

Commission on Global Governance (1995) *Our Global Neighbourhood: The Report of the Commission on Global Governance*. Oxford: Oxford University Press.

Commission on the Social Determinants of Health (2008) *Closing the Gap in a Generation: Health Equity through Action on the Social Determinants of Health*. Geneva: WHO. Available at: www.who.int/social_determinants/thecommission/finalreport/en/index.html (accessed 23.10.2012).

Connell, Raewyn (1987) *Gender and Power: Society, the Person and Sexual Politics*. London: Allen & Unwin.

Connell, Raewyn (2005) *Masculinities* (Vol. 1). Cambridge: Polity Press.

Connell, Raewyn (2009) *Gender: In World Perspective* (2nd edn). Cambridge: Polity Press.

Courtenay, William H. (2000) 'Behavioural factors associated with disease, injury and death among men: evidence and implications for prevention'. *Journal of Men's Studies*, 9: 81–142.

Crawford, Claire, Johnson, Paul, Machin, Steve and Vignoles, A. (2011) *Social Mobility: A Literature Review*. London: Department for Business, Innovation and Skills.

Crinson, Ian (2009) *Health Policy: A Critical Perspective*. London: Sage.

Crompton, Rosemary and Jones, Gareth (1984) *White-collar Proletariat, De-skilling and Gender in Clerical Work*. London: Macmillan.

Crompton, Rosemary and Sanderson, Kay (1990) *Gendered Jobs and Social Change*. London: Unwin Hyman.

Crone, James A. (2011) *How Can We Solve Our Social Problems?* (2nd edition). Los Angeles: Sage.

Cumming Elaine and Henry, William E. (1961) *Growing Old: The Process of Disengagement*. New York: Basic Books.

Dahlberg, John-Thor (1995) 'Sweatshop case dismays few in Thailand'. *Los Angeles Times*, 27 August.

Das Gupta, Monica, Lee, Sunhwa, Uberoi, Patrica et al. (2000) *State Policies and Women's Autonomy in China, India and the Republic of Korea 1950–2000: Lessons from Contrasting Experiences*. World Bank Policy Research Working Paper No. 2497. Available at: www-wds.worldbank.org/servlet/WDSContentServer/WDSP/IB/2001/03/09/000094946_01022705322025/Rendered/PDF/multi_page.pdf (accessed 5.9.2012).

Davey Smith, George, Chaturvedi, Nish, Harding, Seeromanie, Nazroo, James and Williams, Rory (2000) 'Ethnic inequalities in health: a review of UK epidemiological evidence'. *Critical Public Health*, 10 (4): 375–408.

Davis, Kingsley and Moore, Wilbert (1945) 'Some principles of stratification'. *American Sociological Review*, 10: 242–9.

De Grazia, Victoria (2005) *Irresistible Empire: America's Advance through 20th Century Europe*. Cambridge, MA: The Belknap Press of Harvard University Press.

Deere-Birkbeck, Carolyn (2009) 'Global governance in the context of climate change: the challenges of increasingly complex risk parameters'. *International Affairs*, 85 (6): 1173–94.

DEMOS and SCOPE (2006) *Disablist Britain: Barriers to Independent Living for Disabled People in 2006*. London: DEMOS and SCOPE.

Department of Health (1999) *Saving Lives: Our Healthier Nation* (White Paper). London: Department of Health.

Department of Health (2000) *The NHS Plan*. London: Department of Health.

Department of Health (2003) *Tackling Health Inequalities: A Programme for Action*. London: Department of Health.

Department of Health (2005) *Tackling Health Inequalities: Status Report on the Programme for Action*. London: Department of Health.

Department for Work and Pensions (2008) *Transforming Britain's Labour Market: Ten Years of the New Deal*. London: HMSO.

Department for Work and Pensions (2010a) *The Work Programme Framework*. Available at: www.dwp.gov.uk/docs/work-programme-prospectus.pdf (accessed 11.7.2011).

Department for Work and Pensions (2010b) *Universal Credit: Welfare that Works*. Available at www.dwp.gov.uk/policy/welfare-reform/legislation-and-key-documents/universal-credit/ (accessed 11.7.2011).

DIFD (Department for International Development) (2005) *Reducing Poverty by Tackling Social Exclusion: A Policy Paper*. London: DIFD.

DIFD (Department for International Development) (2009) 'Eliminating world poverty: building our common future'. Background paper, DFID Conference on the Future of International Development, London, 9–10 March. Available at: www.odi.org.uk/resources/details.asp?id=3172&title=eliminating-world-poverty-building-our-common-future (accessed 15.8.2012).

Direct Gov (2010) *Tax Credits and Child Benefit*. Available at: www.direct.gov.uk/en/index.htm (accessed 20.10.2012).

Dixey, Rachael (ed.) (2013) *Health Promotion: Global Principals and Practice*. Wallingford: CABI.

Dixon, Anna, Le Grand, Julian, Murray, Richard and Poteliakhoff, Emmi (2003) *Is the NHS Equitable? A Review of the Evidence*. Health and Social Care Discussion Paper 11. London: London School of Economics.

Dorling, Daniel (2009) *Injustice: Why Social Inequality Persists*. Bristol: Policy Press.

Dorling, Daniel (2012) *The No-nonsense Guide to Equality*. Oxford: New Internationalist.

Dorling, Daniel and Thomas, Bethan (2011) *Bankrupt Britain: An Atlas of Social Change*. Bristol: Policy Press.

DuBois, William E.B. (1970 [1896]) *The Suppression of the Slave-Trade to the United States of America, 1638–1870*. New York: Dover.

DuBois, William E.B. (1973 [1899]) *The Philadelphia Negro*. Millwood, NY: Kraus-Thomson.

Esping-Anderson, Gosta (1990) *The Three Worlds of Welfare Capitalism*. Cambridge: Polity Press.

Estes, Carroll L., Biggs, Simon and Phillipson, Chris (2003) *Social Theory, Social Policy and Ageing*. Buckingham: Open University Press.

European Consumer Debt Network (2007) 'Debt advice services'. *Money Matters*, 3: 7.

European Union Fundamental Rights Agency (2011a) *Migrants, Minorities and Employment: Exclusion and Discrimination in the 27 Member States of the European Union (Update 2003–2008)*. Available at: https://fra.europa.eu/fraWebsite/research/publications/publications_per_year/pub_migrants-minorities-employment_en.htm (accessed 3.10.2012).

European Union Fundamental Rights Agency (2011b) *EU-MIDIS 5 Data in Focus Multiple Discrimination*. Available at: https://fra.europa.eu/fraWebsite/research/publications/publications_per_year/pub-multiple-discrimination_en.htm (accessed 3.10.2012).

Evans, Sara (1980) *Personal Politics: The Roots of Women's Liberation in the Civil Rights Movement and the New Left*. New York: Knopf Doubleday.

Evertsson, Marie and Nermon, Magnus (2007) 'Changing resources and the division of housework: a longitudinal study of Swedish couples'. *European Sociological Review*, 23 (4): 445–70.

Farre, Lidia (2011) *The Role of Men for Gender Equality*. World Development Report 2012 Background Paper. Washington, DC: World Bank.

Feacham, Robert G.A. (2001) 'Globalisation is good for your health, mostly'. *British Medical Journal*, 323: 504–6.

Fekete, Liz (2011) *Pedlars of Hate: The Violent Impact of the European Far Right*. London: Institute of Race Relations.

Firebraugh, Glenn (2003) *The New Geography of Global Income Inequality*. Cambridge, MA: Harvard University Press.

Food and Agricultural Organisation (2009) *The State of Agricultural Commodity Markets 2009: High Food Prices and the Food Crisis – Experiences and Lessons Learned*. Rome: The United Nations.

Food and Agriculture Organisation (2010) *The State of Food Insecurity in the World 2010: Addressing Food Insecurity in Protracted Crises*. Rome: The United Nations.

Foster, Peggy (1995) *Women and the Health Care Industry: An Unhealthy Relationship?* Buckingham: Open University Press.

Foucault, Michel (1978) *The History of Sexuality*. London: Penguin.

Fowler, Alan F. (1998) 'Authentic NGDO partnerships in the new policy agenda for international aid: dead end or light ahead?' *Development and Change*, 29: 137–59.

Fox, Kate (2005) *Watching the English: The Hidden Rules of English Behaviour*. London: Hodder Arnold.

Fukuyama, Francis (1999) *The Great Disruption: Human Nature and the Reconstruction of the Social Order*. London: Profile Books.

Gabbatt, Adam (2011) '"Occupy" anti-capitalism protests spread around the world'. *The Guardian*, www.guardian.co.uk/world/2011/oct/16/occupy-protests-europe-london-assange (accessed 19.12.2011).

George, Susan (2010) *Whose Crisis, Whose Future? Towards a Greener, Fairer, Richer World*. Cambridge and Malden, MA: Polity Press.

George, Vic and Wilding, Paul (2009) 'Globalization and human welfare: why is there a need for a global social policy?' in Douglas, J., Earle, S., Handsley, S., Jones, L., Lloyd, C.E. and Spurr, S. (eds), *A Reader in Promoting Public Health*. London: Sage, pp. 27–34.

Giddens, Anthony (1982) *Sociology: A Brief but Critical Introduction*. New York: Harcourt, Brace, Jovanovich.

Giddens, Anthony (1994) *Beyond Left and Right: The Future of Radical Politics*. Cambridge: Polity Press.

Giddens, Anthony (2009) *Sociology* (6th edn). Cambridge: Polity Press.

Gilman, Charlotte P. (1911) *Man Made World or Our Androcentric Culture*. New York: Charlton.

Gilroy, Paul (1987) *"There Ain't No Black in the Union Jack": The Cultural Politics of Race and Nation*. London: Hutchinson.

Girling, Richard (2005) *Rubbish! Dirt on Our Hands and Crisis Ahead.* London: Transworld Publishers.

Gjonca, Aran, Tomassinic, Cecilia, Toson, Barbara and Smallwood, Steve (2005) 'Sex differences in mortality: a comparison of the UK and other developed countries'. *Health Statistics Quarterly 26.* Newport: Office for National Statistics.

Global Poverty Project (2012) *Women and Poverty,* www.globalpovertyproject.com/infobank/women (accessed 5.9.2012).

Gnath, Katherina and Reimers, Niklas (2009) 'Die G8-Gipfelarchitektur im Wandel'. *DGAP Analyse,* 6 (June). [In German, with a summary in English.]

Goldthorpe, John H. and Jackson, Michelle (2007) 'Intergenerational class mobility in contemporary Britain: political concerns and empirical findings'. *British Journal of Sociology,* 58: 525–46.

Gough, Brendan and Robertson, Steve (eds) (2010) *Men, Masculinities and Health: Critical Perspectives.* Basingstoke: Palgrave Macmillan.

Gould, Lara (2008) 'Scandal of recycled rubbish ending up in India'. *The Mirror,* www.mirror.co.uk/news/top-stories/2008/09/07/scandal-of-recycled-rubbish-ending-up-in-india-115875-20727734/ (accessed 19.12.2011).

Graham, Hilary (2000) *Understanding Health Inequalities* (2nd edition). Buckingham: Open University Press.

Graham, Hillary (2010) 'Poverty and health: global and national patterns', in Douglas, J., Earle, S., Handsley, S., Jones, L., Lloyd, C.E. and Spurr, S. (eds), *A Reader in Promoting Public Health.* London: Sage, pp. 39–51.

Greig, Alastair, Hulme, David and Turner, Mark (2007) *Challenging Global Inequality: Development Theory and Practice in the 21st Century.* Basingstoke: Palgrave Macmillan.

Griffin, Penny (2010) 'Global governance and the global political economy'. *Australian Journal of International Affairs,* 64 (1): 88–104.

Grundy, Emily and Bowling, Ann (1991) 'The sociology of ageing', in Jacoby, Robin and Oppenheimer, Catherine (eds), *Psychiatry in the Elderly.* Oxford: Oxford University Press, pp. 24–36.

Guardian (2011a) 'UK consumer confidence slumps'. The *Guardian,* www.guardian.co.uk/business/2011/apr/28/uk-consumer-confidence-slumps (accessed 19.12.2011).

Guardian (2011b) 'Eurozone crisis'. The *Guardian,* www.guardian.co.uk/business/debt-crisis (accessed 19.12.2011).

Gursoy, Akile (1996) 'Abortion in Turkey: a matter of states, family or individual decision'. *Social Science and Medicine,* 42 (4): 531–42.

Halsey, A.H., Lauder, Hugh, Brown, Phillip and Wells, Amy Stuart (eds) (1997) *Education: Culture, Economy and Society.* Oxford: Oxford University Press.

Hamnett, Chris (1994) 'Social polarization in global cities: theory and evidence'. *Urban Studies,* 31: 401–24.

Hamnett, Chris (1996) 'Why Sassen is wrong: a response to Burgers'. *Urban Studies,* 33 (1): 107–10.

Hamnett, Chris (1998) 'Social polarisation, economic restructuring and welfare state regimes', in Musterd, Sako and Ostendorf, Wim (eds), *Urban Segregation and the Welfare State: Inequality and Exclusion in Western Cities.* London: Routledge, pp. 15–27.

Hamnett, Chris (2003) *Unequal City: London in the Global Arena.* London: Routledge.

Hanley, Lynsey (2007) *Estates: An Intimate History.* London: Granta Books.

Hardy, Frances (2011) 'Will this cosseted new generation break the Bank of Mum and Dad?' *Daily Mail*, 19 May, www.dailymail.co.uk/femail/article-1388478/Will-cosseted-new-generation-break-Bank-Mum-Dad.html (accessed 20.9.2011).

Harjes, Thomas (2007) *Globalization and Income Inequality: A European Perspective.* IMF Working Paper 169. Washington, DC: International Monetary Fund.

Harman, Chris (2009) *Zombie Capitalism: Global Crisis and the Relevance of Marx.* London: Bookmark Publications.

Harper, Sarah (2006) *Ageing Societies: Myths, Challenges and Opportunities.* London: Hodder Arnold.

Harrison, Steve and Macdonald, Ruth (2008) *The Politics of Healthcare in Britain.* London: Sage.

Held, David and Kaya, Ayse (eds) (2007) *Global Inequality.* Cambridge: Polity Press.

Held, David and McGrew, Anthony G. (eds) (1999) *Global Transformations.* Cambridge: Polity Press.

Held, David and McGrew, Anthony G. (2002) *Governing Globalization: Power, Authority and Global Governance.* Cambridge: Polity Press.

Helman, Cecil G. (2000) *Culture, Health and Illness* (4th edition). London: Hodder Arnold.

Henry, James S. (2003) *The Blood Bankers: Tales from the Global Underground Economy.* New York and London: Four Walls Eight Windows.

Hill, Kenneth, Thomas, Kevi, Abouzahr, Caral et al. (2007) 'Estimates of maternal mortality worldwide between 1900 and 2005: an assessment of available data'. *Lancet*, 370: 1311–19.

Hill, Michael (1997) *The Policy Process in the Modern Society* (3rd edition). London: Prentice Hall.

Hills, John, Brewer, Mike, Jenkins, Stephen, Lister, Ruth, Lupton, Ruth, Machin, Stephan, Mills, Colin, Modood, Tariq, Rees, Teresa and Riddell, Shelia (2010) *An Anatomy of Economic Inequality in the UK: Report of the National Equality Panel.* London: Centre for the Analysis of Social Exclusion.

Hochschild, Arlie (1983) *The Managed Heart: Commercialisation of Human Feeling.* Berkeley, CA: University of California Press.

Hochschild, Arlie (1989) *The Second Shift: Working Parents and the Revolution at Home.* New York: Avon.

Holton, Robert (2005) *Making Globalization.* Basingstoke: Palgrave.

Home Office (2011) *Racist Incidents, England and Wales, 2010/11.* London: HMSO. Available at: www.homeoffice.gov.uk/publications/science-research-statistics/research-statistics/crime-research/hosf0111/ (accessed 8.10.2012).

Howard, John H., Rechnitzer, Peter A., Cunningham, D.A. and Donner, Allan P. (1986) 'Change in Type A behaviour a year after retirement'. *Gerontologist*, 26 (6): 643–9.

Hudson, John, Kuhner, Stefan and Lowe, Stuart (2008) *The Short Guide to Social Policy.* Bristol: Policy Press.

Humphrey, Alun, Lee, Lucy and Green, Rosie (2011) *Aspirations for Later Life.* Research Report No. 737. London: Department for Work and Pensions.

Hyde, Mark (2000) 'Disability', in Payne, Geoff (ed.), *Social Divisions.* Basingstoke: Palgrave Macmillan, pp. 185–202.

ICLS (International Centre for Lifecourse Studies) (2010) *Ethnicity and Health*, ICLS Briefing Note 2, www.ucl.ac.uk/icls/publication/bn/ethnicity (accessed 1.10.2012).

Jackson, Michelle, Goldthorpe, John H. and Mills, Colin (2005) 'Education, employers and class mobility'. *Research in Social Stratification and Mobility*, 23: 3–33.

Jackson, Stevi (2006) 'Interchanges: gender, sexuality, heterosexuality. The complexity (and limits) of heteronormativity'. *Feminist Theory*, 7: 105–21.

Jackson, Stevi and Scott, Sue (2000) 'Childhood', in Payne, Geoff (ed.), *Social Divisions*. Basingstoke: Palgrave Macmillan, pp. 152–67.

Jackson, Tim (2011) *Prosperity Without Growth: Economics for a Finite Planet*. London: Earthscan.

James, Oliver (2007) *Affluenza*. London: Vermillion.

Jencks, Christopher and Mayer, Susan (1990) 'The social consequences of growing up in a poor neighbourhood', in Lynn, Laurence and McGeary, Michael G.H. (eds), *Inner City Poverty in the United States*. Washington, DC: National Academic Press, pp. 111–86.

Jenkins, Richard (1997) *Rethinking Ethnicity*. London: Sage.

Joseph Rowntree Foundation (2000) *Poverty and Social Exclusion in Britain*. York: Joseph Rowntree Foundation.

Justino, Patricia (2004) 'The impact of collective action on economic development: empirical evidence from Kerala, India'. *World Development*, 34 (7): 1254–70.

Kar, Dev and Cartwright-Smith, Devon (2010) *Illicit Financial Flows from Africa: Hidden Resource for Development*. Washington, DC: Global Financial Integrity.

Kelley, Sarah M.C. and Kelley, Claire G.E. (2009) 'Subjective social mobility data from 30 nations', in Hallier, Max, Jowell, Roger and Smith, Tom W. (eds), *Charting the Globe: The International Social Survey Programme 1984–2004*. London: Routledge.

Kilgour, Maureen A. (2007) 'The UN global compact and substantive equality for women: revealing a well-hidden mandate'. *Third World Quarterly*, 28 (4): 751–73.

Kindhauser, Mary K. (2003) *Communicable Diseases 2002: Global Defence against the Infectious Disease Threat*. WHO/CDS/2003.15. Geneva: World Health Organization.

Kingdon, John W. (1995) *Agenda, Alternatives and Public Policies* (2nd edition). Reading, MA: Addison-Wesley.

Klein, Naomi (2001) *No Logo*. London: Flamingo.

Klein, Naomi (2007) *The Shock Doctrine*. London and New York: Penguin.

Kunst, Anton E., Groenhof, Feikje, Mackenbach, Johan P. and EU Working Group on Socioeconomic Inequalities in Health (1998) 'Mortality by occupational class among men 30–64 years in 11 European countries'. *Social Science and Medicine*, 46 (11): 1459–76.

Labbock, M. and Nazro, J. (1995) 'Breastfeeding: protecting a natural resource'. Washington, DC: Georgetown University. Cited in Macdonald, Theodore (2005) *Third World Hostage to First World Health*. Oxford: Radcliffe Publishing.

Labonte, Ronald (2010) 'Health promotion, globalisation and health', in Douglas, J., Earle, S., Handsley, S., Jones, L., Lloyd, C.E. and Spurr, S. (eds), *A Reader in Promoting Public Health*. London: Sage, pp. 235–45.

Lansley, Stuart (2011) *The Cost of Inequality: Three Decades of the Super-rich and the Economy*. London: Gibson Square.

Laverack, Glenn (2006) *Health Promotion Practice: Power and Empowerment*. London: Sage.

Laverack, Glenn and Whipple, Amanda (2010) 'The sirens' song of empowerment: a case study of health promotion and the New Zealand Prostitutes' Collective'. *Global Health Promotion*, 17 (1): 33–8.

Lawler, Ellis and Nicholls, Jeremy (2008) *The Gap Years: Enterprise and Inequality in England 2002–2006*. London: New Economics Foundation.

Layard, Richard (2011) 'Is a happier society possible?' Joint Joseph Rowntree Foundation/University of York Annual lecture 2011, York, 10 March.

Le Grand, Elias, Hellgren, Zenia and Halldén, Karin (2008) 'Introduction: social stratification in multi-ethnic societies: class and ethnicity', in Halldén, Karin, Le Grand, Elias and Hellgren, Zenia (eds), *Ethnicity and Social Divisions: Contemporary Research in Sociology*. Newcastle: Cambridge Scholars Publishing, pp. 1–22.

Leach, Beryl, Paluzzi, Joan E. and Munderi, Paula (2005) *Prescription for Healthy Development: Increasing Access to Medicines*. London: Earthscan.

Lee, Kelley (1998) 'Shaping the future of global health co-operation: where do we go from here?' *Lancet*, 351: 899–902.

Letwin, Oliver (1988) *Privatising the World: A Study of International Privatisation in Theory and Practice*. London: Caswell Educational.

Lewis, Paul (2011) 'Upskilling the workers will not upskill the work: why the dominant economic framework limits child reduction poverty in the UK'. *Journal of Social Policy*, 40 (3): 535–56.

Lewis, Paul, Taylor, Matthew and Ball, James (2011) 'Kenneth Clarke blames English riots on a "broken penal system"'. The *Guardian*, Monday 5 September, www.guardian.co.uk/uk/2011/sep/05/kenneth-clarke-riots-penal-system (accessed 20.9.2011).

Levitas, Ruth (2006) 'The concept and measurement of social exclusion', in Pantazis, Christina, Gordon, David and Levitas, Ruth (eds), *Poverty and Social Exclusion in Britain: The Millennium Survey*. Bristol: Policy Press.

Levitas, Ruth, Pantazis, Christina, Fahmy, Eldin, Gordon, David, Lloyd, Eva, Patsios, Demi (2007) *The Multi-dimensional Analysis of Social Exclusion*. Bristol: University of Bristol.

Lindsay, Colin (2010) 'Reconnecting with "what employment means": employability, the experience of unemployment and priorities for policy in an era of crisis', in Greener, I., Holden, C. and Kilkey, M. (eds), *Social Policy Review 22: Analysis and Debate in Social Policy, 2010*. Bristol: Policy Press.

Lister, Ruth (2004) *Poverty (Key Concepts)*. Cambridge: Polity Press.

Long, Russ (2012) *Racial and Ethnic Inequality*, http://dmc122011.delmar.edu/socsci/rlong/problems/chap-08.htm (accessed 11.10.2012).

Lorber, Judith (1993) 'Believing is seeing: biology as ideology'. *Gender and Society*, 7: 568–81.

Lorber, Judith (ed.) (1994a) *Paradoxes of Gender*. New Haven, CT: Yale University Press.

Lorber, Judith (1994b) 'Night to his day: the social construction of gender', in Lorber, Judith (ed.), *Paradoxes of Gender*. New Haven, CT: Yale University Press.

Lorber, Judith (1998) *Gender Inequality: Feminist Theories and Politics*. Los Angeles: Roxbury.

Lowe, Stuart G., Searle, Beverley A. and Smith, Susan J. (2012) 'From housing wealth to mortgage debt: the emergence of Britain's asset-shaped welfare state'. *Social Policy and Society*, 11 (1): 105–16.

Lukes, Steven (1974) *Power: A Radical View*. London: Macmillan.

Lupton, Ruth (2003) *Neighbourhood Effects: Can We Measure Them and Does It Matter?* CASE Paper 73. London: Centre for the Analysis of Social Exclusion.

Lynch, John, Davey Smith, George, Kaplan, George A. and House, James S. (2008) 'Income inequality and mortality: importance to health of individual income, psychosocial environment, or material conditions'. *British Medical Journal*, 320: 1200–4.

Macdonald, Theodore (2006) *Health, Trade and Human Rights*. Oxford: Radcliffe Publishing.

Macdonald, Theodore (2007) *The Global Human Right to Health: Dream or Possibility?* Oxford: Radcliffe Publishing.

Macionis, John J. (2001) *Society: The Basics* (8th edition). London and New York: Prentice Hall.

Macionis, John J. and Plummer, Ken (2002) *Sociology: A Global Introduction* (2nd edition). London and New York: Prentice-Hall.

Macionis, John J. and Plummer, Ken (2008) *Sociology: A Global Introduction* (4th edition). London: Pearson; New York: Prentice-Hall.

Macready, Norra (2007) 'Developing countries court medical tourists'. *Lancet*, 369: 1849–50.

Manji, Firozi (2000) 'Collaboration with the South: agents of aid or solidarity?', in Eade, D. (ed.), *Development, NGOs and Civil Society*. Oxford: Oxfam GB, pp. 75–9.

Marcuse, Peter (1993) 'What's so new about divided cities?' *International Journal of Urban and Regional Research*, 17 (3): 355–65.

Marks, Gary (1999) *The Measurement of Socioeconomic Status and Social Class in the LSAY Project*. Technical Paper No. 14. Melbourne: Australian Council for Educational Research.

Marmot, Michael (2004) *The Status Syndrome: How Social Standing Affects Our Health and Longevity*. London: Bloomsbury.

Marmot Review Team (2010) *Fair Society, Healthy Lives: The Marmot Review*. London: The Marmot Review.

Marshall, Gordon. 'Goldthorpe class scheme.' A Dictionary of Sociology. 1998. Encyclopedia.com. available at http://www.encyclopedia.com (accessed 28th February 2013).

Martell, Luke (2010) *The Sociology of Globalization*. Cambridge: Polity Press.

Marx, Karl (1906 [1867]) *Capital: A Critique of Political Economy*. New York: Modern Library.

Mauss, Marcel (1967) *The Gift: The Form and the Reason for Exchange in Archaic Societies*. London: Taylor and Francis.

Mayer, Karl (2009) 'New directions in life course research'. *Annual Review of Sociology*, 35: 413–33.

McCarthy, John D. (1997) 'The globalization of social movement theory', in Smith, J., Chatfield, C. and Pagnuccio, R. (eds), *Transnational Movements and Social Rights*. Syracuse, NY: Syracuse University Press.

McDougall, Dan (2007) 'Waste not, want not in the £700m slum'. *The Observer*, www.guardian.co.uk/environment/2007/mar/04/india.recycling (accessed 19.12.2011).

McQuaid, Ronald W. and Lindsay, Colin (2002) 'The "employability gap": long-term unemployment and barriers to work in buoyant labour markets'. *Environment and Planning C: Government and Policy*, 20 (4): 613–29.

Merton, Robert K. (1949) 'Discrimination and the American Creed', in MacIver, Robert M. (ed.), *Discrimination and National Welfare*. New York: Harper Publishers, pp. 77–145.

Milanovic, Branko (2006) *Global Income Inequality: What is it and Why it Matters?* DESA Working Paper No. 26. New York: United Nations.

Milanovic, Branko (2007) 'Globalisation and inequality', in Held, David and Kaya, Ayse (eds), *Global Inequality*. Cambridge: Polity Press.

Milanovic, Branko (2009) *Global Inequality and the Global Inequality Extraction Ration: The Story of the Past Two Centuries*. Policy Research Working Paper 5044. Washington, DC: World Bank.

Ministry of Justice (2011) *Statistics on Race and the Criminal Justice System 2010: A Ministry of Justice Publication under Section 95 of the Criminal Justice Act 1999*. London: Ministry of Justice.

Mitchell, Daniel J. (2006) *The Moral Case for Tax Havens*. Occasional Paper 24, www.ipd.fnst.org/webcom/show_article.php/_c-1624/_nr-1/_lkm-2243/i.html (accessed 18.11.2011).

Moghadam, Valentine (2005) 'Transnational feminist networks: collective action in an era of globalization'. *International Sociology*, 15 (1): 57–85.

Momani, Bessma (2010) 'IMF rhetoric on reducing poverty and inequality', in Wilkinson, Rorden and Clapp, Jennifer (eds), *Global Governance, Poverty and Inequality*. London: Routledge, pp. 72–89.

Morosanu, Laura (2007) *Back to Europe? Framing Romania's Accession to the European Union in the United Kingdom*. Prague: Multi-Cultural Prague.

Morris, Lydia D. (1993) 'Is there a British underclass?' *International Journal of Urban and Regional Research*, 17 (3): 404–12.

Moynihan, Claire (1998) 'Theories in health care and research: theories of masculinity'. *British Medical Journal*, 317: 1072–5.

Moyo, Dambisa (2009) *Dead Aid: Why Aid Makes Things Worse and How There is Another Way for Africa?* London: Penguin.

Murphy, Craig N. (2000) 'Global governance: poorly done and poorly understood'. *International Affairs*, 76 (4): 789–803.

Murray, Charles (1990) *The Emerging British Underclass*. London: Institute of Economic Affairs.

Naidoo, Jenny and Wills, Jane (2008) *Health Studies: An Introduction*. Basingstoke: Palgrave Macmillan.

Narayan, Deepa (1999) *Bonds and Bridges: Social Capital and Poverty*. Washington, DC: World Bank.

NEF (New Economics Foundation) (2010) *The Great Transition*. London: New Economics Foundation.

Newman, Ines (2011) 'Work as a route out of poverty: a critical evaluation of the UK welfare to work policy'. *Policy Studies*, 32 (2): 91–108.

Newman, Sarah (1997) 'Masculinities, men's bodies and nursing', in Lawler, Jocalyn (ed.), *The Body in Nursing*. Melbourne: Churchill Livingstone, pp. 135–53.

Nikiema, Beatrice, Haddad, Slim and Potvin, Louise (2008) 'Women bargaining to seek health care: norms, domestic practices and implications in rural Burkino Faso'. *World Development*, 36 (4): 608–24.

Nikkhah, Hedayat Allah and Redzuan, Ma'rof (2009) 'Participation as a medium of empowerment in community development'. *European Journal of Social Sciences*, 11 (1): 170–6.

Oakley, Ann (1976) *Woman's Work: The Housewife, Past and Present*. New York: Random House.

Office for National Statistics (2004) *Social Trends 34*. Newport: Office for National Statistics. Available at: www.ons.gov.uk/ons/rel/social-trends-rd/social-trends/no--34--2004-edition/index.html (accessed 22.10.2012).

Office for National Statistics (2010) 'News Release: Healthy life expectancy is shorter in manual social classes'. *Health Statistics Quarterly*, 45. Newport: Office for National Statistics.

Office for National Statistics (2011) *NS-SEC Categories, Sub-categories and Classes*. Newport: Office for National Statistics. Available at: www.ons.gov.uk/ons/guide-method/classifications/archived-standard-classifications/ns-sec/categories--sub-categories-and-classes/index.html (accessed 20.9.2011).

Office for National Statistics (2012) *Migration Statistics Quarterly Report* (August). Newport: Office for National Statistics. Available at: www.ons.gov.uk/ons/rel/migration1/migration-statistics-quarterly-report/august-2012/msqr.html (accessed 16.10.2012).

Ogden, Jane (1996) *Health Psychology: A Textbook*. Buckingham: Open University Press.

Ohmae, Keniche (1990) *The Borderless World: Power and Strategy in the Industrial Economy*. London: Collins.

Ohmae, Keniche (1995) *The End of the Nation State: The Rise of Regional Economies*. London: Free Press.

Oliver, Michael (1990) *The Politics of Disablement*. Basingstoke: Macmillan.

Ollilia, Eeva (2005) 'Global health priorities – priorities of the wealthy?' *Globalisation and Health*, 1 (6): 1–6.

Ortiz, Isabel and Cummins, Matthew (2011) *Global Inequality: Beyond the Bottom Billion. A Rapid Review of Income Distribution in 141 Countries*. New York: United Nations Children Fund (UNICEF).

Orton, Michael (2008) 'State approaches to wealth', in Ridge, Tess and Wright, Sharon (eds), *Understanding Inequality, Poverty and Wealth*. Bristol: Policy Press.

Orton, Michael (2011) 'Flourishing lives: the capabilities approach as a framework for new thinking about employment, work and welfare in the 21st century work', *Employment and Society*, 25 (2): 352–60.

Orton, Michael and Rowlingson, Karen (2007a) 'A problem of riches: towards a new social policy research agenda on the distribution of economic resources'. *Journal of Social Policy*, 36 (1): 59–78.

Orton, Michael and Rowlingson, Karen (2007b) *Public Attitudes to Economic Inequality*. York: Joseph Rowntree Foundation.

Owen, Glen (2010) 'The coalition of millionaires: 23 of the 29 member of the new cabinet are worth more than £1m... and the Lib Dems are just as wealthy as the Tories'. *Mail Online*, 23 May, www.dailymail.co.uk/news/election/article-1280554/The-coalition-millionaires-23-29-member-new-cabinet-worth-1m--Lib-Dems-just-wealthy-Tories.html (accessed 14.9.2011).

Oxfam (2010) *21st Century Aid: Recognising Success and Tackling Failure*. Oxfam Briefing Paper. Oxford: Oxfam International.

Oxfam (2012) *Left Behind by the G20? How Inequality and Environmental Degradation Threaten to Exclude Poor People from the Benefits of Economic Growth*. Oxfam Briefing

Paper 157. Oxford: Oxfam International. Available at: http://policy-practice.oxfam. org.uk/publications/left-behind-by-the-g20-how-inequality-and-environmental-degradation-threaten-to-203569 (accessed 15.8.2012).

Paluski, Jan and Waters, Malcolm (1996) *The Death of Class*. London: Sage.

Parliamentary Office of Science and Technology (2007) *Postnote 276: Ethnicity and Health*. London: Parliamentary Office of Science and Technology.

Parsons, Talcott (1942) 'Age and sex in the social structure of the United States'. *American Sociological Review*, 7 (4): 604–16.

Parsons, Talcott (1960) 'Towards a healthy maturity'. *Journal of Health and Social Behaviour*, 1 (3): 163–73.

Philpott, John (1999 *Behind the 'Buzzword': Employability*. London: Employment Policy Institute.

Piachaud, David (2002) *Capital and the Determinants of Poverty and Social Exclusion*. Case Paper 60. London: Centre for the Analysis of Social Exclusion.

Pierson, Paul (2004) *Politics in Time: History, Institutions and Social Analysis*. Princeton, NJ: Princeton University Press.

Plan International (2007) *Because I am a Girl. The State of the World's Girls 2007*. London: Plan.

Platt, Lucida (2011) *Inequality within Ethnic Groups*. JRF Programme Paper: Poverty and Ethnicity. York: Joseph Rowntree Foundation.

Pogge, Thomas W. (2007) 'Why inequality matters', in Held, David and Kaya, Ayse (eds), *Global Inequality*. Cambridge: Polity Press.

Popay, Jennie, Bennett, Sharon, Thomas, Carol, Williams, Gareth, Gatrell, Anthony and Bostock, Lisa (2003) 'Beyond "beer, fags, egg and chips"? Exploring lay understandings of social inequalities in health'. *Sociology of Health and Illness*, 25 (1): 1–23.

Popay, Jennie and Dhooge, Yvonne (1989) *Unemployment and Health: What Role for Health and Social Services?* London: Polytechnic of the South Bank.

Pope, Vicky (2008) 'Met Office's bleak forecast on climate change: the head of the Met Office Centre for Climate Change Research explains why the momentum on emissions targets must not be lost'. The *Guardian*, www.guardian.co.uk/environment/2008/oct/01/climatechange.carbonemissions (accessed 13.1.2010).

Putnam, Robert D. (2000) *Bowling Alone: The Collapse and Revival of American Community*. New York: Simon & Schuster.

Radnedge, Aidan (2012) 'We've lifted the clouds for disabled'. *Metro*, 10 September.

Razavi, Shahra (2011) *World Development Report 2012: Gender Equality and Development. An Opportunity both Welcome and Missed (An Extended Commentary)*. New York: United Nations Research Institute for Social Development (UNRISD).

Ridge, Tess and Wright, Sharon (2008) 'State approaches to poverty and social exclusion', in Ridge, Tess and Wright, Sharon (eds), *Understanding Inequality, Poverty and Wealth*. Bristol: Policy Press, pp. 283–310.

Rissel, Christopher (1994) 'Empowerment: the holy grail of health promotion?' *Health Promotion International*, 9: 39–47.

Ritzer, George (2008) *The McDonaldization of Society*. Thousand Oaks, CA: Pine Forge Press.

Robertson, Douglas (2011) 'Knowing your place: class identity and its significance in understanding social exclusion'. Paper presented at the HAS Annual Conference, York.

Robinson, Fred, Else, Richard, Sherlock, Maeve and Zass-Ogilive, Ian (2009) *Poverty in the Media: Being Seen and Getting Heard.* York: Joseph Rowntree Foundation.

Rosenau, James N. (1997) *Along the Domestic–Foreign Frontier: Exploring Governance in a Turbulent World.* Cambridge: Cambridge University Press.

Rostow, Walt W. (1978) *The World Economy: History and Prospect.* London: Macmillan.

Rowlingson, Karen and Conner, Stuart (2011) 'The "deserving" rich? Inequality, morality and social policy'. *Journal of Social Policy*, 40 (3): 437–52.

Rowlingson, Karen and McKay, Stephen (2012) *Wealth and the Wealthy: Exploring and Tackling Inequalities between Rich and Poor.* Bristol: Policy Press.

Runciman, Walter G. (1966) *Relative Deprivation and Social Justice.* London: Routledge Kegan Paul.

Sachs, Jeffery D. (2001) *Macroeconomics and Health: Investing in Health for Economic Development.* Report on the Commission on Macroeconomics and Health. Geneva: World Health Organization.

Sachs, Jeffery D. (2005) *The End of Poverty: How We Can Make It Happen in Our Lifetime.* London: Penguin.

Salgado-Pottier, Rayen (2008) 'A modern moral panic: the representation of British Bangladeshi and Pakistani youth in relation to violence and religion'. *Anthropology Matters*, 10 (1): 1–17.

Salway, Sarah, Allmark, Peter, Barley, Ruth, Higginbottom, Gina, Gerrish, Kate and Ellison, George (2009) *Researching Ethnic Inequalities Social Research Update.* Brighton: University of Surrey.

Salway, Sarah, Barley Ruth, Allmark, Peter, Gerrish, Kate, Higginbottom, Gina and Ellison, George (2011) *Ethnic Diversity and Inequality: Ethical and Scientific Rigour in Social Research.* York: Joseph Rowntree Foundation.

Sanders, David (2005) 'Primary healthcare and health system development: strategies for revitalisation'. Paper presented to the People's Health Assembly, Ecuador, July.

Sandhu, Tauqir, Chaudhry, Ayesha, Akbar, Nadeem et al. (2005) 'Effect of socio-economic factors on the female education in rural areas of Faisalabad (Pakistan)'. *Journal of Agriculture and Social Sciences*, 41–42: 1813–2235.

Sarkar, Amarendra N. (2011) 'Global climate governance: emerging policy issues and future organisational landscapes'. *International Journal of Business Insights*, 4 (2): 67–83.

Sassen, Saskia (1991) *The Global City.* Princeton, NJ: Princeton University Press.

Sayers, Janet (1982) *Biological Politics: Feminist and Anti-Feminist Perspectives.* London and New York: Tavistock.

Scherger, Simone and Savage, Mike (2009) *Cultural Transmission, Educational Attainment and Social Mobility.* CRESC Working Paper Series. Working Paper No. 70. Manchester: University of Manchester.

Scholte, Jan Aart (2000) *Globalization: A Critical Introduction.* Basingstoke: Macmillan.

Scholte, Jan Aart (2005) *The Sources of Neo-liberal Liberalisation.* United Nations Research Institute for Social Development, Overarching Concerns – Program Paper No. 8. New York: United Nations.

Scott, John and Marshall, Gordon (eds) (1998) *A Dictionary of Sociology.* Oxford: Oxford University Press.

Scottish Parliament (1999) *Measuring Social Exclusion Research Paper 99/11.* Edinburgh: Scotland Information Centre.

Seckinelgin, Hakan (2010) 'Global social policy and international organizations: linking social exclusion to durable inequality'. *Global Social Policy*, 9: 205–27.

Sen, Amartya (1985) *Commodities and Capabilities*. Oxford: Oxford University Press.

Sen, Amartya (1998) 'Mortality as an indicator of economic success and failure'. *Economic Journal*, 108 (447): 1–25.

Sen, Amartya (1999) *Development as Freedom*. Oxford: Oxford University Press.

Sen, Amartya (2001) 'Many faces of gender inequality'. *Frontline*, 18 (22), 9 November.

Sentamu, John (2011) 'Only shared wealth brings happiness'. *The Independent*, 13 November, www.independent.co.uk/opinion/commentators/john-sentamu-only-shared-wealth-brings-happiness-6261447.html (accessed 16.8.2012).

Sernau, Scott (2011) *Social Inequality in a Global Age* (3rd edition). Los Angeles: Sage.

Shafiq, Najeeb M. (2009) 'A reversal of educational fortune? Educational gender gaps in Bangladesh'. *Journal of International Development*, 21: 137–55.

Sharpe, Rosalind (2010) *An Inconvenient Sandwich: The Throwaway Economics of Takeaway Food*. London: New Economics Fund.

Shavit, Yassi, Arum, Richard and Gamoran, Adam (eds) (2007) *Stratification in Higher Education*. Standford, CA: Stanford University Press.

Shaxon, Nicolas (2011) *Treasure Islands: Tax Havens and the Men Who Stole the World*. London: The Bodley Head.

Simons, Paula (2012) 'Fairness at the heart of all policies would improve health'. *Edmonton Journal*, www.edmontonjourbal.com/story (accessed 21.6.2012).

Singer, Peter (2002) *One World: The Ethics of Globalization*. New Haven, CT: Yale University Press.

Sklair, Leslie (2002) *Globalisation: Capitalism and Its Alternatives* (3rd edition). Oxford: Oxford University Press.

Smith, Dorothy (1987) *The Everyday World as Problematic: A Feminist Sociology*. Boston, MA: Northeastern University Press.

Smith, Dorothy (1990) *The Conceptual Practices of Power: A Feminist Sociology of Knowledge*. Boston, MA: Northeastern University Press.

Smith, Katherine E. (2007) 'Health inequalities in Scotland and England: the contrasting journey of ideas from research into policy'. *Social Science and Medicine*, 64 (7): 1438–49.

Social Exclusion Unit (1997) *Social Exclusion Unit: Purpose, Work Priorities and Working Methods*. London: Office of the Deputy Prime Minister.

Social Exclusion Unit (2002) *Tackling Social Exclusion: Achievements, Lessons Learned and the Way Forward*. London: Office of the Deputy Prime Minister.

Social Exclusion Unit (2004) *Breaking the Cycle: Taking Stock of Progress and Priorities for the Future*. London: Office of the Deputy Prime Minister.

Solomon, Barbara (1976) *Black Empowerment: Social Work in Oppressed Communities*. Columbia, OH: Columbia University Press.

Soubbotina, Tatanya P. (2004) *Beyond Economic Growth: An Introduction to Sustainable Development* (2nd edition). Washington, DC: World Bank.

Stamp, Stuart (2012) 'The impact of debt advice as a response to financial difficulties in Ireland'. *Social Policy and Society*, 11 (1): 93–104.

Stevens, Alex (2011) 'Telling policy stories: an ethnographic study of the use of evidence in policy-making in the UK'. *Journal of Social Policy*, 40 (2): 237–55.

Stewart, Frances (2010) 'Horizontal inequalities and conflict: an introduction and some hypotheses', in Stewart, Frances (ed.), *Horizontal Inequalities and Conflict: Understanding Group Violence in Multi-ethnic Societies*. Basingstoke: Palgrave Macmillan, pp. 3–24.

Stiglitz, Joseph (2002) *Globalization and Its Discontents*. Harmondsworth: Penguin.

Stiglitz, Joseph (2006) *Making Globalisation Work: The Next Steps to Global Justice*. London: Allen Lane.

Stiglitz, Joseph (2012) *The Price of Inequality*. London: Allen Lane.

Stone, David (2009) 'Health and the natural environment', in Griffiths, Jenny, Raos, Mala, Adshead, Fiona and Thorpe, Allison (eds), *The Health Practitioner's Guide to Climate Change: Diagnosis and Cure*. London and Sterling, VA: Earthscan.

Summerhayes, Colin (2010) *Climate Change: An Emerging Issue in Health*. World Health Organization's Global Health Histories Seminar. Geneva: WHO. Available at: www.who.int/global_health_histories/seminars/presentation39a.pdf (accessed 11.10.2010).

Tahir, Tariq (2011) 'World has more obese people than starving'. *Metro*, 23 September.

Telegraph (2011) 'Greek €8bn Eurozone loan expected in November'. *The Daily Telegraph*, www.telegraph.co.uk/finance/financialcrisis/8820128/Greek-8bn-eurozone-loan-expected-in-November.html (accessed 18.10.2011).

The Poverty Site (2012) *Work and Ethnicity*, www.poverty.org.uk/47/index.shtml (accessed 8.10.2012).

Therian, Jean-Phillippe (1999) 'Beyond the north-south divide: two tales of world poverty', in Wilkinson, Rorden (ed.) (2005), *The Global Governance Reader*. London: Routledge.

Thomas, Bethan, Dorling, Danny and Davey Smith, George (2010) 'Inequalities in premature mortality in Britain: observational study from 1921 to 2007'. *British Medical Journal*, 341: 3639.

Thompson, Martha E. and Armato, Michael (2011) *Investigating Gender*. Cambridge: Polity Press.

Townsend, Peter (1999) 'Poverty, social exclusion and social polarisation: the need to construct an international welfare state', in Douglas, J., Earle, S., Handsley, S., Jones, L., Lloyd, C.E. and Spurr, S. (eds), *A Reader in Promoting Public Health*. London: Sage, pp. 81–9.

Townsend, Peter and Davidson, Nick (1982) *Inequalities in Health: The Black Report*. London: Penguin.

Turner, Brian S. (1988) *Status*. Milton Keynes: Open University Press.

Turquet, Laura, Seck, Papa, Azcona, Ginette, Menon, Roshni, Boyce, C., Pierron, N. and Harbour, E. (2011) *Progress of the World's Women: In Pursuit of Justice*. New York: United Nations Women.

UNAIDS (2007) *AIDS Epidemic Update: December 2007*. Geneva: UNAIDS and World Health Organization.

UNICEF (2011) *The State of the World's Children: Adolescence an Age of Opportunity*. New York: UNICEF.

United Human Rights Council (2012) *Genocide in Rwanda*, www.unitedhumanrights.org/genocide/genocide_in_rwanda.htm (accessed 3.10.2012).

United Nations (2005) *Report on the World Social Situation 2005: The Inequality Predicament*. New York: Department of Economic and Social Affairs.

United Nations (2006) *Convention on the Rights of Persons with Disabilities.* New York: United Nations. Available at: www.un.org/disabilities/default.asp?id=150 (accessed 12.9.2012).

United Nations (2007) *Millennium Development Goals Report.* New York: United Nations.

United Nations (2009) *Rethinking Poverty: Report on the World Social Situation 2010.* New York: Department of Economic and Social Affairs.

United Nations (2011a) *Global Issues: Ageing.* New York: United Nations. Available at: www.un.org/en/globalissues/ageing/index.shtml (accessed 22.9.2011).

United Nations (2011b) *Ageing.* New York: Social Policy and Development Division. http://social.un.org/index/Ageing/DataonOlderPersons/BLivingConditionsCharts.aspx (accessed 22.9.2011).

United Nations (2012) *Framework Convention on Climate Change.* New York: United Nations. Available at: http://unfccc.int/kyoto_protocol/items/2830.php (accessed 11.4.2012).

United Nations Development Programme (1995) *Human Development Report 1995. Gender and Human Development.* Oxford and New York: Oxford University Press.

United Nations Development Programme (1998) *Human Development Report 1998: Consumption for Human Development.* Oxford and New York: Oxford University Press.

United Nations Development Programme (1999) *Human Development Report 1999. Globalisation with a Human Face.* Oxford and New York: Oxford University Press.

United Nations Development Programme (2009) *Human Development Programme 2009: Overcoming Barriers: Human Mobility and Development.* Oxford and New York: Oxford University Press.

United Nations Development Programme (2010) *The Real Wealth of Nations: Pathways to Human Development.* Basingstoke: Palgrave Macmillan.

United Nations Development Programme (2012) *The Millennium Development Goals: Eight Goals for 2015.* New York: United Nations Development Programme. Available at: www.undp.org/content/undp/en/home/mdgoverview.html (accessed 10.4.2012).

United Nations Development Programme (2013) *Human Development Report: The Rise of the South, Human Progress in a Diverse World.* New York: United Nations Development Programme. Available at: http://hdr.undp.org/en/media/HDR2013_EN_Statistics.pdf (accessed 24.6.2013).

University of Essex (2012) *The European Socio-economic Classification.* Colchester: University of Essex. Available at: www.iser.essex.ac.uk/archives/esec/user-guide/the-european-socio-economic-classification (accessed 13.8.2012).

Vandenbroucke, Frank (1998) *Globalisation, Inequality and Social Democracy.* London: Institute for Public Policy Research.

Vaughan, Adam (2009) 'Elimination of food waste could lift 1bn out of hunger, say campaigners'. The *Guardian,* www.guardian.co.uk/environment/2009/sep/08/food-waste (accessed 19.12.2011).

Venkatapuram, Sridhar (2011) *Health Justice: An Argument for the Capabilities Approach.* Cambridge: Polity Press.

Verdung, Evert (1998) Policy instruments: typologies and instruments, in M.L. Belemans-Videc, C.L. Rist and E. Verdung (eds), *Carrots Sticks and Sermons – policy instruments and their evaluation.* New Brunswick, NJ: Transaction Publishers. pp. 21–55.

Vivian, Jessica (1994) 'NGOs and sustainable development in Zimbabwe: no magic bullets'. *Development and Change,* 25: 181–209.

Wach, Heike and Reeves, Hazel (2000) *Gender and Development: Facts and Figures.* Report Number 56, prepared for the Department of International Development. Brighton: University of Sussex.

Wade, Robert H. (2007) 'Should we worry about income inequality?' in Held, David and Kaya, Ayse (eds), *Global Inequality.* Cambridge: Polity Press.

Wainwright, David (2009) 'The changing face of medical sociology', in Wainwright, David (ed.), *A Sociology of Health.* London: Sage, pp. 1–18.

Walby, Sylvia (1990) *Theorizing Patriarchy.* Malden, MA: Blackwell.

Wallace, Alison (2012) '"Feels like I'm doing it on my own": examining the synchronicity between policy responses and the circumstances and experiences of mortgage borrowers in arrears'. *Social Policy and Society*, 11 (1): 117–29.

Wallerstein, Nina (2006) *What is the Evidence on Effectiveness of Empowerment to Improve Health?* Report for the Health Evidence Network (HEN). Copenhagen, WHO.

Warhurst, Chris, Hurrell, Scott A., Gilbert, K., Nickson, Dennis, Commander, Johanna and Calder, Isobel (2009) 'Just mothers really? Role stretch and low pay amongst female classroom assistants', in Bolton, S.C. and Houlihan, M. (eds), *Work Matters: Critical Reflections on Contemporary Work.* Basingstoke: Palgrave.

Warner, Jeremy (2011) 'Coalition fiscal policy is under scrutiny because, for all the talk, we're no nearer to the end of this economic crisis'. *The Daily Telegraph*, 18 October, www.telegraph.co.uk/finance/financialcrisis/8769836/Coalition-fiscal-policy-is-under-scrutiny-because-for-all-the-talk-were-no-nearer-to-the-end-of-this-economic-crisis.html (accessed 18.10.2011).

Warwick-Booth, Louise, Cross, Ruth and Lowcock, Diane (2012) *Contemporary Health Studies: An Introduction.* Cambridge: Polity Press.

Weaver, Catherine (2010) 'Reforming the World Bank', in Wilkinson, Rorden and Clapp, Jennifer (eds), *Global Governance, Poverty and Inequality.* London: Routledge, pp. 112–31.

Weber, Max (1946) *From Max Weber: Essays in Sociology.* New York: Oxford University Press.

Weber, Max (1978) *Economy and Society* (Vol. 1). Berkeley, CA: University of California Press.

Weeks, Jeffrey (1986) *Sexuality.* London: Methuen.

Wheeler, Brian (2005) 'Leave chavs alone say MPS'. *BBC News*, Thursday 30 June, http://news.bbc.co.uk/1/hi/uk_politics/4077626.stm (accessed 2.8.2011).

White, Alan, de Souza, Bruno, de Visser, Richard et al. (2011) *The State of Men's Health in Europe.* Brussels: European Commission, Directorate General for Health and Consumers. Available at: http://ec.europa.eu/health/population_groups/docs/men_health_extended_en.pdf (accessed 5.9.2012).

Whitfield, Grahame and Dearden, Chris (2012) 'Low income households: casualties of the boom, casualties of the bust?' *Social Policy and Society*, 11 (1): 81–91.

Wilkinson, Paul (2005) 'Global environmental change and health', in Scriven, Angela and Garman, Sebastian (eds), *Promoting Health: Global Perspectives.* Basingstoke: Palgrave Macmillan, pp. 129–38.

Wilkinson, Richard G. (1995) *The Impact of Inequality. How to Make Sick Societies Healthier.* New York: New Press.

Wilkinson, Richard (1996) *Unhealthy Societies: The Afflictions of Inequality.* London: Routledge.

Wilkinson, Richard (2005) *The Impact of Inequality,* New York: New Press.

Wilkinson, Richard (2011) 'Inequality: the enemy between us?' Talk at the Policy Provocations Event, North Liverpool Academy, Everton, 13 September.

Wilkinson, Richard and Pickett, Kate (2009) *The Spirit Level: Why More Equal Societies Almost Always Do Better.* London: Allen Lane.

Wilkinson, Rorden (ed.) (2005) *The Global Governance Reader.* London: Routledge.

Wilkinson, Rorden and Clapp, Jennifer (2010) 'Governing global poverty and inequality', in Wilkinson, Rorden and Clapp, Jennifer (eds), *Global Governance, Poverty and Inequality.* London: Routledge, pp. 1–23.

Wilmoth, John, Mathers, Colin, Say, Lale and Mills, Samuel (2010) 'Maternal death drop by one-third from 1990-2008: a United Nations Analysis'. *Bulletin World Health Organization,* 88.

Wilson, William J. (1987) *The Truly Disadvantaged.* Chicago, IL: University of Chicago Press.

Wilson, William J. (1996) *When Work Disappears.* New York: Knopf.

Wilton, Nick (2011) 'Do employability skills really matter in the UK graduate labour market? The case of business and management graduates'. *Work, Employment and Society,* 25 (1): 85–100.

Wolf, Martin (2004) *Why Globalization Works: The Case for the Global Market Economy.* New Haven, CT: Yale University Press.

Wolf, Martin (2011) 'The big questions raised by anti-capitalist protests'. *Financial Times,* www.ft.com/cms/s/0/86d8634a-ff34-11e0-9769-00144feabdc0.html#axzz1gygMaHgf (accessed 19.12.2011).

Woodall, James, Warwick-Booth, Louise and Cross, Ruth (2012) 'Has empowerment lost its power?' *Health Education Research,* doi: 10.1093/her/cys064. First published online: June 19, 2012. Available at http://her.oxfordjournals.org/content/27/4/742. extract (accessed 28.3.2013).

World Bank (2002) *Globalisation, Growth and Poverty: Building an Inclusive World Economy.* World Bank Policy Research Report. Washington DC, World Bank and New York: Oxford University Press.

World Bank (2004) 'Global poverty down by half since 1981 but progress uneven as economic growth eludes many countries'. News Release No. 2004/309/S, 23 April, http://go.worldbank.org/R3SKHZRZ30 (accessed 16.4.2012).

World Bank (2005) *Pro-Poor Growth in the 1990s: Lessons and Insights from 14 Countries.* Washington, DC: World Bank.

World Bank (2009a) 'Crisis hitting poor hard in developing countries'. Press release No. 2009/220/EXC, 12 February.

World Bank (2009b) *Reshaping Economic Geography: World Development Report.* Washington, DC: World Bank. Available at: http://web.worldbank.org/WBSITE/EXTERNAL/EXTDEC/EXTRESEARCH/EXTWDRS/0,,contentMDK:23080183~pagePK:478093~piPK:477627~theSitePK:477624,00.html (accessed 15.8.2012).

World Bank (2011) *World Development Report 2012: Gender Equality and Development.* Washington, DC: World Bank.

World Bank, Development Research Group (2009) *PovcalNet Online Poverty Analysis Tool.* Washington, DC: World Bank. Available at: http://go.worldbank.org/NT2a1XUWPO (accessed 25.8.2011).

World Health Organization (1995) *The World Health Report 1995: Bridging the Gaps*. Geneva: WHO.

World Health Organization (2000) *The World Health Report. Health Systems Improving Performance*. Geneva: WHO.

World Health Organization (2005a) 'Climate and health'. Fact Sheet, July. Available at: www.who.int/globalchange/news/fsclimandhealth/en/print.html (accessed 13.1.2010).

World Health Organization (2005b) *Ecosystems and Human Well-being: Health Synthesis*. Report of the Millennium Ecosystem Assessment. Geneva: WHO.

World Health Organization (2007) *World Health Statistics, 2007*. Geneva: WHO.

World Health Organization (2008a) *The Global Burden of Disease: 2004 Update*. Geneva: WHO.

World Health Organization (2008b) *Closing the Gap in a Generation: Health Equity through Action on the Social Determinants of Health*. Commission for the Social Determinants of Health. Geneva: WHO.

World Health Organization (2012) 'Obesity and overweight'. Fact Sheet No. 311. Available at: www.who.int/mediacentre/factsheets/fs311/en/ (accessed 13.8.2012).

World Marriage Patterns (2000) *Wallchart*. New York: United Nations Department of Economic and Social Affairs. Available at: www.un.org/esa/population/publications/worldmarriage/worldmarriagepatterns2000.pdf (accessed 5.9.2012).

World Resources Institute (2000) *World Resources 2000–2001: People and Eecosystems: The Fraying Web of Life*. New York: United Nations Development Programme, United Nations Environment Programme, World Bank, World Resources Institute, September. Available at: www.wri.org/publication/world-resources-2000-2001-people-and-ecosystems-fraying-web-life (accessed 23.10.2012).

Wright, Erik O. (1997) *Class Counts: Comparative Studies in Class Analysis*. Cambridge: Cambridge University Press.

Yeates, Nicola and Holden, Chris (eds) (2009) *The Global Social Policy Reader*. Bristol: Policy Press.

Yodanis, Carrie L. (2004) 'Gender inequality, violence against women, and fear: a cross-national test of the feminist theory of violence against women'. *Journal of Interpersonal Violence*, 19: 655–75.

Young, Iris M. (1990) *Justice and the Politics of Difference*. Princeton, NJ: Princeton University Press.

Yuill, Chris, Crinson, Ian and Duncan, Eilidh (2010) *Key Concepts in Health Studies*. London: Sage.

Zhu, Ying (2000) 'Globalization, foreign direct investment and their impact on labour relation and regulation: the case of China'. *International Journal of Comparative Labour Law and Industrial Relations*, 16 (1): 5–24.

Zimmerman Cathy, Kiss Ligia, Hossain, Mazeda (2011) *Migration and Health: A Framework for 21st Century Policy-Making*. PLoS Med 8(5): e1001034. doi:10.1371/journal.pmed.1001034 (accessed 1.3.13).

INDEX